ADAM SMITH:

MAN OF LETTERS AND ECONOMIST

Books by Clyde E. Dankert

Adam Smith: Man of Letters and Economist
Contemporary Unionism in the United States
An Introduction to Labor

ADAM SMITH
Man of Letters
and Economist

Clyde E. Dankert

**Professor of Economics Emeritus
Dartmouth College**

An Exposition-University Book

Exposition Press   Hicksville, New York

First Edition

© 1974 by Clyde E. Dankert

LIBRARY OF CONGRESS CATALOG CARD NUMBER: 74-80675

ISBN 0-682-48020-7

Printed in the United States of America

Contents

Contents

Preface

In preparing the essays in the present volume I have profited greatly from the works of many writers, six or seven of whom have been particularly helpful. First, of course, there is Adam Smith himself. In the essays I make very extensive use of *The Wealth of Nations* and *The Theory of Moral Sentiments,* and to a lesser degree resort to Smith's minor writings. In two of the essays I draw rather frequently on the famous scholar's belatedly discovered *Lectures on Rhetoric and Belles Lettres.*

Among Smithian students whom I would mention individually are Dugald Stewart, the personal friend of Adam Smith, whose old *Memoir* has been a constant source of information to persons writing about the Scottish economist and moral philosopher—and man of letters; John Rae, whose *Life* (now with a *Guide* by Professor Viner) was for many years the best general biography of Smith, in fact the sole major biography; and, in brief, James Bonar, A. L. Macfie, William R. Scott, and Jacob Viner. I should also mention Edwin Cannan, notably for his famous edition of *The Wealth of Nations;* and George B. Hill and Lawrence F. Powell for their outstanding edition of *Boswell's Life of Johnson,* used principally in Essays 4 and 5. To these scholars I am highly indebted, just as I am also indebted to numerous other writers.

A substantial portion of the material in the essays has already been published, as individual articles in a number of journals, and as the contents of a brochure entitled *Thoughts from Adam Smith.* The journals are *Texas Studies in Literature and Language,* the University of Texas Press, Summer 1961 (Essay 1); the *Queen's Quarterly,* Summer 1961 (Essay 4); *The Dalhousie Review,* Autumn 1962, Spring 1967 (Essays 4 and 6); *The South Atlantic Quarterly,* Duke University Press, Spring 1967 (Essay

3); *Papers on Language and Literature,* Winter 1970 (Essay 5); and the *Dartmouth College Library Bulletin,* January 1959 (Essay 4). I thank the editors of these journals for permission to use copyrighted contributions that first appeared in their publications. I should point out, however, that in the process of moving the articles to their present location I have made many alterations in most of them, including numerous additions and some omissions and transpositions. I have also made a considerable number of alterations in the *Thoughts.*

I should say a few words concerning a type of bibliographical shorthand I have employed. Since I make frequent references to certain books I have used in the essays, all such references in the main text, after the complete footnote citation, I usually give in an abbreviated form. Thus *The Wealth of Nations* becomes WN; *The Theory of Moral Sentiments,* TMS; and the *Lectures on Rhetoric and Belles Lettres,* RBL. In a similar fashion, and both in the main text and the footnotes, I ordinarily refer to Dugald Stewart's sketch of Smith simply as Stewart; to Rae's biography, as Rae; to Scott's study of Smith as student and professor, as Scott or by the title of the study itself; and to Macfie's essays by the title of his collection. In Essays 4 and 5, I refer to the Hill-Powell edition of *Boswell's Life of Johnson* as HP.

The edition of *The Wealth of Nations* I have used is the Cannan edition, published by Random House in its Modern Library series, but issued originally by Methuen & Co. in 1904. (The Cannan text follows that of the old fifth edition of Smith's classic, which was the last one printed during the author's lifetime.) *The Theory of Moral Sentiments* is contained in *The Essays of Adam Smith,* published by Alex. Murray & Son in 1869. (The text here is that of the sixth edition of the *Theory,* published in the last year of Smith's life.) Since the Murray volume may not be readily accessible to the reader, and since my essays contain a great many references (with page numbers) to the *Theory,* some of which the reader may wish to refer to in another edition of the book, it will be helpful to him to know what pages are covered by the various Parts of the *Theory* in the particular source I have used. This information follows:

In writing these essays I have benefited from the book collections of a number of libraries, especially the Baker Library at Dartmouth College. To the Baker reference librarians I owe a debt of thanks. I am also thankful for assistance I have received from the Widener Library and the Houghton Library at Harvard University, and from the Kress Library, with its comprehensive collection of Smith material, in the Harvard School of Business. I have also been aided by a number of other libraries, aid that was channeled through the Inter-Library Loan Service, and for this help too I am grateful.

CLYDE E. DANKERT

ADAM SMITH:

MAN OF LETTERS AND ECONOMIST

1.

Adam Smith—Man of Letters

That unprosperous race of men commonly called men of letters.

—ADAM SMITH

Adam Smith is known today principally for his remarkable contribution to the development of economics. His notable classic, *The Wealth of Nations,* opened up a new era in the history of economic thought and brought its author immense and lasting fame. Indeed, on the basis of having written the book, Smith has often been referred to as "The Father of Political Economy."

But Adam Smith was more than a political economist. He had interests and enthusiasms that extended far beyond "the nature and causes of the wealth of nations," a fact that is evident in the famous treatise itself. He was greatly interested, of course, in moral philosophy. This vast subject, which included "expediency" or political economy, was his central concern as teacher during the years he spent at the University of Glasgow, and in his first book, *The Theory of Moral Sentiments,* he dealt with a segment of the subject. Smith, however, had a still further area of interest, namely literature.

The great economist had a profound and active devotion to literature. This devotion, which manifested itself in a variety of ways, developed early in his career and remained with him as

3

long as he lived. Not only was Smith a reader and admirer of literature but he was a commentator on literature. Furthermore, he produced literature himself. In addition, his interest in literature was accompanied by, and to some extent intertwined with, an interest in the arts in general. Smith's credentials for being admitted to that "unprosperous" group known as men of letters are therefore quite substantial. But the credentials need to be more closely examined, and it is to that task that we shall turn in the present essay.

In June 1740, when he was seventeen years of age, Smith temporarily left his native Scotland to begin his studies at Balliol College. The young student had spent the previous two and a half years at the University of Glasgow. During his sojourn at Oxford, then in a very unexciting period in its history (as one learns from certain remarks that Smith himself makes in his *Wealth of Nations,* as well as from other sources), he devoted his time to various branches of learning, including literature. He gave extended attention to Greek and Latin writers; he read the works of Italian and French authors; and he became better acquainted with English literature itself. At the same time he gave careful attention to his style of writing. As Dugald Stewart reports in his Memoir on Smith, and on the basis of Smith's own statement, he often made translations into English, especially from French, as a means for improving his style.[1] Besides improving his manner of writing, he improved, or at least changed, his manner of talking. We are told that he returned to his home in Kirkcaldy "able to speak with fairly English tones," an achievement beyond the reach of most Scottish intellectuals of the time.[2]

After spending slightly more than six years at Oxford, apparently with no visits home in the interim, Smith went back to Scotland in August, 1746. The country was then entering upon a period of intense intellectual activity. The second half of the century, it has been said, was "the most brilliant epoch" in Scottish literature and science; in no country but France was there "so rich and varied an efflorescence of genius."[3] The names of the geniuses, in varying numbers, have often been cataloged, with Adam Smith invariably included. The period itself has been characterized as the Golden Age of Scotland, the Scottish Renaissance, Scotland's Augustan Age. Edinburgh, the scene of much of the intellectual activity, was referred to as the Athens of the North. Certainly, as the half century advanced it could no longer be said with any justification that Scotland's northern lights were just farthing candles.[4]

Possibly the scholarly and scientific achievements made in Scotland during the latter half of the eighteenth century have been exaggerated, and hence some adjustment in the balance of appraisal may be called for.[5] But that many of the achievements were outstanding, and with a significance that extended far beyond the country's borders, cannot be denied.

Smith spent two quiet years at his home in Kirkcaldy, undoubtedly continuing the process of self-education that had engaged his attention at Balliol. Then, late in 1748, he began a series of public lectures in Edinburgh which continued for three years. In undertaking this venture Smith, it would seem, was encouraged by a number of his friends, particularly by Henry Home (Lord Kames). The lectures were presented to "a respectable auditory" made up principally of students studying law and theology.[6] Not a few of those in the "auditory" were later to achieve prominence in the political and intellectual life of the land. Included in this group were such men as Hugh Blair, Henry Home, William Johnstone, William Robertson, and Alexander Wedderburn.

Smith gave three courses of lectures in all, two of which appear to have been on literature and literary criticism.[7] Before his death in 1790 the Scottish scholar asked that these lectures be destroyed, a request that was duly carried out. For almost a century and three quarters Smithian scholars were without direct knowledge of what he had said in the lectures. But then an important discovery was made. Professor John M. Lothian, in a great stroke of fortune in buying books and papers at sales held in Aberdeen, came into possession of a set of manuscripts with the written title *Notes of Dr. Smith's Rhetoric Lectures*. These

Notes were taken in 1762-1763, the last session that Smith spent at Glasgow previous to his trip to the continent with the young Duke of Buccleuch. Professor Lothian believes that these lectures are "an expanded version" of the ones Smith had given in Edinburgh in 1748-1751. In 1963 the lectures were published under the editorship of Mr. Lothian and with an introduction by him.[8]

Among those who attended Smith's Edinburgh lectures was the Reverend Hugh Blair, as we have already noted. At one time it was felt that Blair had embodied much of Smith's material in his long popular book, *Lectures on Rhetoric and Belles Lettres.* This opinion lacks a solid foundation. Blair himself stated that he had borrowed a number of ideas from the manuscript Smith had used in his lectures. But many of Smith's friends felt that Blair's acknowledgment was not adequate. According to John Rae, the economist's biographer, this feeling was apparently not shared by Smith himself.[9]

In his *Lectures on Rhetoric and Belles Lettres* Smith has a great deal to say on the general matter of literary style, much of it of a very practical nature. This is the central theme of the first lectures, in which some of the chief characteristics of style are discussed. A second group of lectures relates to descriptive style, a third to historical style, a fourth to oratorical style. In his lectures Smith makes numerous references to English, French, Italian, Roman, and Greek authors. Much of the knowledge he exhibits here must have been acquired during his long stay at Oxford.

The *Lectures on Rhetoric and Belles Lettres* supply additional proof that Smith was indeed a true man of letters. But the *Lectures* have an additional significance. Not only did they have an important influence on the many students who heard them—including James Boswell—but they had a notable effect on the development of the theory and practice of rhetoric at the University of Glasgow and in Scotland generally. As Lothian points out (p. xxiii), Smith's lectures distinctly mark the change from the old, traditional study of formal rhetoric at the University to the study of belles lettres.[10] These lectures, Lothian further declares, were so far as is known the first of their kind in Great Britain.

During the time he was lecturing in Edinburgh Smith performed (or *may* have performed) another task that points to his literary interests.[11] He collected and edited the poems of his friend and fellow Scot, William Hamilton of Bangour, author of the long popular "Braes of Yarrow." Hamilton, who was the first translator of Homer into English blank verse and also, apparently, the first of his countrymen in the eighteenth century "to write poetry in good English,"[12] knew nothing of this undertaking. Because of his Jacobite sympathies he was in political disfavor at the time and was on the continent.

In carrying out his work on Hamilton's poems, Rae says (pp. 30, 39-41) that Smith made "a first contribution to English literature himself." The size of the contribution is very modest, however. Collecting and editing the poems was perhaps a sizable task, but not the writing of the preface. The latter runs to only three hundred and fifty words. It contains a few observations on Hamilton's poetry and thus may be looked upon as a small bit of literary criticism.[13]

In 1751 Smith was appointed to the Chair of Logic at the University of Glasgow, a position that included the teaching of rhetoric and belles lettres. He also filled in for the Professor of Moral Philosophy who was ill at the time. In both posts he found his Edinburgh lectures useful. Early in 1752 he received a permanent appointment to the Chair of Moral Philosophy, and in that position he continued to give expression to his literary interests. As one of his pupils, William Richardson, remarked (Rae, pp. 55-56), he gave lectures on taste, the history of philosophy, and belles lettres. Moreover, according to Richardson, Smith enjoyed digressing into literary criticism regardless of the subject of his lectures.

In 1755, in the first number of the original *Edinburgh Review,* of which only two issues were printed, Smith reviewed Samuel Johnson's recently published *Dictionary of the English Language.* The review is a brief one. True, it totals eleven pages, but only two of these pages are devoted to an actual discussion of the *Dictionary.* Smith pays tribute to Johnson's achievement—

e.g., "When we compare this book with other dictionaries, the merit of its author appears very extraordinary"—but he thinks the plan of the *Dictionary* is defective. And to illustrate his point he uses nine pages to show how Johnson deals with the words "but" and "humour," and how he, the reviewer, wishes he had dealt with them. Smith said some fine things about the *Dictionary,* but Johnson was probably displeased with a number of his other statements. Although several well-known authors of the time wrote articles for the two issues of the original *Edinburgh Review,* it would seem that Smith's review of Johnson's *Dictionary* attracted the most attention, "from those best fitted to judge of literary merit."[14]

In the second and final issue of the *Review* Smith contributed an article (in the form of a letter) relating largely to the prevailing condition of European literature. After suggesting to the *Review* that it should give attention to the literature of Europe, Smith comments very briefly on the state of learning and literature in Italy, Spain, and Germany. Then at quite some length he discusses French literature, comparing it with that of England and giving special attention to the work of the Encyclopedists and of Rousseau.

Smith was obviously impressed by the achievements of the Encyclopedists and speaks very highly of their volumes. He believes, however, that the style of some of the contributors is too declamatory. Moreover, he thinks that the Encyclopedists could have left out a few of the articles they included, such as the one on *Amour,* a contribution which "will tend little to the edification either of the learned or unlearned reader." But Smith feels that the inclusion of these unnecessary articles is of no great moment.

In his discussion of Rousseau, Smith refers to Mandeville and his *Fable of the Bees.* Rousseau, we are told, has transformed Mandeville. The latter's principles are "softened, improved, and embellished, and stript of all that tendency to corruption and licentiousness which has disgraced them in their original author." Smith points not only to dissimilarities between the views of the two men, however, but to similarities as well. To furnish the readers of *The Edinburgh Review* with a specimen of Rousseau's "eloquence" the author translated a number of passages from the French writer's *Discourse on the Origin and Foundation of the Inequality of Mankind.*

On the "literary merit" of France and England, Smith makes the following interesting generalization. "If we may pass any judgment concerning the literary merit of these two great rivals in learning, trade, government, and war: Imagination, genius, and invention, seem to be the talents of the English; taste, judgment, propriety, and order, of the French."

Smith was not only keenly interested in literature but was also interested in several other areas of human knowledge which impinge on the field of literature. This fact is well brought out in a letter he wrote in 1785, five years before his death, to the Duc de la Rochefoucauld.[15] After referring to a matter concerning the Duke and *The Theory of Moral Sentiments,* Smith goes on to say in his letter that "I have likewise two other great works upon the anvil; the one is a sort of Philosophical History of all the different branches of Literature, of Philosophy, Poetry and Eloquence; the other is a sort of theory and History of Law and Government." He also states that the materials for both studies have been largely collected and that parts of both studies are in tolerably good order. "But," he adds, "the indolence of old age, tho' I struggle violently against it, I feel coming fast upon me, and whether I shall ever be able to finish either is extremely uncertain."

Unfortunately, these two ambitious projects were never completed. Some of the material that apparently was to go into them was preserved, however, in a number of Smith's essays which were published by his executors after his death. Of the essays the executors (Black and Hutton) state: "When these were inspected, the greater number of them appeared to be parts of a plan he once had formed, for giving a connected history of the liberal sciences and elegant arts."[16] Setting aside any detailed discussion of his two books, *The Theory of Moral Sentiments* and *The Wealth of Nations,* until later parts of the present volume, we shall now describe some of the characteristics of these essays.

The first of the essays in the Black-Hutton volume is entitled "Considerations Concerning the First Formation of Languages." This essay was included in the third edition of *The Theory of Moral Sentiments,* published in 1767 (not in the first edition of 1759, as J. R. McCulloch states, nor in the second of 1761 as Dugald Stewart "believed" it was—and as numerous other writers, who probably obtained their information from Stewart, have asserted). The first appearance of the essay in print, however, goes back beyond 1767, to 1761. In that year there was published a *Philological Miscellany* in which Smith's discussion appears.[17]

The essay "The Formation of Languages" runs to twenty pages and is both informative and interesting. In dealing with his theme, however, the author is forced to dip into the dark and misty past and is consequently driven to a considerable amount of intelligent guesswork. Such expressions as "probably" and "must have" figure in his analysis with some frequency.

Much of Smith's treatment of his subject relates to the relative difficulty of originally forming the chief parts of speech. Starting with "nouns substantive," the introduction of which "would probably be one of the first steps towards the formation of language," he proceeds to discuss at some length "nouns adjective." The "original invention" of the latter would be quite difficult, he declares, but not as difficult however as the invention of prepositions. Since verbs are necessary for the making of statements, they "must necessarily have been coeval with the very first attempts towards the formation of language." Indeed, certain impersonal verbs might even have been the first words in the formation of language.

The breaking down of words into their "elements," and the formation of characters to represent these elements, involved the invention of personal pronouns. These pronouns, the bachelor economist informs us, "are among the last words of which children learn to make use." And for illustrative purposes, Smith states that "A child, speaking of itself, says, *Billy walks, Billy sits,* instead of *I walk, I sit.*"

The author then discusses the intermixture of languages consequent upon the mixture of nations. As a result of the latter development, language "becomes more simple in its rudiments and principles, just in proportion as it grows more complex in its composition." This simplification, however, makes languages "more and more imperfect, and less proper for many of the purposes of language."

In his essay on "The Formation of Languages" Smith ventures into difficult territory, and it ill becomes one who is essentially an economist to pass judgment on the value and the validity of his discoveries. The author himself, we learn from Dugald Stewart, held a high opinion of the essay. Possibly, however, the process he used in his work of exploration in this area is of greater significance than the product of his efforts, a possibility that Stewart regarded as a certainty. Smith was greatly interested in investigating origins, either in terms of the basic attributes of human nature or the objective conditions of society. In other words, he was very fond of using what we now refer to as the genetic method. This fact is clearly evident in his writings. When dealing with the Formation of Languages, however, as we have already noted, he had to rely very largely on conjecture. In this instance, and in others that could be cited, he uses a type of methodological practice—a "species of philosophical investigation"—that Stewart (p. 34) described as *Theoretical* or *Conjectural History*.

Following the discussion of "The Formation of Languages" there are in the Black-Hutton compilation three essays (of sixty, ten, and ten pages respectively) on "The Principles Which Lead and Direct Philosophical Inquiries"—as illustrated first, by the history of astronomy; secondly, by the history of ancient physics; and finally, by the history of ancient logic and metaphysics.

The first of these essays, commonly entitled "The History of Astronomy," was written quite early in Smith's career. This is evident from a remark near the end of the essay about the predictions, made by the followers of Isaac Newton, of the appearance of a number of comets, "particularly of one which is to make its appearance in 1758." Smith is here referring to the remarkable forecast of Edmund Halley. True to the latter's prophecy, this particular "Halley's Comet" made its appearance, being first seen by an amateur astronomer on the night of December 25, 1758, near Dresden.

In a letter he wrote early in 1773 to his good friend David Hume, Smith speaks of his essay on astronomy, referring to it as "a fragment of an intended juvenile work."[18] Two observations may be made about this remark: first, the essay presupposes a rather high degree of knowledge on the part of any "juveniles" who might read it; secondly, it suggests that Smith had plans for a larger work. The latter observation is borne out by a statement made by Dugald Stewart. Stewart (p. 36) declares that he had heard Smith say "more than once" that he had planned, in his earlier years, on writing a history of the other sciences along the same general line that he had used in his work on astronomy. The latter work, it should be added, was not published until after the author's death.

Though relatively few economists, and perhaps few astronomers, are familiar with Smith's essay "The History of Astronomy," it is of interest to observe that one modern scholar, Professor O. H. Taylor, in writing a book on economic thought, has considered it desirable to devote five and a half pages to the essay. Among other things Mr. Taylor points out that Smith's theory of "connecting links," as set forth in the essay, throws light on his two books.[19] In speaking of Smith's essays in general (which "nobody would credit the author of the *Wealth of Nations* with the power to write"), another economist, Joseph Schumpeter, feels that the "pearl" of the group is the essay on astronomy.[20]

Smith's early intention of writing a comprehensive history of the sciences was not carried through. However, there are the other two "fragments" to which we have referred. These were probably in the writing desk or behind "the glass folding-doors of a bureau" referred to by Smith in his letter of April 16, 1773, to David Hume; they were also likely among the papers Smith wanted his friend to destroy in the event of his death. (The publication of the essay on astronomy was left to Hume's discretion—Hume, however, predeceased Smith.) The essay on "The History of the Ancient Physics" is a much smaller fragment than the one on astronomy. So, too, is the third of the essays, the one on "The History of the Ancient Logics and Metaphysics."

Part of this third "fragment" goes back to the very beginning of Smith's teaching career at Glasgow. The part constitutes a portion of the address he gave at the University in January 1751 when, at the age of twenty-seven, he was installed as a faculty member. The address itself was entitled "De Origine Idearum."[21]

The titles of these three historical essays suggest the breadth of Smith's knowledge and interest. They also point to an age in which the division of labor, about which our author wrote so engagingly in *The Wealth of Nations,* was much less developed in the intellectual sphere than it is today.

The next essay in the Black and Hutton volume is entitled "Of the Nature of That Imitation Which Takes Place in What are Called the Imitative Arts." This essay, which well suggests the wide scope of Smith's cultural interests, is thirty pages in length and has appended to it (placed there by the editors) a brief discussion entitled "Of the Affinity between Music, Dancing, and Poetry."

In his essay on the Imitative Arts, Smith attempts to show that to a great extent the pleasure people receive from the various arts is determined by the difficulty of imitation. Speaking of the disparity between "the object imitating, and the object imitated," the author declares that "the pleasure arising from the imitation seems greater in proportion as this disparity is greater." Dugald Stewart (pp. 48-49) advances the opinion that Smith's principle, or theory, was probably suggested by the principle—*difficulté surmontée*—used by certain French critics in their discussion of versification and rhyme.

Smith directs the attention of the reader to a wide variety of specific questions concerning such arts as painting, sculpture, music, poetry, and dancing. Why is it, for example, that drapery (when it is used) is tight on statues and loose in paintings? Why are statues seldom painted and "universally reprobated" when they are? What is to be said concerning the desirability of clipping yew and holly trees "into the artificial shapes of pyramids, and columns, and vases, and obelisks?" What things can poetry express that dancing cannot, or at least cannot express as well? Why is it that the imitative powers of instrumental music "are much inferior to those of Vocal Music?" These are some of the detailed matters that Smith takes up in his discussion of the Imitative Arts.

In his essay Smith gives a great deal of attention to music. Among numerous observations he makes on the subject there is one that points to a type of "harmony of interests" that differs from the kind ordinarily associated with his name. "The sentiments and passions which Music can best initiate are those which unite and bind men together in society." These are the social, decent, virtuous, and other types of passions he mentions. On the other hand, Smith declares, the passions which separate men, "the unsocial, the hateful, the indecent, the vicious passions, cannot easily be imitated by Music." Moreover, the music that "does imitate them is not the most agreeable." (This same theme is touched on in *The Theory of Moral Sentiments,* p. 36.)

A musical novice finds this statement and others that Smith makes quite fascinating. With what authority the moral philosopher and economist speaks on these matters it is not for him to say. It would seem, however, that Smith had considerable knowledge of the scientific aspects of music. Whether or not he was keenly sensitive to the refinements of music is not so certain. The Earl of Buchan, whose sharp view of Smith as a literary critic we shall note shortly, said the economist did not have an ear for music.[22] On this point Smith's other contemporaries unfortunately are silent, and it would seem unjust to make a confident and final pronouncement on the question on the basis of Buchan's opinion alone.

There is an account of an interesting and rather amusing episode relating to Smith and music that has come down to us, and though it does not prove a great deal about Smith's musical sensitivity, as a bit of Smithiana it deserves brief attention.

In 1784, on his tour of England and Scotland, Bartolemy Faujas De Saint Fond visited Edinburgh.[23] There "that venerable philosopher, Adam Smith" (then sixty-one years of age) was the person whom Saint Fond saw most frequently. On one occasion Smith asked his visitor if he was fond of music and received an affirmative reply—if the music was "well executed." Smith thereupon stated that he would take his friend to hear "a kind of music of which it is impossible you can have formed any idea." Moreover, said Smith, "it will afford me great pleasure to know the impression it makes upon you." The two men then set out to hear a bagpipe competition.

Saint Fond, who describes the comments upon the occasion at some length, was not impressed by the music—he felt the performance belonged more to history than to music. Speaking of the players, he writes that he "thought them all of equal proficiency; that is to say, the one was as bad as the other." (To those who enjoy bagpipe music this is indeed a shocking statement.) Though Smith was desirous of getting Saint Fond's opinion of the music itself, we are not told what comments he made to the venerable philosopher.

Smith's interest in the imitative arts extended over a long period of time. From Professor John Millar's letter of August 10, 1790, to David Douglas we learn that the economist read two papers on the theme to the Literary Society of Glasgow, and in addition had a third one in an incomplete form.[24] This was back in the 1750s, or possibly early 1760s. During the first part of the 1780s Smith must have returned once again to this early interest for we find that Sir Joshua Reynolds, in his letter of September 12, 1782, to Bennet Langton, states that Smith "intends publishing this winter an essay on the reason why imitation pleases."[25] This intention was not carried through; the essay was not published until after Smith's death.

Reynolds, it might be pointed out, was also interested in "imitation." He gave two papers on the subject—Discourse VI of 1774 and Discourse XIII of 1786. Not only was he interested in the theme but, what is of greater significance to us in the present discussion, he asked Smith (so he tells us in his letter to Langton) if he would read what he had to say on the question. "I had wrote a great deal on detached slips of paper, which I would put together and beg him to look over it." Smith, who was in the process of finishing his own essay, would not oblige his artist friend. It is possible that he was fearful of being accused of taking some of his ideas from Reynolds, especially since the latter had said that his notions "perfectly agreed" with Smith's. In view of the fact that quite some years before, late in 1759 to be exact, Reynolds had found the recently published *Theory of Moral Sentiments* of some use when he wrote *Idler* No. 82,[26] it might be argued that Smith would have been entitled to some aid from his friend.

Smith's essay on the Imitative Arts was apparently just part of a much larger undertaking the author had contemplated. He envisaged a whole book on the subject.[27] Unfortunately this plan, as well as others that he had in mind, was not carried through.

The next essay in the Black-Hutton volume contains a discussion of the External Senses. In this essay of thirty pages Smith deals with seeing, hearing, smelling, tasting, and touching. Here again he ventures into areas that for the most part are outside the orbit of present-day economists, and again he exhibits his wide learning.

Finally there is in the volume a brief essay, to be referred to shortly, entitled "Of the Affinity Between Certain English and Italian Verses."

Smith's stature as a man of letters is enhanced by his essays, but interesting though these essays are they do not compare in scholarly performance and intellectual influence with the author's two books. In the pages that follow, indeed in our work as a whole, we shall have occasion to refer frequently to these books. Both are notable not only for what they say but how they say it. Both books represent contributions to literature and greatly increase Smith's reputation as a man of letters.

Smith had an enthusiastic and abiding love of poetry. In his personal library he had a wide range of poetry books, in English, French, Italian, Latin, and Greek. In addition he had books about poetry, including a number on the relationship between music and poetry, a matter that interested him. Indeed, he was interested in the nature and interrelationships of all the "imitative arts."

The presence of numerous books on and about poetry in Smith's library does not necessarily prove that the great economist was keenly interested in poetry, nor that he had an extensive knowledge of the works of the poets. These books could have remained as mere fixtures on his shelves. In Smith's case, however, there is ample evidence that he read his books, not only the books on poetry but on the many other subjects represented in his library collection. In his *Lectures on Rhetoric and Belles Lettres* there are many references to poets. The same is true, though to a somewhat lesser degree, of his *Theory of Moral Sentiments.* In some of his essays too he cites various poets, and even in his *Wealth of Nations* he has occasional allusions to poetry.

Though Smith did not produce any extensive piece of writing on poetry, he went beyond casual references to the poets and their works. He discusses the general theme in his essays on "The Imitative Arts" and "The Affinity Between Certain English and Italian Verses." He also touches on the theme in a fragment of an essay, "The Affinity Between Music, Dancing, and Poetry." In addition there are sizable segments—a paragraph or more in each instance—in his *Theory of Moral Sentiments* that deal specifically with poetry.

One final bit of evidence concerning Smith's interest in poetry is found in the ability he had to quote it. In his older years when, as Dugald Stewart (p. 9) phrased it, "after all the different occupations and inquiries in which his maturer faculties had been employed," the writings of the Roman, Greek, French and Italian poets retained a strong hold on his memory.[28] And as for English poetry, not only could he refer to a variety of passages but, as Stewart informs us, he could repeat the passages correctly. One of the places at which he repeated poetry was at the Edinburgh Customs House—Smith became a customs official in 1778, two years after the publication of his *Wealth of Nations*. To wile away some of the dull times at this establishment, he and a fellow commissioner often quoted long selections from the classics.[29] During his declining years his love of the classics was particularly marked. In fact, he appears largely to have spent his leisure time reading these writings, acting on the basis of his theory that "the best amusement of age" is "to renew acquaintance with the writers who were the delight of one's youth."[30] And some of these writers were poets.

Closely allied to his interest in poetry was Smith's interest in drama and plays in general. While he was in Paris, as tutor to the young Duke of Buccleuch, he often went to see plays. He was very fond of the French playwrights and had an especially high regard for Racine's *Phaedra*. The Greek and Roman dramatists appealed to him throughout his adult life, and he had a wide knowledge of their works. His opposition to the establishment of a playhouse in Glasgow was by no means an expression of any lack of interest in plays—just a lack of interest in, and objection to, those theatrical productions which involve "scandal or indency." Other types, other "dramatic representations and exhibitions," he would have the government foster by adopting a hands-off policy with respect to the endeavors of self-seeking promoters.[31] In speaking of Smith's interest in plays it might be observed that he was an associate of David Garrick in the famous London Literary Club.

In addition to being interested in "ordinary" plays, Smith was also interested in opera, both serious and comic. In his essay on "The Imitative Arts" he briefly discusses operas and opera actors. "Nothing can be more deeply affecting," he declares among other observations, "than the interesting scenes of the serious opera, when to good Poetry and good Music, to the Poetry of Metastasio and the Music of Pergolese, is added the execution of a good actor."[32]

With his strong interest in poetry it would not be strange if Smith himself had tried to write in that medium. Indeed, the evidence points to the fact that he found the writing of blank verse (a type of poetry that stood low in his estimation) very easy, though the composition of verse that rhymes was beyond his powers. In one of his conversations, in 1780, with a friend and admirer who wrote under the pen name *Amicus,* Smith declared that "I myself, even I, who never could find a single rhime in my life, could make blank verse as fast as I could speak."[33] Unfortunately, none of Smith's rapidly written blank verse has come down to us.

Today Smith is not looked upon as an authority in literary criticism. Yet he made ventures into this field, just as he ventured into other areas of intellectual activity. His critical opinions, which are sometimes quaint and surprising, and expressed with considerable vigor, are interesting even when they are not expressive of the best judgment.

As we have already observed, Smith strongly disliked blank verse, though he made an exception for Milton's. "They do well," he said to *Amicus,* "to call it *blank,* for blank it is." Smith's attitude, it would seem, was based on his view concerning the test of literary beauty, namely that such beauty is proportionate to the degree of perceived difficulty to be overcome.[34] The difficulty in the way of writing blank verse was, in his opinion, not great. In his strictures on this type of verse Smith adds that "nothing but laziness hinders our tragic poets from writing, like the French, in rhime."

Smith's strong predilection for poetry that rhymes, a sentiment that was shared by his contemporary and acquaintance Samuel Johnson, is affirmed by Boswell in an account of one of his conversations with Johnson. The latter, we are told, had been enlarging "very convincingly upon the excellence of rhyme over blank verse in English poetry." Boswell's thoughts went back to his attendance at Smith's lectures in Glasgow a few years before, and he told Johnson that Smith "had maintained the same opinion strenuously." He also mentioned some of the arguments Smith had advanced in defense of his view. Johnson (in a frequently quoted passage) thereupon stated, "Sir, I was once in company with Smith, and we did not take to each other; but had I known that he loved rhyme as much as you tell me he does, I should have HUGGED him."[35]

Smith made critical observations—in his writings and in his lectures on rhetoric and belles lettres—on numerous writers. To describe all these observations would take us too far afield, but a brief analysis of his remarks on a number of English writers is feasible.

Smith held very positive ideas concerning Shakespeare, of whom he was not a great admirer. He felt that Shakespeare had great scenes but not one good play. Had the famous playwright made a more extensive use of rhyme in his plays, however, they would have been greatly improved. This conclusion is suggested by a statement Smith makes about Dryden. "Dryden," he declared to *Amicus,* "had he possessed but a tenth part of Shakespeare's dramatic genius, would have brought rhyming tragedies into fashion here as well as they are in France." Smith rated Shakespeare's tragedies below Racine's *Phaedra,* for he speaks of this production, in his *Theory of Moral Sentiments* (p. 111), as "the finest tragedy, perhaps, that is extant in any language."

With further reference to Shakespeare (and especially with reference to Johnson), another remark of Smith's should be mentioned. Smith spoke in highly complimentary terms of the Preface Johnson included in his famous edition of Shakespeare. It was, he said, "the most *manly* piece of criticism that was ever published in any country."[36] This view may be exaggerated, but the merit of the Preface, and of Johnson's edition of Shakespeare in general, has been recognized.

Smith was fond of Milton's "L'Allegro" and "Il Penseroso" but felt, so *Amicus* again tells us, that "all the rest of Milton's short poems were trash." Gray aroused Smith's enthusiasm. He believed, *Amicus* further reports, that Gray's odes were "the standard of lyric excellence." Much earlier (TMS, p. 111) he had spoken of Gray as a poet "who joins to the sublimity of Milton the elegance and harmony of Pope, and to whom nothing is wanting to render him, perhaps, the first poet in the English language, but to have written a little more." His view, however, that Gray's slender poetic output in his later years was because of the injury he felt at the publication of two parody odes (on "Oblivion" and "Obscurity") is apparently without foundation.[37]

Smith rated Dryden high, and he liked Pope's works. He referred to Pope as "the most correct, as well as the most elegant and harmonious of all the English poets" (TMS, p. 111). Smith, *Amicus* tells us, had no use for his private character, however, feeling that Pope was all affectation. "Of Swift," *Amicus* says that "Dr. Smith made frequent and honourable mention." Had he had the inclination, Swift could have become "one of the greatest of all poets."

In his lectures on rhetoric and belles lettres (given over a period of years, and relatively early in his career(Smith made numerous references to the writers just mentioned, especially to Milton, Pope, Shakespeare, and Swift, and to many others, both English and non-English, both modern and ancient. In his linking together of rhetoric and belles lettres he found his extensive knowledge of literature not only useful but indispensable.

The account *Amicus* gives of Smith's views on some of Samuel Johnson's writings is of interest. Smith, we are informed, "was no admirer of *The Rambler* or *The Idler,* and hinted that he had never been able to read them." This statement is not quite correct since Smith had made comments on *The Rambler* back in his Glasgow days. The political pamphlets of Johnson, and particularly one of them, aroused Smith's admiration. "But, above all," says *Amicus,* "he was charmed with that respecting Falkland's Islands, as it displayed, in such forcible language, the madness of modern wars." (The "madness of modern wars" was thus recognized long before the Atomic Age.)

Amicus conveys to us Smith's views on a number of other writers and also his opinion of the *Reviews.* For the latter publications he had a thorough dislike, declaring that he had never looked at them nor knew the names of their publishers.[38]

Smith's stature as a literary critic was by no means outstanding. While Leslie Stephen has said that he "held the ordinary opinions of the leading critics of his time,"[39] other commentators have passed severe judgment on Smith in this role. Alexander Carlyle stated that "With respect to taste, we held David Hume and Adam Smith inferior to the rest"—the rest being, apparently, Adam Ferguson, William Robertson, and Henry Home (Lord Kames). Hume and Smith, Carlyle continued, "were both prejudiced in favor of the French tragedies, and did not sufficiently appreciate Shakespeare and Milton. Their taste was a rational act, rather than the instantaneous effect of fine feeling."[40] The Earl of Buchan declared that Smith did not have "any perception of the sublime or beautiful in composition, either in poetry or language of any kind." Buchan attributed the great economist's lack of taste to the fact that he was "too much of a geometrician," though he added that Smith "had the greatest perception of moral beauty and excellence."[41] The editor of *The European Magazine,* who in 1791 reprinted most of the *Amicus* letter which appeared earlier in the year in *The Bee,* stated that on the subject of poetry Smith seemed "not to have been endowed with a gleam of taste." "Almost all his opinions," the editor added, "are erroneous and contemptible."[42]

It was Wordsworth, however, whose opinion is most frequently cited. Smith, he said, was "the worst critic, David Hume not excepted, that Scotland, a soil to which this sort of weed seems natural, has produced."[43] It seems probable that Wordsworth's opinion was based largely on the observations made by *Amicus,* as reprinted in *The European Magazine,* and not on a knowledge of the content of Smith's lectures on rhetoric and belles lettres as delivered first in Edinburgh and later at the University of Glasgow. (These lectures were heard by many persons, though they were not given general circulation until 1963). *The European Magazine* had been a favorite of Wordsworth's for a long time.[44] Had Wordsworth had the opportunity of examining Smith's lectures, his opinion of the Scottish scholar as a literary critic might have been less extreme.

Is it possible that in his very adverse criticism of Hume and Smith, Wordsworth was motivated by anti-Scottish sentiments?

Ernest C. Mossner thinks this was the case. Mossner declares that the two Scotsmen were "men of letters of a breadth incomprehensible to Wordsworth," and that "only blind anti-Scottish prejudice could have produced such absurdity."[45] This conclusion is difficult to believe. Wordsworth visited Scotland a number of times; Sir Walter Scott was one of his friends; he wrote poetry about Scotland (including three poems about Yarrow, and "The Solitary Reaper"); he was keenly interested in Robert Burns, bemoaned the fact that he had not met him, and wrote an elegy to him; he referred to William Hamilton's "Braes of Yarrow" as "the exquisite Ballad of Hamilton." In the light of these facts and of a highly significant circumstance now to be noted, one should say that Wordsworth instead of having an anti-Scottish prejudice had an anti-Jeffrey prejudice.

Francis Jeffrey, the editor of *The Edinburgh Review,* had been highly critical of Wordsworth's poetry and philosophy, and this criticism could well have been in the back of the poet's mind when he made his derogatory observation about Hume and Smith. Jeffrey looked upon Wordsworth—the *young* Wordsworth, it should be empasized—as a social menace.[46]

Carrying speculation a step farther, it might be added that Wordsworth's attitude toward Smith as literary critic might have been influenced somewhat by the latter's highly flattering views concerning Thomas Gray. (This, of course, assumes that Wordsworth knew what Smith's views were, which may be a large assumption.) Wordsworth looked upon Gray's poetry as the outstanding example of a weakness in eighteenth-century verse: its creation of "a special diction" far removed from that of prose; he felt that poetry should steer clear of all such diction "and employ the language really used by men."[47]

The size and scope of Smith's library, to which some reference has already been made, suggest the breadth of our author's intellectual interests. Though one would expect any man of letters to be fascinated by books, in Smith's case the degree of fascination was particularly marked. Dugald Stewart (p. 6) refers to the economist's early "passion for books." The Earl of Buchan declares that "The three great avenues to Smith, were his mother, his books, and his political opinions"; and our author himself once stated that *"I am a beau in nothing but my books."*[48]

The excellence of Smith's collection of books (which he built up largely after he left the University of Glasgow) is revealed in a number of studies that have been made of the contents of his library. In his pioneer analysis of Smith's library, which was published in 1894, James Bonar lists approximately 1,000 titles, covering 2,200 volumes.[49] Though this listing is far from complete, a fact which the compiler recognized, a classification of the books that Bonar made at the time is of interest. Omitting a few volumes of a miscellaneous nature, he found that, roughly, Smith's books could be divided about equally among the following five categories:

> Literature and Art
> Latin and Greek authors and commentators
> Law, Politics, and Geography
> Political Economy and History
> Science and Pholosophy

In 1932 a revised and enlarged edition of Bonar's *Catalogue* appeared, and in 1967 Mizuta's study of the contents of Smith's library was published.[50] Mizuta added a substantial number of new titles to the Bonar list, but there are still some titles missing. However, from the extensive information we now have of Smith's collection of books, it is clear that the great economist and moral philosophy had very wide intellectual interests, including a keen interest in literature. This fact is also suggested by the variety of illustrations and allusions found in *The Wealth of Nations* and his other writings, and also by those in his *Lectures on Rhetoric and Belles Lettres.*

John Rae, who had seen Bonar's 1894 *Catalogue,* noted (p. 328) "the almost complete absence" of books on theology and fiction in Smith's library.[51] Since that date, as the existence of still further books of Smith's has been discovered (by Bonar himself,

Mizuta, and others) additions have been made in these categories —including more sermons by Bishop Massillon, "the eloquent and philosophical bishop of Clermont," Smith calls him (TMS, p. 149), to supplement the fifteen-volume set mentioned by Bonar. The general observation made by Rae, however, though now somewhat extreme, remains essentially true.

Smith not only enjoyed being in the "company" of books but he was also fond of being in the company of intellectually stimulating persons. In the course of his life he belonged to a variety of clubs and societies, a number of which he helped to establish and some of which were of a literary nature.[52] In Glasgow he was associated with the Political Economy Club, the Literary Society, and Mr. Robin Simson's Club (or the Anderston Club). Of the last-mentioned of these, James Watt, who was a member of the group, states that "Our conversations then, besides the usual subjects with young men, turned principally on literary topics, religion, morality, belles lettres, etc."[53] In Edinburgh Smith belonged to the Philosophical Society, the Select Society, the Poker Club (established to stir things up, to enliven Scottish culture, not to promote a card game), the Oyster Club, and the Royal Society. It need hardly be mentioned that he did not belong to all of these clubs simultaneously. In London he probably attended a dining club made up mostly of Scotsmen, and we know, of course, that he was a member of the famous Literary Club (more accurately, The Club). Elected to the membership of the latter organization in 1775, when he was in London finishing his *Wealth of Nations*, Smith came into contact with many of the great figures of the period, men who were outstanding in the field of literature and other areas. Johnson, Goldsmith, Boswell, Reynolds, Garrick, Burke, and Gibbon were among the club's members. Living in a "clubable" age, his attachment to these various groups afforded him an excellent opportunity to cultivate and give expression to his interest in literature and other subjects.

In one or two instances the clubs afforded Smith an opportunity to present papers or ideas that were later to be embodied in his writings. The Earl of Buchan declared, perhaps a bit too positively, that the literary Society at Glasgow to which he had been elected a member in 1763, "gave origin" to Smith's essay on "The Formation of Languages" and to his *Theory of Moral Sentiments*.[54] Some of the material that was later to be included in *The Wealth of Nations* and in some of his other essays was undoubtedly discussed also at these clubs.

In discussing "Adam Smith Among His Books," James Bonar, in a delightfully informative fantasy, has "Victorian" say to the shade of the great economist (on the basis of the known books in his library): "your prime favourite among studies was not philosophy, not political economy, but literature."[55] Literature indeed had a special appeal to Smith. His interest in the subject was a very active one. It went beyond the mere reading of the works of others. In his conversation, his teaching, and his writing he frequently dealt with literary matters.

On the basis of the evidence we have considered it is certain beyond question that Smith belonged to what he himself referred to as "That unprosperous race of men commonly called men of letters" (WN, p. 131). It should be added, however, that in the present age of mass sales the members of the race are now not always unprosperous.

Appendix
The Authority and Identity of Amicus

The editor of *The Bee*, James Anderson, an early writer on the theory of rent and on other economic questions, states that the *Amicus* letter was turned over to him "under the strongest assurances of authenticity." Anderson further declares that he had no doubt about its authenticity since certain views of Smith as expressed in the letter coincided with opinions that "he himself had heard maintained by that gentleman." In the present essays we shall assume that Smith actually expressed the opinions attributed to him by *Amicus,* or views resembling them.

The identity of *Amicus* is a matter of uncertainty. Rae devotes several pages to the *Amicus* communication, but expresses no opinion on who the writer was. However, he identifies *Ascanius,* who commented on the *Amicus* letter and on Smith generally, in the June 8, 1791, issue of *The Bee,* as the Earl of Buchan (pp. 51-52, 370). He says, moreover, that the Earl contributed to *The Bee* under various pen names. Other biographical writers on Smith—Macpherson, Haldane, Scott, Fay—similarly fail to identify *Amicus.*

On the other hand a number of writers, including James Bonar and John M. Lothian, imply or say that *Amicus* was the Earl of Buchan. And one writer, A. W. Currie, provides interesting evidence (*Notes and Queries,* July 1962, p. 269) that the reader might take as proof that *Amicus* was Francis Maseres.

It is impossible for us to discuss further the mystery surrounding the identity of Amicus. We shall content ourselves by saying that the question is still an open one.

NOTES

1. *The Collected Works of Dugald Stewart,* ed. by Sir William Hamilton, 10 vols. and supplementary vol. (Edinburgh: Constable, 1854-1860), X, p. 8.

2. Henry G. Graham, *Scottish Men of Letters of the Eighteenth Century* (London: Black, 1901) p. 150. At one of the meetings of the Select Society of Edinburgh, a club to which Smith belonged, Charles Townshend teased the members about being unable to speak English—though they could write it. Mischievously, he suggested they should use an interpreter. Some time later the Society set up a committee to promote "the reading and speaking of the English language in Scotland." See William L. Mathieson, *The Awakening of Scotland* (Glasgow: Maclehose, 1910), pp. 201-202.

3. Mathieson, p. 203.

4. This remark was made by Samuel Johnson. Quoted by John De Lancey Ferguson, *Pride and Passion, Robert Burns* (New York: Oxford University Press, 1939), p. 31.

5. David Kettler is surely extreme and inaccurate, however, when in association with some complimentary remarks he declares that the period "produced no profound scholars and very few original thinkers." *The Social and Political Thought of Adam Ferguson* (Ohio

State University Press, 1965), p. 35. See also David Daiches, *The Paradox of Scottish Culture: The Eighteenth Century Experience* (London: Oxford University Press, 1964), Lecture III.

6. Alexander Fraser Tytler (Lord Woodhouselee), *Memoirs of the Life and Writings of the Honourable Henry Home of Kames*, 2 vols. (Edinburgh: Cadell and Davies, 2nd ed., 1814), I, p. 266.

7. The question of Smith's lectures is discussed at length by William R. Scott in *Adam Smith as Student and Professor* (Glasgow: Jackson, Glasgow University Publications, XLVI, 1937), Chapter V.

8. *Lectures on Rhetoric and Belles Lettres* (London: Nelson, 1963). An appreciative but critical review of Lothian's work, especially his Introduction to the volume, by Ernest C. Mossner, can be found in *Studies in Scottish Literature*, January 1965, pp. 199-208. Among other things Professor Mossner discusses the assumption that the lectures as delivered were copied down by a student (he believes the notes are "not all of a piece"), and the relationship between the Edinburgh and Glasgow lectures. Despite the difficulties that exist concerning these two matters, we shall assume in our references to the *Lectures* in the present essays that in general they reflect Smith's opinions, at least during the period involved.

9. *Life of Adam Smith* (London: Macmillan, 1895), pp. 32-34.

10. Did Smith's interest in rhetoric have methodological significance? Was this interest given expression not only in his lectures on the theme but in all of his thinking and writing—as an Italian scholar, Allesandro Giuliani, seems to believe? See the review, by Vincent M. Bevilacqua, of an article by Giuliani relating to the issue, *The Quarterly Journal of Speech*, December 1964, pp. 445-447.

11. The question involved here is discussed in Essay 2.

12. *18th-Century Scottish Books*, Catalogue of an Exhibition at the Signet Library, Edinburgh Festival of Britain, 1951 (Cambridge: Cambridge University Press, 1951), p. 79. Source of observation not given.

13. Nelson S. Bushwell states that the Preface marks the beginning of "reputable criticism" of Hamilton's work. *William Hamilton of Bangour* (Aberdeen: The University Press, 1957), p. 107. The "beginning" is represented by very few statements.

14. Tytler, p. 234. Not all persons spoke favorably of the review, however. One writer declared that the "specimen" Smith had given of the *Dictionary* was "dark and almost unintelligible." See Scott, p. 117. Further discussion of Smith's review will be found in Essay 4.

15. The letter is reproduced in *The Economic Journal*, March 1896, pp. 165-166.

16. *The Essays of Adam Smith*, ed. by Joseph Black and James Hutton (London: Murray, 1869). In the "Advertisement by the Edi-

tors" in this volume there is the following remark about Smith: "It is long since he found it necessary to abandon that plan as far too extensive." According to the letter referred to in the previous footnote, however, Smith still had such a plan in mind in 1785.

17. This bit of information is supplied by William R. Scott, in a posthumously published discussion of Smith. See *Proceedings of the British Academy, 1940* (London: Milford), p. 274.

18. The letter is reprinted in the *Works of Henry, Lord Brougham, 10 vols.* (London and Glasgow: Griffin, 1855-1857), I (*Lives of Philosophers of the Time of George III*), pp. 286-287.

19. *A History of Economic Thought* (New York: McGraw-Hill, 1960), pp. 51-56. More recently Andrew S. Skinner has given extended attention to Smith's essay on astronomy, with special reference to the great economist's "method," in his article on "Adam Smith: Philosophy and Science," in the *Scottish Journal of Political Economy*, November 1972, pp. 307-319.

20. *History of Economic Analysis* (New York: Oxford, 1954), p. 182.

21. Glenn R. Morrow, in *Adam Smith, 1776-1926* (Chicago: University of Chicago Press, 1928), p. 158.

22. *The Bee* (or *Literary Weekly Intelligencer*), June 8, 1791, p. 166. Buchan writes under the pen name *Ascanius*.

23. *A Journey Through England and Scotland To The Hebrides*, ed. by Sir Archibald Geikie, 2 vols. (Glasgow: Hopkins, 1907), 2, pp. 245-251.

24. Millar's letter is reprinted in Scott, *Adam Smith as Student and Professor,* pp. 311-313.

25. *Portraits by Sir Joshua Reynolds,* ed. by Frederick W. Hilles (New York: McGraw-Hill, 1952), pp. 174-175.

26. Frederick W. Hilles, *The Literary Career of Sir Joshua Reynolds* (New York: Macmillan, 1936), pp. 17, 20-21. Hilles refers to, and agrees with, G. L. Greenway's view on the matter.

27. Rae, p. 214. Rae looks upon Smith's essay as "one of the most finished pieces of work he ever did."

28. Stewart refers a number of times to Smith's remarkable memory. See pp. 6, 47, 77.

29. Scott, p. 40.

30. Rae, pp. 23, 333. The actual words quoted are from Rae, who obtained his information from Stewart (p. 311).

31. *An Inquiry into the Nature and Causes of The Wealth of Nations,* ed. by Edwin Cannan, Modern Library (New York: Random House, 1937) p. 748. Smith recommended the same policy for painting, poetry, music, and dancing, the object being to aid in the correction of "whatever was unsocial and disagreeably rigorous in the morals

of the little sects" found in the country. For a detailed account of the Glassgow playhouse episode and for a discussion of Smith's views on the French theaters, see Rae, pp. 79-83, 210-214.

32. *The Essays of Adam Smith*, pp. 420-422. See also Rae, pp. 214-215.

33. The conversation with *Amicus*, along with an editorial introduction, was printed in *The Bee*, May 11, 1791, pp. 1-8. For a brief discussion of the identity of *Amicus*, see the Appendix to the present essay.

34. Rae, p. 34. See also Stewart, pp. 48-49.

35. *Boswell's Life of Johnson*, ed. by George B. Hill, revised and enlarged edition by Lawrence F. Powell, 6 vols. (Oxford at the Clarendon Press, 1934-50), I, pp. 427-428. This set of books includes not only Boswell's *Life* but his *Tour of the Hebrides* (which we shall have occasion to use later) and Johnson's *Journey into North Wales*. Hereinafter references to, and quotations from, these volumes will be identified by the designation HP, or Hill-Powell.

36. *Johnsoniana*, ed. by John Wilson Croker (Philadelphia: Carey and Hart, 1842), p. 241. The statement is from William Seward's *Anecdotes*.

37. See Robert Halsband's article, "A Parody of Thomas Gray," in the *Philological Quarterly*, July 1943, especially pp. 263-264.

38. In considering Smith's views as reported by *Amicus*, it would seem well to bear in mind an observation made by Dugald Stewart. Stewart (p. 78) declares that Smith's opinions on books and on speculative matters—hazarded "in the thoughtlessness and confidence of his social hours"—were "liable to be influenced by accidental circumstances, and by the humour of the moment, and when retailed by those who only saw him occasionally, suggested false and contradictory ideas of his real sentiments." But even at such times, "there was always much truth as well as ingenuity in his remarks."

39. *The Dictionary of National Biography*, article on Adam Smith.

40. *Autobiography of the Rev. Dr. Alexander Carlyle* (Boston: Ticknor and Fields, 1861), p. 230.

41. *The Bee*, June 8, 1791, p. 166.

42. *The European Magazine*, August 1791, p. 133.

43. *Wordsworth's Prefaces and Essays on Poetry*, ed. by A. J. George (Boston: Heath, 1892), p. 73.

44. For a more detailed discussion of the issue here presented, see Paul M. Zall's article in the *Bulletin of the New York Public Library*, April 1966, pp. 265-269.

45. *Studies in Scottish Literature*, January 1965, p. 208.

46. Zall, p. 265, deeclares that Wordsworth's remark "must of course be read in the context of his running battle with *The Edin-*

burgh Review." For a brief account of this "battle," see George Mc-Lean Harper, *William Wordsworth,* 2 vols. (London: Murray, 1916), II, pp. 134-141, 240-243.

47. R. L. Brett, *The Third Earl of Shaftsbury* (London: Hutchinson's University Library, 1951) p. 213; Northrop Frye, *The Well-Tempered Critic* (Bloomington: Indiana University Press, 1963), p. 94.

48. *The Bee,* June 8, 1791, p. 165; *The Wealth of Nations,* ed. by John Ramsay McCulloch (Edinburgh: Black, new ed., 1870), p. xvii. McCulloch quotes Smith's statement from William Smellie's *Literary and Characteristical Lives.*

49. *A Catalogue of the Library of Adam Smith* (London: Macmillan, 1894) pp. viii, xxviii. A small number of miscellaneous volumes, mainly biographical in nature, were left out of the calculation. Less than half the books included in this survey are in English. In the 1932 edition of his *Catalogue* (p. xxxiii) Bonar omits the "one fifth" fraction noted in the text and to the subjects mentioned above he adds Language, Biography, and Travels.

50. Hiroshi Mizuta, *Adam Smith's Library,* "A Supplement to Bonar's Catalogue with a Checklist of the Whole Library" (Cambridge at the University Press, 1967).

51. Rae mentions a number of Smith's books in each of the categories, however. Though Smith apparently did not have any of Samuel Richardson's novels in his library, he briefly alludes to him in *The Theory of Moral Sentiments,* p. 124.

52. For a discussion of these clubs see Rae, Chapters VII, VIII and pp. 267-268, 334-338, 375-377; and the article by J. F. Bell on "Adam Smith, Clubman" in the *Scottish Journal of Political Economy,* June 1960, pp. 108-116.

53. Samuel Smiles, *Lives of Boulton and Watt* (London: Murray, 1865) p. 112. Rae, pp. 98-99, declares that Watt was probably wrong in including religion among the topics discussed.

54. See David Murray, *Robert and Andrew Foulis and the Glasgow Press* (Glasgow: Maclehose, 1913), p. 38.

55. *The Tables Turned* (London: Macmillan, 1931) p. 31. To what extent Smith's interest in literature was "pure" it is difficult to say. According to Dugald Stewart (p. 48), Smith's "taste for the Fine Arts" was probably associated very significantly with an ulterior purpose—the usefulness of the arts in connection with the examination of "the general principles of the human mind." Stewart's view seems rather extreme. He does say, however, that Smith was "by no means without sensibility" to the beauties of the fine arts.

2.

Adam Smith and the Poets

A well-written poem may last as long as the world.
—ADAM SMITH

The relationship between economists and poetry is closer than that between economics and poetry. The reason is simple. Economists are interested not only in the production, distribution, and consumption of wealth—not only in the "study of mankind in the ordinary business of life"—not only in the allocation of scarce resources, and their full employment—not only in the algebraic and geometrical characteristics of various types of equilibria. They are interested, as ordinary human beings, in a great variety of non-economic matters. Among some economists these other matters include poetry.

A few economists occassionally quote poetry in their writings. This practice will probably become still less common as quantification continues its steady progress and as the language of economics continues to shift from words to equations and graphs. Some economists write poetry. Very little of this work, however, meets the public eye. A few economists though have written poetry for publication. By way of illustration one can mention Stephen Leacock's slender volume *The Hellements of Hickonomics,* and Kenneth Boulding's clever verses at the beginning of the chapters in his *Principles of Economic Policy.* Going back more

33

than two and a half centuries (and using the term "economist" in a very flexible manner) one can add "the lively and humorous, though coarse and rustic eloquence of Dr. Mandeville" (TMS, p. 273), as exhibited in "The Fable of the Bees." In the prose writing of some economists, including Adam Smith, there are sentences and paragraphs that read like poetry.

On the relationship between economics and poetry, the poets seem to have nothing to say, and the economists almost nothing. A book has been written (by Scott Buchanan) on *Poetry and Mathematics,* another has been written (by Thomas Woods) on *Poetry and Philosophy,* and at least two have been written (by M. J. Adler and C. W. Bowra) on *Poetry and Politics.* But no book entitled *Poetry and Economics* has so far appeared, nor is any such book likely to appear. The fact of the matter is that there is no *close* relationship between poetry and economics.

But if one looks carefully enough it is possible to detect at least a remote relationship. The two economists who are the best guides in this matter are Philip H. Wicksteed and Alec L. Macfie. The former, with his fascinating discussion of marginalism in its manifold aspects, suggests a principle that can be applied to poetic style—and to prose style as well. Long before Wicksteed's time, however, Jonathan Swift defined "style" in a way that points to the "marginal test," and in a way that would have met with Wicksteed's approval. The "true definition of a style," said Swift, is to have "proper words in proper places."[1]

The point Swift had in mind is well brought out in a comment made by a modern writer, A. C. Ward, on Thomas Gray's *Elegy Written in a Country Churchyard,* "The *Elegy,*" Ward declares, "is a triumph of poetic art and atmosphere: every word appears both inevitably right and in its inevitably right place."[2] No better general statement of the ideal-allocation principle, so dear to the heart of the economist, especially if he possesses neoclassical sympathies, could be made.

Under Swift's definition, and Gray's practice, there would be no wastage of words. In terms of effect there would be "equality at the margins of use." In poetry (as in economics), however, any such configuration of words (or productive resources), is based on a set of assumed tastes. If the tastes are not proper, if they are not ideal, then the allocation configuration that is based upon them is not ideal. To say, now, that we should go on to discuss the determinants of taste, indicates further the logical complexities of the issue we have raised.

Wicksteed placed the prophet and the poet on a higher level than the economist. The former "may regenerate the world without the economist, but the economist cannot regenerate it without them."[3] But still Wicksteed felt the economist had a contribution to make. "If he can give no strength he may save strength from being wasted." The tie that binds economics and poetry (poetic style), then, is their common interest in avoiding waste. In one case it is the waste of wealth, in the other the waste of words.

Among present-day economists, Professor Macfie, who obviously is keenly interested in poetry and has a fine knowledge of it, has had most to say on the "common interest" to which reference has just been made.[4] Macfie maintains that economy is not only a value but is "a universal aspect of human conduct." Included in human conduct is the production of literature. "It is an old canon of appreciation," Macfie states, "that in the highest power of poetry or prose no word can be added, no word taken away, without a sensible loss of power." This statement is very similar in its meaning to the one we quoted from Swift.

Difficulties arise in applying the concept of economy to the writing of poetry and prose, especially when one raises the issue of sound and sense, and of emphasis and meaning. But the general point of the preceding analysis is clear: there is a relationship between poetry and economics, however slight it may be.

Adam Smith did not develop this relationship. Had he been acquainted with the tools of marginal analysis perhaps he would have probed into the question. Exercising a little imagination, however, one can detect in his writings a faint glimmer of marginalism, and interestingly enough he applied the notion to poetry and painting. We "are said to do injustice to a poem or a picture,"

he declares (TMS, p. 240), "when we do not admire them
enough, and we are said to do them more than justice when we
admire them too much." In these two situations one can notice,
in rather nebulous form, an element of "waste," which, as we
have observed, is so important a part of marginalism.

If we cannot say that the Father of Political Economy took us
very far into the relationship between economics and poetry, we
can at least say that he had a great interest in poetry and a very
wide knowledge of it. It is to that interest and to that knowledge
that we shall direct most of our attention in the present essay.

Nothing definite appears to be known about Smith's interest
in poetry previous to the time when, at the age of seventeen, he
began his studies at Oxford. It would seem likely, however, that
during his younger years such an interest existed. During his sojourn of somewhat more than six years at Balliol the study of
literature—English, French, Italian, Latin, and Greek—occupied
a great deal of his attention, and much of this literature was
poetry. Similarly, during the two years that elapsed between his
return from Oxford and the beginning of his public lectures in
Edinburgh he undoubtedly continued his study of literature. Certainly, if we may judge from his *Lectures on Rhetoric and Belles
Lettres* (as reported by a student in 1762-63 but supposedly much
the same as his lectures on the same general theme earlier at
Edinburgh), his knowledge of poetry at the time was quite wide.

In the preceding essay we noted that while he was giving his
lectures in Edinburgh, Smith presumably collected and edited the
poems of his friend, William Hamilton of Bangour. The poems
were published in 1748 by Robert and Andrew Foulis of Glasgow, under the title *Poems on Several Occasions*. Interestingly
enough, however, neither Hamilton's name nor Smith's name was
on the title page. The poems were reprinted in 1749, again without Hamilton's or Smith's name on the title page. In both print-
ings the Preface, which Smith supposedly wrote, is the same. In
1758 the poems were reissued in a new edition, this time however

with Hamilton's name attached. The Preface, though carried over from the earlier edition, still does not bear Smith's name. This edition has added to it a dedication of about one hundred and fifty words to William Craufurd (Crawford), which Smith again is supposed to have written. At the time this edition was under consideration Sir John Dalrymple suggested to Robert Foulis that Smith should write the Inscription to Crawford—"with all the eloquence & all the feelingness which he, above the rest of mankind, is able to express."[5] In 1760 a new and enlarged edition of the peoms was published, with Hamilton's name on the title page. The old Preface is now replaced by a note "To the Reader," which differs from the first Preface in length and especially in content.

In 1850 Hamilton's poems were reedited by James Patterson and published under the title *The Poems and Songs of William Hamilton of Bangour*. Patterson states that the Preface ("To the Reader") in the 1760 edition was written by David Rae, who later became Lord Eskgrove. He also says that the Preface to the first (1748) edition of Hamilton's poems was written by "the celebrated Dr. Adam Smith." Moreover, Patterson reproduces in his volume the Smith and Eskgrove Prefaces.

Did Smith (at the behest of some of the poet's other friends) initially collect the poems of Hamilton and write the Preface to the collection? Opinion on the question is somewhat divided. Leslie Stephen declares that Smith "probably" edited the poems; and C. R. Fay makes a cautious statement on Smith's having written the first Preface to the collection "If the ascription is correct."[6] A number of other writers, however, state positively that Smith edited the poems. At least some of these writers follow the lead of John Rae, the economist's biographer. Rae (pp. 39-41) in giving an affirmative answer to the question bases his judgment chiefly on manuscript information supplied by "the accurate and learned David Laing" though stating that Laing does not reveal the source of his facts. Professor N. S. Bushnell, in his study of Hamilton, agrees with Rae.[7] Bushnell, who also makes use of the Laing material, quotes a remark (set down by George Chalmers in 1794) that Andrew Lumisden had made in which he asserted

that Smith had written the Preface to the poems. Lumisden had
been a close friend of the poet and his statement, if recorded
accurately, would seem to be conclusive. This is how we shall
regard it. One cannot avoid expressing regret, however, that Smith
did not leave some record concerning the matter.

Early in his career Smith was interested in the work of William
Hamilton, now a largely forgotten poet. Late in his career he was
interested in the writing and economic well-being of another Scottish poet who was to achieve lasting renown. This was Robert
Burns.

The relationship between Smith and Burns, whose ages differed markedly, is a fascinating one. A condition of mutual esteem existed between the two men. In his letter of May 13, 1789,
to Robert Graham, the Scottish bard speaks of "that extraordinary
man, Smith" and, in reference to *The Wealth of Nations,* he declares that "I could not give any mere *man,* credit for half the
intelligence Mr. Smith discovers in his book."[8] Burns also thought
a great deal of *The Theory of Moral Sentiments.* When he turned
over a copy of this book to his friend, Robert Riddell, he stated
poetically in an inscription:

> Had I another friend more truly mine,
> More lov'd, more trusted, this had ne'er been thine.

Burns's acquaintance with *The Theory* goes back at least to
1783, for in September of that year he declared that "I entirely
agree with that judicious philosopher Mr. Smith in his excellent
Theory of Moral Sentiments, that Remorse is the most painful
sentiment that can embitter the human bosom."[9] To Burns the
remorse following actions for which one is himself responsible is
especially hard to bear ("with manly firmness") when, at the
same time, one has "a proper penitential sense of our misconduct." This situation calls forth "a glorious effort of self-command." It is interesting to note that in his *Theory of Moral Sentiments* Smith emphasized the importance of self-command.

Burns apparently held in very high regard an important personage in Smith's book, the so-called "impartial spectator." This imaginary being, who was characterized by the author in a variety of ways—"the great judge and arbiter of our conduct," "the great demigod within the breast," "the abstract and ideal spectator of our sentiments and conduct," and so on—played a highly significant part in Smith's system of morals. Professor Macfie ventures the opinion,[10] and it would seem to be a sound one, that certain lines from *The Theory*—"If we saw ourselves in the light in which others see us, or in which they would see us if they knew all, a reformation would generally be unavoidable"—must surely have inspired Robert Burns's famous words:

> O wad some Pow'r the giftie gie us
> To see oursels as others see us!

If Burns was interested in Smith and his writings, the great economist and moral philosopher was interested in the young Scotsman and in his future as a poet. This fact is clearly brought out in a letter, dated March 29, 1787, that Burns received from his good friend Mrs. Dunlap.[11] In her letter Mrs. Dunlap states that Smith, who "has through life been a friend to unfriended merit," thought that a position as Salt Officer might be obtained for Burns (whose plans for employment at the time were uncertain). Moreover, she refers to Smith's efforts to bring Burns's name before the public in Edinburgh, when his book of poems was published. Mrs. Dunlop also declares that her son had said that according to what he had heard, Smith was the person who was taking the most interest in the poet's future—"wishing to procure you leizure to write," she tells Burns in her letter, "which he said was all you wanted to insure your figure and fortune."

Though the old economist and the young poet held each other in high esteem, they did not meet, a fact that seems a little strange. In 1786 the Kilmarnock edition of Burns's poems, previously referred to, had been published, and fame came rapidly to him. In the latter part of the year he went to Edinburgh where he was acclaimed, and where he met such men as Lord Monboddo, Wil-

liam Robertson, Hugh Blair, Dugald Stewart, and Adam Ferguson. (He also met persons of less renown but of more jovial spirits,
whose company he particularly enjoyed.) Burns visited Edinburgh
again in 1781 and 1788. Early in the former year he went to call
on Smith, bearing an introduction from Mrs. Dunlop, but he was
not at home. A very ill man, Smith had left for London to seek
medical attention from Dr. William Hunter, whose lectures he,
with his friend Edward Gibbon, had attended back in the 1770s.
It is unfortunate that Burns had not made additional attempts to
meet Smith, when his famous countryman was at home. Smith
was ill these years but, in light of Mrs. Dunlop's letter concerning his keen interest in Burns's book of poems, would undoubtedly
have been glad to see him. The young poet, it would seem, was
guilty of negligence.[12]

There was another Scottish poet in whom Smith was person-
ally interested. This was William Wilkie, whose *Epigoniad* was
published in 1759, and whose *Fables* appeared in 1768. Smith
had both of these books in his library. Though David Hume spoke
highly of Wilkie's achievements as a poet, this view was not
widely shared. Certainly there was no solid basis for his being
referred to as "the Scottish Homer." Wilkie was a member of the
Edinburgh group of celebrities, and Rae (p. 102) tells us that
Smith had a special fondness for him. He was an eccentric person and a lively conversationalist. Interestingly enough, Wilkie
has been compared to a most notable person of whom Smith was
not especially fond, namely Samuel Johnson.[13] No evidence exists
concerning Smith's opinion of Wilkie as a poet; the likelihood is,
however, that his fondness for the man was greater than his fondness for the poet.

Following the time of Smith's early interest in William Hamilton and the delivery of his public lectures in Edinburgh, a period
of four decades in the great economist's life was to pass. During
these years his continuing interest in poetry was manifested in a
variety of ways and places: in his lectures at the University of
Glasgow, especially those on rhetoric and belles lettres; in his
"letter" on the prevailing condition of European literature, in the

Edinburgh Review; in his *Theory of Moral Sentiments,* first published in 1759; in a number of his essays, especially those on "The Imitative Arts," "The Affinity Between Certain English and Italian Verses," and "The Affinity Between Music, Dancing, and Poetry." From 1767, when he returned to Kirkcaldy after a sojourn in Europe as tutor to the young Duke of Buccleuch and a six months' stay in London, until 1776 Smith worked intensively on his *Wealth of Nations.* During these years he probably gave less attention to poetry than he had given to it previous to this period, and as he was to give to it after the period was over. His great treatise itself contains few direct references to poetry. Because of the subject matter of the work, this is not surprising. However, for one who was well aware of the fact that the wealth of a nation is not the same as the welfare of a nation (though contributing very substantially to it), Smith might have said a bit more about poets and poetry. He was not averse to making digressions, and he could well have departed from the main path of his discourse to consider such matters as the relationship between poetry and the well-being of the people, the economics of poetry publication, and the connection between wealth or poverty and the writing of poetry. He could also have made more allusions to poetry, and also used a few quotations from the poets—including Goldsmith's lines about the land "where wealth accumulates, and men decay."

But Smith, covering an immense range of knowledge in his book and dealing with a vast quantity of materials, apparently felt that all this was not necessary. However, it seems safe to assume that though the decade preceding the publication of *The Wealth of Nations* was a period of highly concentrated effort, the author found some time during these years to devote to poetry.

One of the reasons for making such an assumption is the fact that in his personal library Smith had a great many books on and about poetry. These books were in a number of languages: English, French, Italian, Latin, and Greek. Such well-known English poets as Butler, Chaucer, Dryden, Goldsmith, Gray, Milton, and Pope are represented; in some instances by numerous volumes. Still other poets, of varying degrees of prominence, are also represented. Among the latter are Akenside, Cowley, Dyer, Logan, Lyttleton, Parnell, Prior, Thomson, and Waller. Included too in Smith's library were several collections of poems, among which were a six-volume set edited by Robert Dodsley, and Thomas Percy's *Reliques of Ancient English Poetry.* Smith was interested, of course, in the poetry of his native Scotland, and had books of poetry by individual Scottish authors as well as collections of Scottish ballads.

The relationship between music and poetry interested Smith, as one would gather from his essay on "The Imitative Arts," as well as from his essay fragment on "The Affinity Between Music, Dancing, and Poetry" (which might have been planned as part of the former essay). This fact is also borne out by the presence in the great economist's library of a number of books on poetry and music, including John Brown's *Dissertation on the Rise, Union, and Power of Poetry and Music,* and François Jean Chastellux's *Essai sur l'union de la Poésie et de la Musique.* His library also contained Jean-Baptiste Du Bos' *Réflexions critiques sur la Poésie et sur la Peintre,* and William Hayley's *Poems and Painting.* It is obvious that Smith approached poetry not as an independent art but as one related to such other arts as music, painting, and dancing.

The number of French, Italian, Latin, and Greek poets represented in Smith's collection of books was large. Not only did such famous writers as Dante and Tasso and Homer find a place on his bookshelves but a great many more. Indeed, poetry books constituted a very sizable portion of the foreign-language volumes in his library.

Though Smith worked very diligently on his *Wealth of Nations* during the ten years preceding the book's publication, there is every reason for believing that for mental relaxation he often turned to the poets. That his interest in poetry and the poets was at a high level after his classic was finished is suggested by the many vigorous observations he made to *Amicus* in 1780. During the more leisurely years he served as Commissioner of Customs at Edinburgh (1778-1790), he must have spent many of his spare hours with his poetry books. In fact, during this period he added to the size of his collection of books on poetry.

In addition to expressing opinions on individual poets, some of which we noted in the previous essay, Smith discussed a variety of issues relating to poets in general and to poetry itself. Some of his observations may be noted.

Our author makes an interesting distinction between mathematicians and natural philosophers on the one hand and poets and "fine" prose writers on the other (TMS, p. 112).[14] The distinction is based on the different degrees of independence of the two groups to the force of public opinion. The members of the first group, in order to build up their own reputation or to lower the reputation of their rivals, are under no strong temptation to form "factions or cabals."[15] It is different with those in the second group. They are very likely, says Smith, to divide themselves into factions, "each cabal being often avowedly, and almost always secretly, the mortal enemy of the reputation of every other, and employing all the mean arts of intrigue and solicitation to preoccupy the public opinion in favour of the works of its own members, and against those of its enemies and rivals." In making this point Smith gives examples from France and Britain. While it seems that there are still cabals among poets today, it would appear that the intrigues and solicitations in which they engage are not as extensive as they were in the eighteenth century.

Despite the danger of cabals among poets, Adam Smtih was strongly "for" poetry. It was his belief, indeed, that the government (toward which he exhibited no small amount of distrust) should help to promote poetry (WN, p. 748). In this case, however, the nature of the help was negative. It involved the granting of "entire liberty" to all those persons who, acting out of self-interest, would endeavor, "without scandal or indecency," to provide amusement and diversion for the people. The forms of this amusement and diversion included not only poetry but painting, music, dancing, and all kinds of dramatic productions. It was Smith's belief that these diversions, along with the study of science and philosophy—which the state could make "almost universal among all people of middling or more than middling rank and fortune"—would correct "whatever was unsocial or disagreeably rigorous in the morals of all the little sects into which the country was divided." The sects Smith had in mind were the small religious sects of the day, which were characterized by frenzy, superstition, and "enthusiasm." Apart from dramatic presentations, the author does not mention the forms in which the self-seeking promoters of poetry would "market" their wares, but he might have had in mind such practices as the singing of ballads, of which Scotland possessed many, or the recital of narrative poems.

In the presentation of poetry and the other forms of amusement and diversion to the public, Smith felt that "scandal and indecency" should be ruled out. On a lower level of undesirability he would also have probably excluded the very ordinary, the improper, the impolite. The ideal of "polite" poetry, and of "polite" culture in general appealed to him,[16] a fact that is suggested by some remarks he made to *Amicus* in 1780. In discussing Allan Ramsay and his play, *The Gentle Shepherd,* a play that did not arouse his enthusiasm, Smith declared that "It is the duty of a poet to write like a gentleman." He said he disliked "that homely style which some think fit to call the language of nature and simplicity, and so forth." Bishop Percy's famous *Reliques of Ancient English Poetry* also came in for criticism: "a few tolerable pieces are buried under a heap of rubbish."[17] One wonders what Smith would have thought of some of the poems that his young friend Robert Burns was later to produce.

Smith's predilection for polite poetry and culture, however, did not prevent him from occasionally using some very impolite terms himself. In *The Theory of Moral Sentiments* he uses some expressions as "impudent blockhead," "mere dialectical pedant," "empty coxcomb" (pp. 231, 257, 274). In *The Wealth of Nations,* in referring to legislators who are motivated by momentary considerations and not by general and permanent principles, he points to "that insidious and crafty animal, vulgarly called a statesman or politician"; he speaks of the "sneaking arts of underling tradesmen"; he refers to "the undiscerning eye of giddy ambition" (pp. 435, 460, 593).

Smith had some noteworthy observations to make on the influence of custom and fashion on poetic form or structure (TMS, pp. 171-174). According to the ancient rhetoricians, we are told, appropriateness in verse form was determined by the predominant "character, sentiment, or passion" to be expressed. But modern experience contradicts this seemingly sound rule. For example, what is burlesque verse in English, he says, turns out to be heroic verse in French, and the burlesque verse in French is closely similar to ten-syllable heroic verse in English. This general condition, according to Smith, reflects the influence of custom.

But in the arts, "eminent" persons can exert a profound influence; they can introduce new fashions into writing, music, and architecture. Not only are the merits of these artists imitated but their weaknesses as well. "After the praise of refining the taste of a nation," Smith asserts, "the highest eulogy, perhaps, which can be bestowed upon any author, is to say, that he corrupted it." In his own age—the eighteenth century—Pope and Swift introduced new styles into rhythmic poetry, which produced profound effects. Swift's plainness superseded Butler's quaintness, and "The rambling freedom of Dryden, and the correct but often tedious and prosaic languor of Addison" gave way as objects of imitation to the long verses currently being written "after the manner of the nervous precision of Mr. Pope."

In general, while recognizing the very significant influence of custom over "the productions of the arts," including poetry, Smith felt that the force of custom could be lessened. Great writers, for example, such as those just mentioned, could set out in new directions, they could introduce new forms and practices into their art. In Smith's opinion this was a desirable situation, as long as it occurred within the limits of propriety.

With his strong interest in poetry, it would not be strange if Smith had tried to express himself in that medium. A number of

writers have stated that this was indeed the case. In his satire entitled *Hypocricy,* published in 1812, Charles Caleb Colton alludes
to Smith's poetical efforts and the failure that attended them.

> Unused am I the muse's path to tread,
> And cursed with *Adam's* unpoetic head;
> Who, though, the pen he wielded in his hand
> Ordained the "wealth of nations" to command,
> Yet, when on Helicon he dared to draw,
> His draft returned, and unaccepted saw
> If then, like him, we woo the Nine in vain,
> Like him we'll strive some humbler prize to gain.

Colton does not tell us the source of his information about
Smith's poetical ambitions, and one may wonder about the truth
of his contention. It seems strange that none of Smith's intimate
friends, including Dugald Stewart, says anything about his efforts
at writing poetry.

There are one or two places, however, where Colton may have
learned about the great economist's "unpoetic head." In his conversation in 1780 with *Amicus,* to whom reference has already
been made, Smith declared, so we are told, that "I myself, even I,
who never could find a single rhyme in my life, could make blank
verse as fast as I could speak." This statement, if true, not only
points to the great economist's adeptness in composing blank verse
but implies that he had attempted to write poetry that rhymes—
the kind that Colton must have had in mind.[18] Again, there is
Smith's view that the writing of Latin verse was not a major
undertaking. In his *Theory of Moral Sentiments* (p. 221) he refers
to Jean de Santeuil (an acquaintance, he tells us, of Nicholas
Boileau, "the great French poet") as one who wrote Latin verses
"and who, on account of that school-boy accomplishment, had the
weakness to fancy himself a poet." Smith had been a very capable
schoolboy, and it would appear from this statement that he at
least had the ability to write Latin verses.

Under any circumstances, none of Smith's poetry, whether of
the rhyming variety or of the blank-verse type, has survived. Peri-

odically, and after many years, notes taken by Smith's students of lectures he delivered have been unearthed and published. It seems unlikely, however, that any of his poetical contributions will yield either to chance discovery or diligent research.

That Smith possessed, to some degree, the temperament of a poet is suggested by certain aspects of his style of writing, particularly his use of similes and metaphors. Here reference is made to those figures of speech that are easily recognizd as similes or metaphors, not to those that have become an inseparable, unrecognizable part of ordinary language—"fossilized poetry," they have frequently been called.[19] Though Smith declared, in his *Lectures on Rhetoric and Belles Lettres* (p. 29), that simplicity in style was highly desirable—"the most beautiful passages are generally the most simple"—he did not feel that simplicity ruled out the use of figurative language. But the latter had to serve a useful purpose. Metaphors, for example, had to add not only verbal strength to whatever was being described but do it in a more striking and interesting fashion. If this is not the case, the metaphors "carry us to bombast on the one hand, or into burlesque on the other" (p. 26).

The most famous of our author's metaphors is his allusion to "the invisible hand," found in both of his books. Smith had a certain liking for "invisible" and uses the word in a number of connections in his various writings. In addition to speaking of "the invisible hand" he uses such expressions as "the invisible Power," "a chain of invisible objects," "the invisible hand of Jupiter," and "invisible features."

Our author found the mundane subject of money and banking well suited to metaphorical expression. In *The Wealth of Nations* (p. 305) he states that the judicious operation of the banking system provides "a sort of waggon-way through the air," thereby contributing to the national wealth. But, continuing in his metaphorical mood, he points to the danger of having commerce and industry suspended—"as it were"—"upon the Daedalian wings of paper money." At another point (p. 517) he speaks of the work of the mint as being "somewhat like the web of Penelope." In less picturesque language he refers on a number of occasions to money as "the great wheel of circulation," and to part of the money in a bank's coffers as resembling a "water pond," with a "stream" running into it and one out of it.

Smith's use of figurative language is well brought out in the many terms he adopts in his *Theory of Moral Sentiments* for the Deity and the "impartial spectator." For the former he uses such expressions as "the Author of nature," "the great Judge of hearts," "the great Director of the universe," "the great Physician of nature," and the "all-wise Architect and Conductor" (pp. 85, 96, 209, 255). For the "impartial spectator" he introduces such alternative terms as "this demigod within the breast," "the great judge and arbiter of our conduct," "the man within the breast," "the abstract and ideal spectator of our sentiments and conduct," and "that equitable judge" (pp. 115, 120, 134, 202).[20] In his *Theory* Smith shows a certain fondness for using the word "machine" in a metaphorical sense. He speaks of "the great machine of the universe" (a popular notion of the time), he alludes to "the wheels of the political machine," he refers to human society as "an immense machine" (pp. 19, 163, 280).[21] Our author uses the word "system" in a similar fashion, including "the great system of the universe" (pp. 210, 245). He also speaks of the "love of system"—of "the same regard to the beauty of order, of art and contrivance," and of "the spirit of system" (pp. 163, 164). Smith emphasized the great importance that man, in his thinking, attaches to well-contrived "machines" and "systems"; to means— beautiful, orderly, harmonious, regular, fit—as distinct from ends. This preoccupation with "machines" and "systems," however, can sometimes lead one astray.[22]

It might be added that though the Deity and the impartial spectator, with their various descriptive titles, are not found in *The Wealth of Nations,* the "machine" (especially in the form of "machinery") is. The word is always used in a nonmetaphorical sense, however.

In his use of figurative language Smith sometimes links a number of figures together. Thus in his *Theory of Moral Sentiments*

(p. 79) he speaks of human society as a building, of beneficence as the ornament that embellishes the building, and of justice as "the main pillar that upholds the whole edifice." In another part of the *Theory* (p. 280), where he makes use of the "machine" concept, he compares human society to "an immense machine," virtue to "the fine polish to the wheels of society," and vice to "vile rust" which makes the wheels "jar and grate upon one another."

Many of Smith's figurative expressions, however, exist singly, with the individual figures exhibiting great variation. For example, in his *Theory* he speaks of "that feeble spark of benevolence" (p. 120); of "the great school of self-command" (p. 126); of "Time, the great and universal comforter" (p. 131); of "enormous and operose machines," in referring to power and riches (p. 161).

Not all of Smith's figurative language is fresh and poetical. His remark about the secretive person who "seems, as it were, to build a wall about his breast" (p. 301) is not especially clear and felicitous. Nor is his reference on the previous page to "the gates of his breast."

Smith's poetic temperament is suggested by a statement he makes in his *Theory* (p. 111) concerning poetry and prose. "Those men of letters," he declares, "who value themselves upon what is called fine writing in prose, approach somewhat to the sensibility of poets." Smith himself engaged in a great deal of fine writing. Not only does he use similes and metaphors and other figures of speech, but he employs additional stylistic techniques, especially in his *Theory of Moral Sentiments*. Frequently he makes contrasting and balancing statements. Very often he resorts to multiple terms and expressions, occasionally to excess. Sometimes, especially in his *Theory,* he presents very colorful character sketches. His descriptions of the prudent man and of the poor man's ambitious son are especially fascinating, but he has vivid portrayals of still other men.

It is possible that Smith's poetical temperament was reflected in his lectures, including those on rhetoric and belles lettres. John Millar, who was a close friend and colleague of Smith's, as well as a former student of his, describes the lectures our author gave when he was Professor of Logic. With Smith's approach and his lectures in mind, Millar declares that there is "no branch of literature more suited to youth at their first entrance upon philosophy than this, which lays hold of their taste and their feelings" (Stewart, p. 11). John M. Lothian (RBL, p. xvi) interprets Millar's remarks as implying that Smith "deliberately proposed to make an emotional rather than an intellectual appeal" to his students, "to stimulate their feelings and their aesthetic sense, rather than their powers of reasoning." This is possibly an extreme interpretation of the approach Smith used in these particular lectures, but on the whole the point Lothian makes seems well taken.

In directing so much of his attention to the taste and feelings of his students, Smith was using an essentially poetical technique. It need hardly be added that in his other lectures he stressed more "practical" considerations and gave a great deal of attention to the power of reasoning (including resort to common sense, a quality for which he himself is well known).

In concluding this part of our discussion it might be observed that a remark that was once made (rather unjustly) about Thomas Warton could be made with considerable justice about Adam Smith. "Tom Warton," a writer in *Blackwood's Magazine* declared, "was one of the finest fellows that ever breathed—and the gods had made him poetical, but not a poet."[23]

If one cannot find any samples of poetry composed by Smith, he can find poems in which the famous economist figures.[24] Caleb Colton's couplets have already been quoted, but these couplets are less familiar than the verse written by Dr. Barnard, Bishop of Derry. Dr. Barnard (described in Goldsmith's poem *Retaliation* as a man "who mix'd reason with pleasure, and wisdom with mirth") was one of the members of the famous Literary Club of London. On one occasion he and Samuel Johnson had discussed the question of whether or not a person over forty-five years of age could achieve improvement in himself. Johnson thought he could, but was rather uncivil in presenting his case. It was out of this "pretty smart altercation," as Boswell calls it, that Dr. Barnard's poem grew.[25] The eighth stanza of the poem, which includes the names of some of the most celebrated members of The Club, is as follows:

If I have thoughts and can't express 'em
Gibbon shall teach me how to dress 'em
   In terms select and terse;
Jones teach me modesty—and Greek;
Smith how to think; Burke how to speak,
   And Beauclerk to converse.

The relationship between Robert Burns and Adam Smith has already been commented upon, and the likelihood that a key idea of Smith's was embodied in two of Burns's best-known lines was noted. The concept of an "impartial spectator" and the principle of sympathy play key roles in *The Theory of Moral Sentiments,* a book to which Burns alludes at least twice in poetical terms. When he turned over a copy of the *Theory* to one of his friends he wrote the couplet we quoted in our essay. Similarly, when he sent the same book and one by Thomas Reid to another friend, he wrote the following verse (from his epistle "To James Tennant of Glenconner"):

I've sent you here, by Johnie Simson,
Twa sage philosophers to glimpse on:
Smith wi' his sympathetic feeling,
An' Reid to common sense appealing.

Lord Sidmouth (Henry Addington) wrote a sonnet addressed to Smith, near the end of the great economist's life. Smith visited London in 1787, and on one occasion was entertained at dinner by William Pitt. Sidmouth was present and, as his biographer states, "It was probably on this occasion that Mr. Addington paid his poetical tribute to the merits of the great philosophical financier."[26] The tribute begins:

Oh! welcome thou! whose wise and patriot page
   The road to wealth and peace hath well defin'd.

As a famous son of the University of Glasgow and as one of the greatest Scotsmen of all time, Adam Smith has probably been mentioned and extolled in verse by a considerable number of his admiring countrymen (in addition to Robert Burns). Two examples can be given. In a sixty-verse poem on Glasgow, John Mayne (1759-1836) refers to Smith and to a number of other native celebrities.[27]

> Here great BUCHANAN learnt to scan
> The Verse that makes him mair than man!
> CULLEN and HUNTER here began
>   Their first probations;
> And SMITH, frae Glasgow, form'd his plan,
>   "The Wealth o' Nations!"

Like many thinkers (including such economists as Alfred Marshall and Wesley Mitchell, and such poets as Wordsworth and Tennyson) Adam Smith was fond of walking. And as he walked he was often, if not usually, immersed in deep thought. While at the University of Glasgow he often strolled in the garden of the University. David Murray suggested the possibility that it was there that he "thought out" his review of Samuel Johnson's *Dictionary*. At any rate, in 1801 a local poet wrote some *Elegiac Lines on an aged Elm, which fell in Glasgow College Garden, 1st Sept., 1799,* including the following lines:[28]

> Here view'dst thou (else unseen) the lonely walks
> Of Genius; inspiring thoughts sublime,
> By thy majestic form, till Fancy glow'd,
> And Science struck her diamonds from the mine—
> Saw'st Hutcheson, Smith, Reid, collect the gems
> That, sparkling bright, illuminate the age.

Wordsworth does not refer to Smith in his group of poems on Scotland, but in *The Prelude* he alludes (it would seem) to Smith's great classic. In the original version of the poem the words in the title of the book are used, but only the word "nation" is capitalized. In the revised poems, however, published about fifty years later, the actual title is adopted.[29]

> And having thus discerned how dire a thing
> Is worshipped in that idol proudly named
> "The Wealth of Nations," *where* alone that wealth
> Is lodged, and how increased . . . .

The influence of Adam Smith was far-reaching, and it is possible that reference to him and his works can be found in the poetry of numerous countries outside the British Isles. We know definitely that this is true in the case of Russia. In that country Smith's influence was early felt. Not only was *The Wealth of Nations* known in Russia in the latter part of the eighteenth century, but during the years 1802 to 1806 the treatise was translated into Russian. Moreover, among the foreign students attracted to Smith's classes at the University of Glasgow were two Russians who later became professors at the Imperial Moscow University, one of them doing a great deal to propagate Smith's economic ideas.[30] It is not exactly surprising, therefore, to find Alexander Pushkin referring to Smith in his famous play *Eugene Onegin*. Eugene was keenly interested in the Scottish economist, as we learn in verse 7 of Chapter (Canto) I:

> Homer, Theocritus disdaining,
> From Adam Smith he sought his training
> And was no mean economist;
> That is, he could present the gist
> Of how states prosper and stay healthy
> Without the benefit of gold,
> The secret being that, all told,
> The *basic staples* make them wealthy.
> His father failed to understand,
> And mortgaged the ancestral land.[31]

The Australian poet, Douglas B. W. Sladen, refers to Smith and his treatise in his poem, *Confessio Amantis, Amater: Amater:*

Mater;[32] and Stephen Leacock, the British-born Canadian economist and humorist, has a two-page poem on Smith, entitled "A
Resurrection of Adam Smith," in his *Hellements of Hickonomics.*

One final reference to "Adam Smith and Poetry" may be
noted. James Bonar declared that in the Revised Version of the
Bible the title of Smith's great work may have been used in the
new translation of the fifth verse, the sixtieth chapter of Isaiah.[33]
In a very extensive change from the Authorized Version, this
verse now reads: "The wealth of the nations shall come to thee."

NOTES

1. W. K. Wimsatt, Jr., *The Prose Style of Samuel Johnson* (New
Haven: Yale University Press, 1941), p. 1.
2. *Illustrated History of English Literature,* 3 vols. (London:
Longmans, Green, 1953-1955), 2, pp. 217-218.
3. *The Common Sense of Political Economy,* 2 vols. (London:
Routledge, 1933), I, pp. 123-124.
4. *An Essay on Economy and Value* (London: Macmillan, 1936)
pp. 46-74. Macfie discusses the principle of economy with reference
to all purposive activity in which the element of scarcity exists.
5. David Murray, *Robert and Andrew Foulis and the Glasgow
Press* (Glasgow: Maclehose, 1913), p. 52.
6. *The Dictionary of National Biography,* article on Smith;
Charles R. Fay, *Adam Smith and the Scotland of His Day* (Cambridge at the University Press, 1956), p. 21.
7. Rae, pp. 30, 39-41; Nelson S. Bushnell, *William Hamilton of
Bangour* (Aberdeen: The University Press, 1957), pp. 6, 53, 132. It
seems a little strange that Dugald Stewart makes no mention of
Hamilton's poems and the Preface that Smith supposedly wrote for
the collection.
8. *The Letters of Robert Burns,* ed. by John De Lancey Ferguson,
2 vols. (Oxford at the Clarendon Press, 1931), I, p. 335.
9. *Common Place Book* (Edinburgh: Privately Printed, 1872),
p. 7. Burns's statement, and an accompanying verse, can be found in
The Poems and Songs of Robert Burns, ed. by J. Kingsley, 3 vols.
(Oxford at the Clarendon Press, 1968), I, p. 37.
10. *The Individual in Society* (London: Allen & Unwin, 1967),
p. 66. Some years earlier James Bonar quoted both Smith's statement
and Burns's lines—the complete verse. See *Moral Sense* (New York:
Macmillan, 1930), p. 223.

11. *Robert Burns and Mrs. Dunlop,* ed. by William Wallace (London: Hodder and Stoughton, 1898), pp. 16-18.

12. Hans Hecht blames Burns: "Through his own negligence Burns failed to come into personal contact with Adam Smith." *Robert Burns* (Edinburgh: Hodge, Second revised ed., 1950), p. 109. A more charitable view will be found in John De Lancey Ferguson's *Pride and Passion, Robert Burns* (New York: Oxford University Press, 1939), p. 206.

13. See Alexander B. Grosart, *Robert Fergusson* (Edinburgh: Oliphant, Anderson & Ferrier, 1898), pp. 56, 63. See also *Dictionary of National Biography,* article on Wilkie.

14. Rae (p. 96) claims that it was Smith's impressions of Robin Simson, Professor of Mathematics at Glasgow and an upright, simple, and charming person, that formed the basis of his exhalted view of mathematicians.

15. At a later point in his discussion (p. 188) Smith seems to enlarge the area in which cabals are found. This time he speaks of their presence in the "superior arts and sciences," and in terms similar to but less strong than those he applied to the cabals mentioned above.

16. For a detailed discussion of "The Establishment of 'Polite' Culture" in Scotland, see David Craig's *Scottish Literature and the Scottish People* (London: Chatto & Windus, 1961), Chap. II.

17. *The Bee,* May 11, 1791, p. 6.

18. Rae (p. 34) declares that "Smith . . . seems to have had dreams of some day figuring as a poet himself." Thomas Seccombe, possibly drawing on Rae, goes even further by declaring positively that Smith "dreamed of becoming a poet himself." *The Age of Johnson* (London: Bell, 6th ed., revised, 1926), p. 89.

19. Isaac Goldberg, *The Wonder of Words* (New York: Appleton-Century, 1938), p. 94.

20 Smith really resorts to two main types of "spectators." First there is the spectator envisioned as external to yourself, and secondly there is you yourself—the internal spectator. The second type in turn takes two forms, one involving your imagination of how the external spectator would react to your actual or prospective behavior, and the other involving your own judgment—the judgment of "the man within your breast." These distinctions are made by Jacob Viner in his article on Smith in the *International Encyclopedia of the Social Sciences.* A. L. Macfie, who looks upon the introduction of the impartial-spectator concept as Smith's special contribution to ethical theory, carefully discusses this hypothetical personage in Essay 5 and on pp. 51-52 of his book, *The Individual in Society.* Referring to Smith's treatment of the impartial spectator, R. F. Brissenden remarks

that "This dynamic account of the social origins of conscience has a great deal in common with Freud's notion of the super-ego," a general point to which Professor D. D. Raphael earlier referred. *Texas Studies in Literature and Language,* Summer 1969, pp. 950, 951.

21. The machine concept has great significance in Smith's moral theory. He stressed the beauty, the fitness of "well contrived machines" in producing agreeable effects, in contrast to their products—a distinctly nonutilitarian notion. For a more detailed discussion of this point see Macfie, pp. 45-46, 56, 69.

22. See "Thought" No. 46 in Essay 7.

23. Quoted in Charles W. Moulton, *The Library of Literary Criticism,* 8 vols. (Buffalo: Moulton, 1901-1905), IV, p. 78.

24. James Bonar first brought a number of these verses together in his book *The Tables Turned* (London: Macmillan, 1931), p. 31.

25. The complete poem, and an account of the various versions of the altercation and of the poem's lines, will be found in *Boswell's Life of Johnson, Hill-Powell,* IV, pp. 115, 431-433.

26. From George Pellew, *The Life and Corespondence of the Right Hon. Henry Addington, First Viscount Sidmouth,* 3 vols. (London: Murray, 1847), I, p. 151. It was at this time that Smith said to Sidmouth (as the latter reported), "What an extraordinary man Pitt is —he makes me understand my own ideas better than before." It is not clear when Sidmouth actually composed his sonnet.

27. The complete poem can be found in *Glasgow, Ancient and Modern,* ed. by J. F. S. Gordon, 4 vols. (Glasgow: Tweed, 1872), I, pp. 28-33.

28. The lines are from (Alexander Molleson) *The Sweets of Society: A Poem, and A few Miscellaneous Poems,* and are quoted by David Murray in *Memories of the Old College of Glasgow* (Glasgow: Jackson, Wylie, Glasgow University Publications III, 1927), p. 417.

29. *Wordsworth's Prelude,* ed. by Ernest De Selincourt, Second ed. revised by Helen Darbishire (Oxford at the Clarendon Press, 1959) pp. 456, 457.

30. Most of the facts presented above are from Norman W. Taylor's article "Adam Smith's First Russian Disciple," in *The Slavonic and East European Review,* July 1967, pp. 425-438.

31. From the book *Eugene Onegin* by Alexander Pushkin. Translated with an introduction and notes by Walter Arndt. Dutton Paperback edition. Published by E. P. Dutton & Co., Inc., and reprinted with their permission.

32. See Charles W. Moulton, *The Library of Literary Criticism,* IV, p. 68.

33. *A Catalogue of the Library of Adam Smith* (London: Macmillan, 1932) p. 27.

3.

Adam Smith as Literary Stylist

He has been too much left to the economists, so that
that mysterious creature called the General Reader
has never realized how great a master of English style
he has missed in failing to read his Adam Smith.
—SIR ALEXANDER GRAY

Adam Smith's *Inquiry into the Nature and Causes of the Wealth
of Nations* has long been looked upon as the most outstanding
contribution to the literature of economics. But *The Wealth of
Nations* has also been regarded as a notable literary achievement,
and over the years glowing tributes have often been paid to it on
that score. In the middle of the last century Lord Brougham, for
example, in referring to Smith's classic declared that "There is not
a book of better English to be anywhere found." Furthermore,
said Brougham, "Besides its other perfections, it is one of the
most entertaining of books. There is no laying it down after you
begin to read."[1] A later observer, L. L. Price, expressed the view
that first among the claims of Smith's book to enduring fame he
would place its quality as "a piece of literary workmanship as well
as a scientific treatise."[2] And a still later commentator, Sir Alexander Gray, asserted that "it is no small matter that a masterpiece
of reasoning and thought should also be a masterpiece of literary
style."[3]

Smith's other book, *The Theory of Moral Sentiments,* has likewise been acclaimed for its literary style. Shortly after the publication of the book, Edmund Burke declared that Smith's language "is easy and spirited, and puts things before you in the fullest light; it is rather painting than writing."[4] Lord Brougham matches his lofty tribute to *The Wealth of Nations* with generous praise of *The Theory.* He speaks of "The admirable felicity, and the inexhaustible variety of the illustrations" in the book, and of "The beauty of the illustrations, and the eloquence of the diction" found in it. Smith's style, he further states, is "peculiarly good" and "his diction is always appropriate and expressive."[5] Professor James McCosh also spoke of the eloquence of the book's language (which explains why it "has commonly been a favorite with students").[6]

As examples of literary workmanship both books, however, have been subject to some criticism. Alexander Carlyle, who described *The Theory of Moral Sentiments* as "the pleasantest and most eloquent book on the subject," found *The Wealth of Nations* "tedious and full of repetition."[7] Charles Fox, we are told by a Miss Berry (whose statement was presented to the public by Harriet Martineau), "used to wonder that people could make such a fuss about that dullest of new books—Adam Smith's *Wealth of Nations.*"[8] And the young Stanley Jevons (aged twenty-two) thought that Smith's treatise was "perhaps one of the driest on the subject."[9]

Lord Brougham, Alexander Carlyle, and Professor McCosh all spoke admiringly of the eloquence of *The Theory of Moral Sentiments.* Another writer, however, John H. Millar, characterized the book as "the most distressing manifestation of 'eloquence' in the worst sense of the word."[10] Walter Bagehot, who, like Millar, pays tribute to the style and merit of *The Wealth of Nations,* stated that in *The Theory* there is "a certain showiness and an 'air of the professor trying to be fascinating,' which are not very agreeable."[11] A more recent writer feels that the rhetoric of the book—"so much admired in its day"—today "rather palls."[12]

Confronted with such a complexity of conflicting views concerning Smith's stature as a literary craftsman, one is inclined to ask (with Alexander Pope, one of the great economist's favorite poets) "Who shall decide when doctors disagree?" The proper answer in this case is, of course, "the individual reader himself."

On approaching Smith, however, particularly for the first time, the reader might be aided by having before him an analysis of background facts concerning Smith's style and of some of the writing practices our author followed. To such an analysis we shall now turn.

In writing his two books Smith was primarily concerned with content, but he was by no means indifferent to form. The matter of literary style was an issue to which he gave no small amount of attention, and it can safely be said that whatever stylistic virtues, or characteristics, his books possess, they were not wholly or even largely accidental attainments. To a very considerable degree they were the results of conscious endeavor.

The factors that determine or condition an author's style of writing may be placed in two categories, those that are activated by the author's own intentions and which exert their influence more or less directly, and those that are not consciously cultivated with any such purpose in view and which thus exert their influence indirectly. Both sets of factors were operative in Smith's case.

While he was a student at Oxford, Smith, according to Dugald Stewart (p. 8), used a technique for improving his style of writing that he often recommended to others: he frequently translated the works of continental writers, and especially French authors, into English. This practice unquestionably influenced his style, at the same time that it greatly broadened his knowledge of literature. It is interesting to note that the same general method for improving one's literary style was used by the Scottish historian and churchman, William Robertson, who was a friend of Smith's.[13] A related method was used by another one of Smith's friends, Edward Gibbon. The style of the *Decline and Fall of the Roman Empire* was greatly influenced by a long study of the best English, French, Latin, and Greek writers.[14]

Smith's general reading of the works of various authors undoubtedly had an effect on his literary style. No one has carefully probed into this matter, however, and little information on the question exists—a condition that, quite understandably, is in sharp contrast to that surounding the style of Smith's contemporary and acquaintance, Samuel Johnson. There is at least one writer, however, whose influence on Smith seems to have been definite. This is Conyers Middleton, the English divine, controversialist, and *Protobibliothecarius* at Trinity College, Cambridge. According to J. R. McCulloch, Smith looked upon the works of Middleton as representing the best examples of English prose. Furthermore, says McCulloch, he suggested a careful reading of Middleton's *Life of Cicero* "to all who wished to write easily, perspicuously, and in correct English."[15]

Dugald Stewart (p. 8) ventures the opinion that the effect of Smith's early liking for Greek geometry may be noticed "in the elementary clearness and fullness, bordering sometimes upon prolixity, with which he frequently states his political reasonings." This contention may well be true. Certainly Smith's works, particularly *The Wealth of Nations,* exhibit both clearness and fullness. Smith's youthful predilection for Greek geometry, however, did not lead to any use on his part of geometrical techniques in explaining economic behavior and processes. *That* would have been too much to expect from such an economic pioneer.

In his *Lectures on Rhetoric and Belles Lettres* (pp. 31, 36) Smith links up a writer's character and his literary style. "The style of an author," he says, "is generally of the same stamp as their character," and he uses Addison and Warburton as examples. In a little-known essay on Smith, entitled "An Old Master," Woodrow Wilson (who wrote long before the student's notes of Smith's lectures were discovered) makes a similar point with specific reference to the famous Scotsman. "The charm about the man consists," says Wilson, "for those who do not regard him with the special interest of the political economist, in his literary method, which exhibits his personality so attractively and makes his works so thoroughly his own, rather than in any facts about his eminency among Scotchmen."[16] Using a modicum of imagination, and some flexibility in terminology, a reader can see illustrated in Smith's style some of the personal characteristics that marked him as a man. The care with which he analyzed the topics he discusses suggests the attribute of patience; the great profusion of his illustrative material points to the immense breadth of his knowledge; the sharp expressions he sometimes uses indicate that he was quite capable of departing from his usual composed and mild temperament; the prolixity of his style in some parts of his analysis possibly reflects his proverbial absentmindedness, or at least his great powers of mental concentration. If Smith's personal characteristics were a "cause," leading to various effects on his style of writing, they were, of course, also an "effect," the result of a wide variety of still other influences.

In his writing Smith apparently tried, and with success, to avoid the use of Scotticisms. It would seem, however, that he did not go as far as James Beattie and David Hume in protecting himself against such a danger;[17] he did not make a list of Scotticisms to guard against. It was Sir James Mackintosh's belief that Smith handled the English language "with a freer hand and with more native ease than any other Scottish writer."[18]

Adam Smith was a slow, deliberate writer—he did not "dash off" his works with the speed that John Stuart Mill, for example, wrote his *Principles of Political Economy*. Dugald Stewart (p. 73) relates that shortly before his death, in 1790, Smith told him that despite all his practice he still wrote as slowly and with as much difficulty as he did originally.

The same fact is also well brought out in a letter Smith wrote to Thomas Cadell in March 1788, when he was working on a new edition of his *Theory of Moral Sentiments*. "I am a slow, very slow workman," he states, "who do and undo everything I write at least half a dozen times before I can be tolerably pleased with it."[19] From this letter it is clear that Smith's slowness in composition was due largely to intellectual fastidiousness. He set high standards for himself.

Some of Smith's writing was done longhand by himself. He wrote very legibly, as is clearly seen in the facsimiles contained in Professor Scott's scholarly study, *Adam Smith As Student and Professor.* James Bonar characterized the handwriting of Smith as "a large, bold, schoolboy hand."[20] A comparison of some of the samples of Smith's writing would seem to indicate that it became somewhat larger and bolder and more "schoolboyish" as he became older. (Compare, for example, his various signatures on p. 367 of Scott; or the copy of his resignation of the Snell Exhibition, 1749 with the copy of his letter of 1788 to Thomas Cadell or with his letter of 1789 to Henry Dundas—also in Scott, pp. 366, 374-378.) It is hazardous, however to generalize dogmatically on this matter.

For Smith the physical process of writing was slow, as one might surmise from the nature of his handwriting. This was probably one of the reasons why he made such extensive use of amanuenses. It may also have had something to do with his dislike for writing letters, as J. M. Keynes has suggested.[21]

Though Smith sometimes wrote in longhand, much of his writing took the form of dictation. When engaged in the process of composition, Dugald Stewart (p. 73) again informs us, Smith usually dictated to a secretary, at the same time walking back and forth in his apartment.

Did the practice of dictation, it might be asked, have any effect on the great economist's style of writing? It is possible that it did. Stewart, who contrasts Smith's practice with that of David Hume (whose works, Stewart had been assured, were written by hand), declares that "A critical reader may, I think, perceive in the different styles of these two classical writers, the effects of their different modes of study." J. R. McCulloch thought that Smith's method of composition might help to account for "that repetition and diffuseness of style which is so observable in both his books, but especially in the *Wealth of Nations.*"[22] (*The Theory of Moral Sentiments,* according to McCulloch, was not dictated, however.)

Another observer, Archibald Alison, author of *Essays on*

Taste, and who as a relatively young man had in 1790 received an inscribed complimentary copy of the sixth edition of *The Theory,* found a relationship between Smith's practice of dictation and the length of his sentences. The sentences in *The Wealth of Nations,* we are told, each have as "much" in them (as one might say) as the secretary or amanuensis could write down while Smith walked from one end of the room to the other—hence they are nearly all the same length![23] Mr. Alison, if he was reported correctly, could hardly have been serious in his remark. Smith's sentences vary a great deal in length. In the first chapter of *The Wealth of Nations,* for instance, they run from nine words to two hundred and fifty-eight words (the latter being the longest sentence in the book), and in between these extremes are sentences of widely varying lengths.

That walking, even within the narrow limits of one's home, can be conducive to thought and creative effort is demonstrated by Smith. Much, if not most, of *The Wealth of Nations* was composed (though not "researched") in this way. Smith's review of Samuel Johnson's *Dictionary of the English Language* was also composed as he walked, not in his house in this case but in the garden at the University of Glasgow.[24]

If much of *The Wealth of Nations* was actually composed as Smith walked back and forth in his study, there can be little doubt that some of the ideas found in the book flashed upon the author's inward eye as he strolled outside of his home. While working on his masterpiece at Kirkcaldy, Smith frequently went out for walks along the nearby coast. In a letter written in 1767 to David Hume he states that "My amusements are long solitary walks by the sea side."[25] On these strolls he may sometimes have been in vacant rather than in pensive mood, but it seems reasonable to assume that he was usually engaged in deep thought.

Before discussing some of the general characteristics of Smith's literary style, we shall note a few observations that Smith himself made on the question of style. In his lectures on rhetoric and belles lettres, both in Edinburgh and at the University of Glasgow, he had much to say about writing. He was keenly interested in improving the writing style of his students; to teach them, as Professor Lothian remarks in his Introduction to Smith's *Lectures on Rhetoric and Belles Lettres* (p. xvii), "to write a simple and direct style, without ornament."

In one of his *Lectures* (p. 38) Smith declares that there are four requisites for making a person a good writer: he must be well versed in his subjects, he must arrange his material in proper sequence, he must present his ideas in the most proper and expressive fashion. (Either Smith or the student who made the notes of Smith's lectures failed to include the fourth requirement.) In another lecture (p. 51) he points out that perfect style involves the expression of the author's thought in "the most concise, proper, and precise manner," and in the manner which best conveys to the reader "the sentiment, passion, or affection" that the author feels, or pretends he feels, as a result of his thoughts. In rhetorical fashion Smith then says to his students, "This, you'll say, is no more than common sense," and he answers "indeed it is no more."

Smith strongly emphasizes the importance of clarity—of "perspicuity"—in writing, and to this end he makes a number of specific suggestions (Lecture 2). He recommends the use of unambiguous expressions and of native, rather than foreign, words; he points to the desirability of placing words in their proper order, and of using "a natural order of expression" with no parentheses and unnecessary words; he feels that in general short sentences are preferable to long ones, though he recognizes certain dangers in the use of such sentences; he speaks against the excessive use of pronouns.

Another factor contributing to "perspecuity" is the avoidance, or at least the very moderate use, of ornamental or flowery language. Smith refers to the danger of such language, and points to Lord Shaftesbury as one who had fallen a victim to the danger. Ornamental language is "very apt to make one's style dark and perplexed," and the studious effect to vary the nature of given expressions often leads one "into a dungeon of metaphorical obscurity." Smith did not like the "pompous diction" Shaftesbury often used, and he felt that "When Shaftsbury is disposed to be in a rhapsody, it is always unbounded, over-violent, and unsupported by the appearance of reason" (pp. 5, 6, 56).

Earlier in our essay we spoke of content and form with reference to Smith's books. These two elements are not completely unrelated, as we shall see later. Smith was aware of this fact, though the proof of his awareness that we shall cite is of a somewhat different nature than what one might expect. In a harsh remark about Shaftesbury, he states (p. 54) that "As he was of no great depth in reasoning, he would be glad to set off by the ornament of language what was deficient in matter."

Though Smith made various suggestions in his lectures for improving one's style, he was of the opinion that any rules directed toward that end must be rather general in nature. He makes this point in a fascinating contrast he draws in his *Theory of Moral Sentiments* (p. 155 and also pp. 290-291) between the rules of justice and those of other virtues—prudence, charity, friendship, etc. The rules of the former he compares to the rules of grammar; those of the latter to "the rules which critics lay down for the attainment of what is sublime and elegant in composition." And then, using a number of stylistic practices with which *The Theory* abounds, he goes on to declare that "The one, are precise, accurate, and indispensable. The other, are loose, vague, and indeteminate, and present us rather with a general idea of the perfection we ought to aim at, than afford us any certain and infallible directions for acquiring it."

It wil be of interest to observe as we now consider some of the characteristics of his style that Smith did not always follow his own rules. What he taught by precept he did not always demonstrate by example.

In considering some of the features of Smith's style it is not to be assumed that these features were unique in any way. Our author lived in an age of "fine" writing, in an age when rhetorical expression was a recognized and honored art. In the general matter of literary style Smith reflected his times.

One of the general characteristics of Smith's style to which tribute has long been paid is the clarity with which he writes.

Gibbon, for example, spoke of *The Wealth of Nations* as containing "the most profound ideas expressed in the most perspicuous language."[26] Many years later Edwin R. A. Seligman stated that Smith's classic, in its external characteristics, "is both remarkably lucid and exceptionally interesting."[27]

Not all persons have shared the view of Gibbon and Seligman, however. William Cobbet found *The Wealth of Nations* not lucid but inscrutable (chiefly, it would seem, the parts relating to the Bank of England, taxation, and the national debt). Cobbett declared that he had read "the work of that old Scotch tax-gatherer Adam Smith" and that he "could make neither top nor tail of the thing."[28] Most readers would not share this extreme opinion.

Smith was interested in achieving clarity in his writing. But this purpose at times interfered with his rule that a writer should aim at conciseness. Where the two objectives were in conflict, Smith favored the former, that of clarity. As he himself stated in *The Wealth of Nations* (p. 29), "I am always willing to run some hazard of being tedious in order to be sure that I am perspicuous." He was aware of the danger involved, the danger of tiring his reader's patience, and on a number of occasions he writes in an apologetic or in an explanatory fashion to justify his action.[29] Smith did not always succeed in avoiding the hazard of tediousness. The most outstanding example is the sixty-five-page "Digression on Silver" found in *The Wealth of Nations.* But there are other instances in the same treatise in which the patience of the reader—the modern, general reader—is put to a very severe test. Among these instances is the latter part of the author's discussion of "Real and Nominal Price," much of his chapter on Money, and his very long chapter "The Sources of the General or Public Revenue of the Society." The general reader is justified in skimming over some substantial sections of *The Wealth of Nations,* and even omitting certain parts altogether. These are segments of the book that only the highly specialized economist can be expected to examine carefully.

But within the dull parts of the book one will sometimes find interesting and exciting statements. For example, the chapter on

Money contains some of Smith's finest metaphors. The reader runs the risk of missing such statements if his perusal of the book is excessively hasty. The same is true of significant generalizations, such as the author's famous Canons of Taxation, that are sometimes embodied in masses of detail.

Another outstanding feature of *The Wealth of Nations,* and also of *The Theory of Moral Sentiments,* is the immense amount of illustrative material the author uses. This feature too has long attracted the attention of observers. One of the early editors of Smith's economic classic, Edward Gibbon Wakefield, declares that the book "is full of pictures, like the Penny Magazines of our day." Moreover, he remarks, the author "is a teller of stories about political economy."[30] Thomas Brown thought that "In its minor details and illustrations," *The Theory of Moral Sentiments* "may be considered as presenting a model of philosophic beauty."[31]

Many of the illustrations used by Smith are historical in nature. In fact, there is so much history in general in *The Wealth of Nations* that Walter Bagehot described the book as "a very amusing book about old times."[32] The element of amusement in Smith's treatise is not substantial, though, as we shall see shortly, it is there; but the amount of material relating to old times is vast.

A great many of Smith's illustrations are historical in nature. There are also many, however, that relate to the contemporary world of the eighteenth century. In both types the illustrations are drawn from numerous fields of human knowledge. The same is true of the more general material found in the author's two books. Smith was a man of very wide learning. Nassau William Senior thought that in the scope and accuracy of his knowledge, the Scottish scholar was perhaps unequaled since Aristotle.[33] This is a great tribute to one living at a time when there were other outstanding giants of learning, men such as Johnson, Burke, and Gray.

In his writing, including his use of illustrations, Smith adopted a method of analysis that reflects his wide knowledge. This method involved an eclectic, philosophical-sociological-historical approach to problems. The method was not original with him, however;

though in his hands it reached a high point of development. The method was, and to some extent still is, characteristic of Scottish scholars. Indeed, it has been referred to as the Scottish method.[34] The use of this method, particularly in *The Wealth of Nations,* helps to account for the detail with which Smith analyzes various topics, at the same time that it explains the great breadth of his approach to these topics. In the author's economic classic the reader is taken not only into the area of economics but also into the areas of politics, geography, sociology, anthropology, philosophy, psychology, education, literature, and history (including religious and military history).

Smith had a very keen interest in history; and his attitude toward it went beyond mere respect. "It is rather reverence for antiquity," he says in one of his lectures (RBL, p. 59), "than any great regard for the beauty or usefulness of the thing itself which makes me mention the ancient divisions of rhetoric." Our author was not only interested in history but he had a keen historical imagination, which made it possible for him to place himself, as it were, in the midst of past events and in the company of, or in the place of, long-deceased persons. "We transport ourselves in fancy," he says in one of his historical references (TMS, p. 68), "to the scenes of those distant and forgotten adventures, and imagine ourselves acting the part of a Scipio or a Camillus, a Timoleon or an Aristides." This power of imagination is not strange, of course, in one whose moral theory rested so heavily on "sympathy" and on the concept of "the impartial spectator."

Smith's preoccupation with history, including its very early phases, helps to account for the great and at times tiresome length with which he deals with some of his topics, especially in *The Wealth of Nations.* One wonders, indeed, if he was not one of those Scottish scholars whom Sydney Smith had in mind when he made his irreverent remark about the propensity of Scotsmen to go back to the beginning of things and then recount events in detail.[35]

As we shall emphasize in Essay 7, dictionaries of quotations have usually done less than justice to Adam Smith. While our author cannot compete with Shakespeare and Pope and Johnson in making epigrammatic statements, nevertheless one can find no small number of statements of a "quotation" character in his two books. There is no need to repeat here, however, any of the epigrams that will be presented in Essays 7 and 8.

There is another important aspect of Smith's style, one that was discussed in Essay 2, namely his use of figurative language, including similes and metaphors. Such language, which we associated with Smith's poetic temperament, is common in both of his books.

Smith was a very serious writer, one not given to flippancy or levity. Yet, whether he intended it or not, there are elements of humor in his writings; and, as can be gathered from a number of statements made by several writers whom we have already quoted, Smithian scholars have sometimes pointed to this feature of his style. Walter Bagehot, as we noted a few pages back, referred to *The Wealth of Nations* as "a very amusing book about old times"; Lord Brougham applied the adjective "entertaining" to it, a word also used by Edward Gibbon Wakefield—Smith's book, said Wakefield, "entertains those even whom it does not instruct, and instructs others by means of entertaining them"; Professor Seligman referred to the "imperturbable good humour" of *The Wealth of Nations.* These expressions of opinion are rather strong, but there is some basis for them.

One can derive a certain amount of enjoyment out of the sharp statements Smith quite often makes about the members of certain groups in society, including monopolistic tradesmen and manufacturers.[36] His numerous observations on human behavior in general, including those in his fascinating character sketches in *The Theory of Moral Sentiments,* are sometimes entertaining. And one may even smile at some of his illustrations. In his *Theory* (pp. 16-17) Smith makes a number of observations concerning jokes and laughter—he is indisputably correct when, in one of his less profound observations, he says that "He who laughs at the same joke, and laughs along with me, cannot well deny the propriety of my laughter." As a further bit of testimony on the point, one might mention the fact, to be noted in Essay 7, that Smith is represented in at least two dictionaries of humorous quotations.

One does not ordinarily think of Smith as a man given to indignation, and yet the great economist was capable of being indignant both in his actions and in his writing. In his *Theory of Moral Sentiments* Smith emphasized the importance of self-command, but he felt that such an admirable human characteristic did not rule out "just" indignation; in fact, this characteristic embodies it. Just indignation, he tells us (p. 213), is "nothing but anger restrained and properly attempered to what the impartial spectator can enter into." Moreover, he states more positively (p. 216), "The want of proper indignation is a most essential defect in the manly character, and, upon many occasions, renders a man incapable of protecting either himself or his friends from insult and injustice."

That Smith could be indignant in his personal contact with others is obvious from his quarrel with Samuel Johnson, which will be discussed in the next essay. Indeed, it would seem that in this instance Smith went beyond "just" indignation: his anger was not restrained nor, it appears, would the impartial spectator have approved it. The examples of indignation (and of strong disapproval) found in his two books, however, are more moderate in tone though some of them might not have passed muster before "the great judge and arbiter of our conduct."

Smith's indignation as expressed in *The Wealth of Nations* and *The Theory of Moral Sentiments* takes the form of vigorous epithets and harsh statements. A variety of such utterances can be found in each of the books. In the former, the author refers to party pamphlets as "the wretched offspring of falsehood and venality" (p. 327); he speaks of "that insidious and crafty animal, vulgarly called a statesman or politician" (p. 435); he describes a notion as "silly" and a policy as "savage" (pp. 515, 600). In a milder fashion he speaks of "upstart greatness" (p. 672), of "upstart fortunes" (p. 854), and of "the undiscerning eye of giddy ambition" (p. 593). Some of Smith's strongest words, however, are aimed at two groups of persons. Merchants and manufacturers fare badly on occasion at his hands. He alludes to "the sneaking arts of underling tradesmen" (p. 460); he speaks of "the impertinent jealousy of merchants and manufacturers" and of their "mean rapacity," their "monopolizing spirit," their "interested sophistry" (pp. 460, 461); he points to certain laws which "the clamour of our merchants and manufacturers has extorted from the legislature, for the support of their own absurd and oppressive monopolies" (p. 612). Certain religious leaders or adherents are also castigated by Smith. He declared that some accounts relating to China have been composed by "stupid and lying missionaries" (p. 688); he attaches the principle, "no plunder, no pay," to the mendicant orders (p. 742); he speaks of "those contemptuous and arrogant airs which we so often meet with in the proud dignitaries of opulent and well-endowed churches" (p. 762). (Complimentary remarks are made about the members of the Presbyterian clergy who are "of small fortune.")

The indignant or harsh expressions in Smith's *Theory of Moral Sentiments* are probably not as severe as those in his great economic treatise, though some of them are by no means lacking in force. He speaks of "that impertinent and foolish thing called a man of fashion" (p. 58); of "some impudent blockhead" (p. 231); of "the empty coxcomb," "the silly liar," "the foolish plagiary" (p. 274). Philosophy and philosophers are the targets of some of Smith's verbal darts. He refers to "some splenetic philosophers" (p. 114); to "those whining and melancholy moralists" (p. 121); to "the ingenious sophistry" of Mandeville's reasoning (p. 276). He speaks of "metaphysical sophism," and of "the abstruse syllogisms of a quibbling dialectic" (pp. 124, 126).

On occasion Smith indulges in sarcasm, as in the following examples from *The Wealth of Nations*. He speaks of the "wisdom" of France and Britain in adopting economically disadvantageous trade policies (p. 463); he refers to what he thought was an unwise monetary policy of Mercantilism as "one of its many admirable expedients for enriching the country" (p. 522); he alludes to an excess of imports over exports as being "to the unspeakable comfort of those politicians who measure the national prosperity by what they call the balance of trade" (p. 833). Smith's celebrated, and often quoted, statement about shopkeepers, which we shall discuss in Essay 8, should also be cited as an example of his use of sarcasm.

A number of Smith's remarks that are somewhat allied to his harsh words and statements are those that bear a strong resemblance to certain terms used by Thorstein Veblen. Though he did not speak of "conspicuous consumption" and "pecuniary emulation," Smith knew what these expressions meant and he talked about them in both of his books.

In his *Theory of Moral Sentiments* he has much to say about vanity and the vain man, about wealth and greatness, and in his discussion of these themes he speaks of the conspicuous consumption of the rich. "We make parade of our riches, and conceal our poverty" he says (p. 47) because man is inclined "to sympathize more entirely with our joy than with our sorrow." Moreover, we often "see the respectful attentions of the world more strongly directed towards the rich and the great, than towards the wise and the virtuous" (p. 57). Man has an inclination to admire, and hence to imitate, the rich and the great, and this tendency enables the latter to set the fashion. "Their dress," says Smith (p. 59), "is the fashionable dress; the language of their conversation, the fashionable style; their air and deportment, the fashionable behavior." "Even their vices and follies are fashionable," he adds.[37]

In *The Wealth of Nations* Smith refers to the conspicuous consumption of the rich with some frequency. One of his best remarks concerning this Veblenian concept is his declaration that "With the greater part of rich people, the chief enjoyment of riches consists in the parade of riches, which in their eye is never so complete as when they appear to possess those decisive marks of opulence which nobody can possess but themselves" (p. 172).[38]

Smith felt that power and riches, greatness and wealth, were fragile possessions. As he states in his *Theory of Moral Sentimennts* (p. 161), they are "enormous and operose machines contrived to produce a few trifling conveniencies to the body," a machine made of springs which, despite all the attention we give to them, "are ready every moment to burst into pieces and to crush in their ruins their unfortunate possessor." And yet, despite the poor record that power and riches make when compared with wisdom and virtue, and regardless of the great uncertainty concerning their continuance and permanency, Smith believed that they were an essential ingredient in human society. Power and riches are the great incentives to industrial progress, and hence necessary. Thus, though we are deceived by their blandishments, this deception is desirable. "It is well, says Smith (p. 162), "that nature imposes upon us in this manner."[39]

In his two books there are certain words and expressions that are favorite ones with the author, and which the attentive reader will probably discern. In both books Smith makes frequent use of what might be described as "cautious" terms. The two most popular are "perhaps" and "seems," Other expressions are "appears," "must have," "probably." In those cases where he reaches conclusions on the basis of scanty or nonexistent information, and there are many such instances, he is forced to use such words. Smith, with his bent for accuracy, would have preferred certainty to conjecture, but he frequently had no alternative in the matter. It is possible, however, if one may resort to conjecture, that he slightly overused such words as we have indicated.[40]

There is no major word that Smith uses more frequently— certainly in *The Wealth of Nations*—than "naturally." The word has various meanings but the OED definition that is applicable most often in Smith's volume is "as might be expected from the circumstances." Occasionally Smith uses the expression "naturally, or rather necessarily." This suggests that the word "naturally" does not involve the notion of absolute inevitability. It implies the idea of probability, however. A somewhat different interpretation of our author's use of "naturally" is given by Kenneth Boulding. Whenever Smith uses the term, says Boulding, it means that "his insightful mind has skipped over several stages in the argument which he has not bothered to make explicit."[41] If this is the case, Smith has saved himself an immense amount of effort and space.

But quite often when he introduces the word he is not engaged in any particular argument. He is just making a simple statement.

In both of his books Smith quite often has recourse to the expression "If I may say so," or some variant of it. An example from *The Theory* (p. 68) and one from *The Wealth of Nations* (p. 579) will illustrate his use of the term. "Such actions seem to deserve, and, if I may say so, to call aloud for, a proportionable punishment"; "Foreign capitals are every day intruding themselves, if I may say so, more and more into the trade of Cadiz and Lisbon." Generally the phrase is either preceded or followed by figurative words or expressions. Our author also uses the phrase "as it were," but with considerably less frequency. Here again the phrase is associated with figurative language.

Smith did not develop any theories about the place of uncertainty in economics—a matter to which more recent economists have given attention—but in his *Wealth of Nations* he shows a certain fondness for the term "lottery." He makes a number of generalizations about lotteries (pp. 108, 870), and uses the word, in a metaphorical sense, in relation to a variety of occupations. He speaks of the lottery of the law (p. 106); the lottery of the sea and of the army (p. 109); the lottery of the church (p. 131); the lottery of mining—the search for new gold and silver mines he considered as "perhaps the most disadvantageous lottery in the world" (pp. 170, 529); and "the great state lottery of British politics" (p. 587). He does not appear to use the word "lottery" in his *Theory of Moral Sentiments,* but he refers (pp. 130-131) to "the most unequal of all games of hazard," that of trying to change our "situation" when both prudence and justice are not in favor of any such attempt.

The word "odious" was popular with Smith, and in his *Theory* he uses the adjective on a considerable number of occasions, applying it to both persons (in a nonspecific manner) and to things. It is in *The Wealth of Nations,* however, that the best-known employment of the word is found. In Book V of his treatise, Smith associates the word with the work of tax collectors. Indeed, in at least five instances in his book he uses the expression "the odious visit and examination of the tax-gatherer" or variations of the expression. In another case (p. 880) he varies his terminology and speaks of "the mortifying and vexatious visits of the tax-gatherers."

A word that was very appropriate in Smth's day but which seems quaint today is "equipage." Our author uses the word in both of his books, and usually in its literal sense. At least once, however, in *The Wealth of Nations,* he employs it in a figurative sense. With the American colonies in mind, he states (p. 899) that countries that support the empire neither by taxes nor military aid "may perhaps be considered as appendages, as a sort of splendid and showy equipage of the empire."

There were certain types of words and certain literary practices that Smith looked upon with disfavor. For one thing, he was opposed to the use of foreign words unless there was good reason for introducing them. "These foreign intruders," he says (RBL, pp. 1, 24), "should never be received but when they are necessary to answer some purpose which the natives cannot supply." It was his belief that though foreign words should have the same meaning as native words they do not have the same force as words with which we are acquainted and the origin of which we can trace.

Smith was also opposed to the use of compound words, the linking of words together, unless greater conciseness is achieved. Though, he says (p. 25), some persons think that such words contribute great majesty to language, they are generally used "rather by the middling than the upper class of authors." Words like *un-come-at-able* and *Pull-off-the-crown-of-Christ* heresy had no appeal to him.

In his lectures on rhetoric our author speaks out against the use of parentheses and superfluous words. A "natural order of writing," the absence of this undesirable practice, contributes very significantly to perspicuity. What is called "easy writing" is achieved; the reader does not have to "hunt backwards and forwards" in order to discover the author's meaning (p. 4). Smith himself did not always act upon this particular piece of advice.

Without much trouble the reader can find in Smith's books examples of writing that are not "easy."

Smith apparently did not favor the use of alliteration. Instances seem rather rare in his writings. His famous word-grouping of "butcher, baker, brewer," is an example of mild alliteration. One might also cite "the clamorous complaints" coming from merchants and manufacturers, the "extraordinary exportation" of corn, and the "cool and candid and consistent" attitude of individuals toward themselves. In general, however, Smith did not strive for alliterative effects.

One would not expect to find puns in Smith's books, and there does not appear to be any. In speaking of puns as "the lowest species of wit," Smith expresses a sentiment very similar to the view stated by Samuel Johnson. Our author, however, does not completely exclude the use of puns in writing. They "are never wholly agreeable," he says (p. 42), "but when there is some contrast betwixt the ideas they excite."

One will find certain words in Smith's books that have either gone out of fashion completely or are seldom used today. "Operose," "piacular," "chirurgical," and "trepanned" are examples from *The Theory of Moral Sentiments;* "apothecaries," "allodially," "assentation," "multure," and "fiars" (two Scottish legal terms) are examples from *The Wealth of Nations.* For the most part, however, Smith's language is highly modern; that is, in the words used. In the words *not* used, however, and here reference is made especially to his famous economic treatise, it is rather old-fashioned. There one will look in vain for such terms as marginal cost, oligopoly, monopsony, multiplier, input-output analysis.

In addition to the characteristics of Smith's style that we have just described there are others of a more technical nature. These characteristics point to the structure of the author's writing rather than to its meaning. First, there is the matter of sentence length. Short sentences, Smith affirms, are usually more "perspicuous"—a favorite word of his—than long sentences. But he recognized a danger in their use: they may lead to the omission of connecting words and thus contribute greatly to verbal obscurity. For historians who set forth the bare facts of history and didactic writers, "concise expressions and short-turned periods" are proper; but they are not proper for orators or public speakers. Long sentences, says Smith, are "generally inconvenient," and they are not likely to be used by anyone "who has his thoughts in good order." This does not mean, however, that one should strive for undue brevity (RBL, pp. 5, 20).

In his books Smith uses sentences that vary greatly in length. A few are quite short, of four, five, and six words. There are somewhat more that are quite long. In both *The Wealth of Nations* and *The Theory of Moral Sentiments* sentences of over one hundred words can be found without too much difficulty; and in the author's famous discussion of the division of labor there is one sentence of more than two hundred and fifty words. No one has performed the laborious task of discovering the average sentence length in Smith's books, as has been done with Macaulay's *History of England*.[42] However, a small sampling of twenty-five sentences at the beginning, near the middle, and at the end of each of the two books reveals that in *The Theory of Moral Sentiments* the average length is thirty-nine words, and in *The Wealth of Nations* it is thirty-eight words. Without having concrete evidence on the point, it seems safe to say that present-day economists use sentences that, on the average, are shorter than Smith's.

Though our author used sentences that varied widely in length, on the whole he preferred sentences of moderate length. Possibly he was influenced here by Addison, whose *Works* he had in his library and about whom he makes some interesting observations. "His sentences are neither long nor short," says Smith, "but of a length suited to the character he has of a modest man, who naturally delivers himself in sentences of a moderate length and with a uniform tone." Long sentences are suitable for declamations, in which Addison does not indulge, or they "bespeak a confusion of ideas," something of which Addison is not guilty. On the other hand, the modest man—Mr. Addison—does not use short sentences since "that would appear like a snip-snap, or the language of presumption and a dictating temper." Smith feels, however, that Addison's sentences are "so uniform in their manner that we read them with a sort of monotony" (RBL, p. 49).

Our author's paragraphs, like his sentences, vary greatly in length, though here again the average length seems moderate. In both of his books one can find one-sentence paragraphs, however; and at the other extreme there are paragraphs that run to more than a page in length. Indeed, there is one in *The Wealth of Nations,* in the chapter "The Expenses of the Sovereign or Commonwealth," that covers more than six pages.

One of the most outstanding features of Smith's style is his very frequent use of "multiples." Instead of using, for example, only one adjective in a given connection he will use two or three or more, as in "their universal, continual, and uninterrupted effort." Not only does he use adjectives in this multiple fashion but nouns, verbs, adverbs, phrases, clauses, and sentences as well. Sometimes the multiples are combined, as when a duplicate is associated with a triplicate. Quite often a duplicate will involve an antithesis, as when two adjectives, or two statements, are opposite in nature. Many of the duplicates, including those involving an antithesis, possess the characteristic of balance. Sometimes, moreover, the multiples are characterized by a certain cadence.

The number of examples of multiples in Smith's two books is vast, but a few examples will indicate their general nature. In *The Theory of Moral Sentiments* (p. 132) we read: "Faction, intrigue, and cabal, disturb the quiet of the unfortunate statesman. Extravagant projects, visions of gold mines, interrupt the repose of the ruined bankrupt." In this example there is a duplicate, a triplicate, and the element of balance. Smith uses duplicates a great deal, sometimes in tandem as in the following excerpt (p. 24): "As taste and good judgment, when they are considered as qualities which deserve praise and admiration, are supposed to imply a delicacy of sentiment and an acuteness of understanding not commonly to be met with; so the virtues of sensibility and self-command are not apprehended to consist in the ordinary, but in uncommon degrees of those qualities."

While our author was very fond of using duplicative terms and expressions, he also had a strong liking for triplicates. Some of the best-known expressions in *The Wealth of Nations* are of this nature: "truck, barter, and exchange," the "butcher, baker, and brewer." These triplicates are very simple, but there are others that are more complex. Thus in describing in his famous treatise the evil that will befall a member of parliament who has authority enough to thwart the lobbying activities of monopolists, Smith says (p. 438), "neither the most acknowledged probity, nor the highest rank, nor the greatest public service, can protect him from the most infamous abuse and detraction, from personal insults, nor sometimes from real danger, arising from the insolent outrage of furious and disappointed monopolists." Here there are duplicates and balance as well as a triplicate. At another point (p. 348) Smith refers to "the wonderful accounts of the wealth and cultivation of China, of those of ancient Egypt, and of the antient state of Indostan." It should be added that Smith uses both "antient" and "ancient" in his book.

Quadruplicates are sometimes found in Smith's writing. A good example, with two duplicates included, is his descriptive statement in *The Theory of Moral Sentiments* (p. 266) concerning his old teacher, "the never-to-be-forgotten Dr. Hutcheson," and his moral theory or system in which virtue is based on benevolence: "But of all the patrons of this system, ancient or modern, the late Dr. Hutcheson was undoubtedly, beyond all comparison, the most acute, the most distinct, the most philosophical, and what is of the greatest consequence of all, the soberest and most judicious."

On occasion our author also uses quintuplicates. A good example is a remark in *The Theory* (p. 269) concerning certain characteristics of self-interest: "The habits of economy, industry, discretion, attention, and application of thought, are generally supposed to be cultivated from self-interested motives." Even sextuplicates can be found in Smith's writing.

In Smith's use of duplicates the element of balance, to which we have already referred, is often found, sometimes with the element of antithesis. The following statement from *The Theory* (p. 57) illustrates the joint use of these two techniques as well as a number of other stylistic practices. It even includes a favorite Veblenian word. In general the excerpt is a good sample of the rhetorical aspect of Smith's writing. "Two different characters," says our author, "are presented to our emulation; the one, of proud ambition and ostentatious avidity; the other, of humble modesty and equitable justice. Two different models, two different pictures, are held out to us, according to which we may fashion our own character and behaviour; the one more gaudy and glittering in its colouring; the other more correct and more exquisitely beautiful in its outline: the one forcing itself upon the notice of every wandering eye; the other, attracting the attention of scarce any body but the most studious and careful observer."

Sometimes Smith's practice of using multiples is carried to excess, with the multiples falling from the author's pen in great profusion. Sometimes the multiples appear to be unnecessary because of the highly similar nature of the words they contain. In each of the following examples, from *The Theory of Moral Sentiments,* one of the words could be omitted with little or no loss of meaning: "faculties and powers," "best and most perfect," "congruity and fitness," "separated and detached." The same observation could be made concerning the following multiples from *The Wealth of Nations:* "complete and entire," "assistance and co-operation," "pillage and plunder," "judgment and discretion." In other instances, however, the multiples are all necessary in order to give full expression to what Smith has in mind. In many cases the multiples though not all absolutely necessary, nevertheless give greater fullness to what the author is saying.

A very different technical feature of Smith's style relates to his use of footnotes and source references. In the words of Dugald Stewart (pp. 169-170), "he considered every species of note as a blemish or imperfection; indicating, either an idle accumulation of superfluous particulars, or want of skill and comprehension in the general design." Further evidence on the point is furnished by James Boswell. When he was approaching the completion of *The Wealth of Nations,* Smith told Boswell that "he was now convinced that a Book should be complete and without references to other Books." Boswell, it is interesting to note, later saw his friend Topham Beauclerk and remarked to him that this policy was hard on one's readers, since they were compelled to pay for what others had said. Beauclerk did not agree with this opinion, pointing out on the contrary that the policy was "cheaper than, by referring, to make them buy all the Books."[43]

In justice to the great economist it should be added that in *The Wealth of Nations,* Smith refers to almost one hundred books, either by title or author. Moreover, he inserted a considerable number of footnote notations in the second edition of his work, which was published three years after Boswell and Beauclark discussed the "economics" of his policy of neglecting source references.

There has been some criticism of *The Wealth of Nations* on the score of its structural features. Even such an admirer as J. B. Say, who did much to popularize Smith's book on the continent, and who paid high tribute to its merits, nevertheless referred to "the celebrated work" as an "immethodical assemblage" and as "an irregular mass of curious and original speculations, and of known demonstrated truths."[44] Preferences in the matter of book structure certainly vary, and Say's own *Treatise* differed greatly from Smith's. But *The Wealth of Nations* is by no means without structural merit. There is a logical sequence in much of the work. In one or two instances there could be smaller groupings of chapters, and in a number of cases chapters could be shifted to other positions. Perhaps the most advantageous change would have been a narrowing of the structure, achieved by the omission or compression of some of the material. Smith had a strong desire "to tell the whole story," including its historical aspects. The result was the production of a book that is much longer than necessary. The digressions in particular could have been cut down, especially the one relating to silver (pp. 176-242). But other parts too could well have been reduced in length. Cases in

point are the author's discussion of standing armies versus militias
(pp. 659-669), and his analysis of religious instruction (pp.
740-766). Dugald Stewart, who praised the arrangement of
Smith's book, nevertheless declared (p. 87) that some of the
author's "incidental discussion and digressions might have been
more skillfully and happily incorporated with his general design."
Thorold Rogers, who thought the arrangement of Smith's treatise
"inartificial," suggested that some of the material should have
been placed in footnotes or in an appendix; and Francis Horner
went so far as to suggest that Smith would have been well advised
to have written separate essays rather than to have attempted a
general, systematic presentation.[45]

Such structural changes as those that have just been mentioned
would have increased the readability of *The Wealth of Nations,*
especially for the impatient general reader of today. At the same
time they would have detracted little, if at all, from those outstanding features of the book that have made it a classic.

In taking an overall view of Smith's books the observer will
probably note a major difference in their general style. *The
Theory of Moral Sentiments* is more rhetorical in nature than
The Wealth of Nations. It is characterized by a higher degree
of literary eloquence. How can one account for this difference?

Professor Macfie ascribes it to a background element in the
two books. *The Theory* is more rhetorical, he says, because it
was given as lectures to "very young students," students who
were between fourteen and sixteen years of age. To transform
these young lads into an intelligent group it was highly essential
for Smith to hold their interest, and to this end there were a
number of techniques at hand. The first, which was common in
the eighteenth and nineteenth centuries, was rhetoric; the second
was "various forms of rather facile humour."[46]

This argument seems quite plausible, but its force is lessened
by a number of considerations. Smith's lectures on Moral Philosophy, one has reason for believing, were subject to revision in
the process of their preparation for publication in book form.

Moreover, his *Lectures on Rhetoric and Belles Lettres,* as reported by one of his Glasgow students, are on the whole not nearly as rhetorical as the chapters in his *Theory of Moral Sentiments.* These lectures were also delivered to very young students (as well as to some not so young, in Edinburgh). On the same general point one might add that his *Lectures on Justice, Police, Revenue and Arms,* again as reported by a student, are not any more rhetorical in style than *The Wealth of Nations,* much of which was dictated to an amanuensis. (One might contend, of course, that students taking down or transcribing notes would omit some of the verbal ornamentation.) Finally, it should be noted that some of our author's finest writing, including a number of his outstanding character sketches, is found in Part VI of his *Theory,* a part that was added to the sixth edition of the book which appeared in 1790, the last year of Smith's life. This was long after he had given up his teaching duties. It might be argued, however, that this part was simply a modest revision of old lectures he had given three decades earlier; or, perhaps a bit more convincingly, that in writing Part VI Smith attempted to preserve a high degree of uniformity in the style of the new edition. To the extent that these arguments are true, Macfie's position on Smith's style in *The Theory* is strengthened; to the degree that they are not true, it is weakened.

It might be contended that as Smith grew older he adopted a more restrained style. His *Theory of Moral Sentiments* was published in 1759, when he was thirty-six years of age. His *Wealth of Nations,* though very long in preparation, was not published until 1776, when Smith was over fifty. There may be some truth in this contention, though, as we first noted, Smith wrote some highly rhetorical prose at the end of his life.

One of the best reasons for the difference in the style of the two books is suggested by Smith himself, and it relates to subject matter. In his *Theory* (p. 292) our author declares that ethics is of all the sciences "the most susceptible of all the embellishments of eloquence." It is certainly easier to soar to high levels of eloquence when discussing such moral issues as sympathy, self-command, and virtue than when dealing with real and nominal price, money, and taxes on consumable commodities. There are parts of *The Wealth of Nations,* to be sure, where Smith rises to considerable eloquence. His discussion of the division of labor and the education of youth are examples. But this does not disprove the general argument. It simply means that subject matter must be thought of in a wide as well as in a narrow sense.

As a final explanation for the differences in the style of the two books we may note an observation made by J. R. McCulloch. *The Wealth of Nations,* McCullough declared, is "exceedingly diffuse" because Smith dictated it, whereas *The Theory of Moral Sentiments,* which the author wrote by hand, is "admirable in style."[47]

Whatever the reason, or reasons, may be, *The Theory* is a more highly embellished book, a more eloquent treatise, a much more rhetorical production than *The Wealth of Nations.* The latter, however, is by no means lacking in those literary touches and techniques that characterize many of the writings of the eighteenth century. These touches and techniques have now largely gone out of fashion—completely out of fashion in those quantitative and econometric studies that now occupy the central place in economic literature—although there are still some persons who look upon the fine writing of Smith's time with considerable enjoyment and even a certain amount of admiration.

NOTES

1. *Works of Henry, Lord Brougham,* 10 vols. (London and Glasgow: Griffin, 1855-1857), I *(Lives of Philosophers of the Time of George III),* p. 263.

2. *The Economic Journal,* June 1893, p. 240.

3. *Adam Smith* (London, Historical Association Publications, General Series: G 10, 1948), p. 27.

4. *The Annual Register, 1759* (London: Otridge and others, 8th ed., 1802), p. 485. Similarly, in his letter of September 10, 1759, to Smith, Burke tells his friend that "there is so much elegant Painting of the manners and passions" in his book. *The Correspondence of Edmund Burke,* ed. by Thomas W. Copeland, 8 vols. (Cambridge at

the University Press, 1958-1969), I, p. 130.

5. *Works,* I, p. 201.

6. From Charles W. Moulton, *The Library of Literary Criticism,* 8 vols. (Buffalo: Moulton, 1901-1905), IV, p. 59.

7. *Autobiography of the Rev. Dr. Alexander Carlyle* (Boston: Ticknor and Fields, 1861), p. 228.

8. From George B. Hill, *Johnsonian Miscellanies,* 2 vols. (New York: Barnes & Noble, reprint, 1966), II, p. 424. Though Fox may have felt that Smith's work was very dull, and though he did not subscribe to the basic principles of policy set forth in it, he neverthe-less was the first person to mention the book in the House of Commons. See Rae, pp. 289-290. Refering to an "excellent book upon the Wealth of Nations," he alludes to Smith's view concerning the way to individual and national riches: managing things so that income exceeds outgo.

9. *Letters & Journals of W. Stanley Jevons,* ed. by His Wife (London: Macmillan, 1886), p. 101.

10. *A Literary History of Scotland* (London: Unwin, 1903), p. 321. At another point (p. 343) Millar speaks of *The Theory as* "flaccid and invertebrate."

11. *Biographical Studies,* ed. by Richard H. Hutton (London: Longmans, Green, 1881), p. 272.

12. Glenn R. Morrow, in *Adam Smith,* 1776-1926 (Chicago: University of Chicago Press, 1928), p. 173.

13. Stewart, p. 106. See also the article on Robertson in *The Dictionary of National Biography.*

14. Harold Bond, *The Literary Art of Edward Gibbon* (Oxford at the Clarendon Press, 1960), p. 137.

15. *The Wealth of Nations,* ed. by John Ramsay McCulloch (Edinburgh: Black, new ed., 1870), p. xvii. McCulloch does not give the source of his information.

16. *An Old Master and Other Political Essays* (New York: Scribners, 1893), pp. 6, 7.

17. John H. Millar, *Scottish Prose of the Seventeenth & Eighteenth Centuries* (Glasgow: Maclehose, 1912), p. 181.

18. Preface to 1818 reprint of the two copies of the original *Edinburgh Review,* 1755, p. ix.

19. *The Economic Journal,* September 1923, p. 427.

20. *Malthus and His Work* (New York: Macmillan, 1924), p. 431.

21. *Economic History,* February 1938, pp. 45-46.

22. *The Wealth of Nations,* ed. by John Ramsay McCulloch, p. XVII. See also Rae, p. 260-261.

23. Rae, p. 261.

24. C. R. Fay, *Adam Smith and the Scotland of His Day* (Cambridge at the University Press, 1956, p. 66. David Murray, on whom Fay may have based his statement, says, regarding the notion that Smith prepared *The Wealth of Nations* while he walked in the College garden at Glasgow, that "It is more probable that in his walks in the College garden he thought out his article on Johnson's Dictionary." *Memories of the Old College of Glasgow* (Glasgow: Jackson, Wylie, 1927), p. 417.

25. Henry, Lord Brougham, *Works,* I, p. 285.

26. *The Letters of Edward Gibbon,* ed. by J. E. Norton, 2 vols. (London: Cassell, 1956), 2, p. 101. David Hume, in a letter to William Strahan, the publisher, expressed the view (which he had conveyed to Smith), however, that his countryman's work "requires too much thought to be as popular as Mr. Gibbon's" (the first volume of whose great history was also published in 1776, and also by Strahan & Cadell). Strahan himself declared that *The Wealth of Nations* "required much thought and reflection . . . to peruse to any purpose." J. A. Cochrane, *Dr. Johnson's Printer* (Cambridge: Harvard University Press, 1964) p. 162.

27. *The Wealth of Nations,* Everyman's Library ed., 2 vols. (London: Dent, 1910), I, p. viii.

28. *The Progress of a Plough-Boy to a Seat in Parliament,* ed. by William Reitzel (London: Faber & Faber, 1933), pp. 150-151.

29. WN, pp. 417-418, 455, 490. The "occasions" relate to long explanations or to digressions.

30. *The Wealth of Nations,* ed. by Edward Gibbon Wakefield, 4 vols. (London: Knight, 1835-39), I, p. vii.

31. *Lectures on the Philosophy of the Human Mind,* 4 vols. Edinburgh: Tait, Second ed., 1824), IV, p. 105. It is of passing interest to note that Thomas De Quincey used the same words with reference to "the total architecture" of *The Wealth of Nations*—no "systems," no 'aggregate of doctrines" approach Smith's book in "philosophic beauty." *The Collected Writings of Thomas De Quincey,* ed. by David Masson, 14 vols. (London: Black, 1896-1897), IX, pp. 115, 116.

32. *Biographical Studies,* ed. by Richard H. Hutton, p. 273.

33. *Selected Writings on Economics* (New York: Kelley, Reprints of Economic Classics, 1966), "Four Introductory Lectures on Political Economy," p. 5.

34. A. L. Macfie in *The Individual in Society* (London: Allen & Unwin, 1967), pp. 21-23.

35. "The Scotch, whatever other talents they may have, can never condense; they always begin a few days before the flood, and come *gradually* down to the reign of George the third, forgetful of nothing but the shortness of human life, and the volatility of human attention."

The Letters of Sydney Smith, ed. by Nowell C. Smith, 2 vols. (Oxford at the Clarendon Press, 1953), I, p. 327. The specific incident the theologian-humorist had in mind when he made his remark was the publishing of "an article of endless length" in the *Edinburgh Review*.

36. For a detailed analysis of some of these statements, see Arthur H. Cole's whimsical article "Puzzles of the *Wealth of Nations*," in *The Canadian Journal of Economics and Political Science*, February 1958, pp. 1-8.

37. Other statements of a Veblenian nature can be found on pp. 48, 60, 158, 161, and 274 of *The Theory*.

38. Other references in *The Wealth of Nations* relating to conspicuous consumption are on pp. 205, 329, 331, 332, 364, 389, 649, 794, 854.

39. See Essay 10 for further discussion of this point.

40. Speaking of qualifications in general—including not only "perhaps" but "generally" and "in most cases"—and thus raising a larger issue, Jacob Viner expresses a somewhat different view. He considers it arguable, by those who stress realism more than analytical rigor and elegance, that on the whole both of Smith's books are better because of his numerous qualifications, and that they would have been still better (though still more untidy) had he used qualifying adjectives and phrases even more liberally. See *International Encyclopedia of the Social Sciences*, article on Adam Smith.

41. *Economic Analysis*, 2 vols. (New York: Harper & Row, Fourth ed., 1966), I, p. 53.

42. Professor L. A. Sherman found the average was 23.43. See W. K. Wimsatt, *The Prose Style of Samuel Johnson* (New Haven: Yale University Press, 1941), p. 24.

43. *Private Papers of James Boswell from Malahide Castle*, ed. by Geoffrey Scott and Frederick A. Pottle, 18 vols. (Privately printed, 1928-1934), 10, pp. 175-176.

44. *A Treatise on Political Economy* (Philadelphia: Lippincott, Grambo, New American ed., 1853), p. xix. William Letwin, in contrast to Say, pays tribute to the basic structural merits of Smith's book. See *The Origins of Scientific Economics* (London: Methuen, 1963), pp. 226-227.

45. *The Wealth of Nations*, ed. by James E. Thorold Rogers, 2 vols. (Oxford at the Clarendon Press, Second ed., 1880), I, pp. xxi-xxii; James Bonar, *The Tables Turned* (London: Macmillan, 1931), p. 39.

46. Article on the Smith in *Chamber's Encyclopedia*, and *The Individual in Society*, pp. 42-43.

47. *Memoirs, Journal, and Correspondence of Thomas Moore*, ed. by Lord John Russell, 8 vols. (London: Longman, Brown, Green, and

Longmans, 1853-1856), VI, p. 198. Another observer (perhaps Edmund Burke) gives a different reason why Smith's style in *The Wealth of Nations* "may be sometimes thought diffuse." "It must be remembered," he tells us, "that the work is didactic, that the author means to teach, and teach things that are by no means obvious." *The Annual Register, 1776,* Section on "Account of Books for 1776" (London: Dodsley, 4th ed., 1788), p. 241.

4.

Adam Smith, James Boswell, and Samuel Johnson

That happy facility which Mr. Adam Smith allows
me to possess is of vast value.

—JAMES BOSWELL

Sir, I was once in company with Smith, and we did
not take to each other; but had I known that he
loved rhyme as much as you tell me he does, I should
have HUGGED him.

—SAMUEL JOHNSON

The names of Adam Smith and James Boswell are not commonly
linked together, certainly not by economists. Yet there were a
number of bonds that tied the two men together. Not only were
they both Scotsmen, but they were contemporaries. Their lives
overlapped for a period of fifty years. Furthermore, they were
acquaintances. Though it would not be accurate to call Smith
and Boswell intimate friends, they were friends nevertheless, and
over the years the two celebrities occasionally met. It is with this
relatively unfamiliar aspect of the careers of the great economist
and the renowned biographer and diarist that we shall primarily
concern ourselves in the first part of the present essay. In the
remainder of the essay we shall deal principally with the relationship between Smith and Samuel Johnson.

In November 1759, Boswell, then nineteen years of age, entered the University of Glasgow to study civil law. His stay at the university was quite short, however. In the spring of 1760 he temporarily discontinued his studies and went off for three months of varied experiences in London.

During his brief sojourn at Glasgow Boswell came into contact with Adam Smith. This was long before the appearance of *The Wealth of Nations,* which was not published until 1776. It was in the same year, however, that *The Theory of Moral Sentiments* appeared, the book that first brought Smith into prominence. Smith had been at Glasgow since 1751. In that year he was appointed to the Chair of Logic, a post that included the teaching of rhetoric and belles lettres, and he also filled in for the indisposed Professor of Moral Philosophy. Early in 1752 he received a permanent appointment to the Chair of Moral Philosophy, and he was in that position when Boswell first met him. The subject of Moral Philosophy was a very broad one and included Natural Theology, Ethics, Jurisprudence (Justice), and Political Economy (Expediency). In addition to teaching these subjects Smith gave lectures on rhetoric and belles lettres, taste, and the history of philosophy. The lectures on rhetoric and belles lettres, which Boswell said he attended, were probably of more interest to the young Scottish student than those on moral philosophy, and had a greater influence on him.[1]

At Glasgow Smith had established an enviable reputation as a lecturer, a reputation that extended beyond his native Scotland. "Apart from his own master Hutcheson," J. M. Keynes declared,[2] he "was perhaps the first and greatest of the teachers who have taught a modern subject in a modern way." In view of Smith's standing as a lecturer it is not surprising that numerous students, some coming from distant countries, were attracted to his classes.

Boswell made the acquaintance of Smith at the University of Glasgow in the latter part of 1759. That was about three and a half years before the highly important date of May 16, 1763, when, in the back parlor of Thomas Davies, the actor and bookseller, Boswell first met Samuel Johnson.[3] It might also be noted, as a further point of modest significance, that Smith met Johnson before Boswell did, the two men coming together in London in 1761. Boswell's brief sojourn at the University of Glasgow was apparently not of his own choosing. His father, it would seem, felt that Glasgow was a safer place for his lively son than Edinburgh, where he had been attending the university.[4]

Early in 1760, while he was at Glasgow, Boswell wrote a letter to his friend John Johnston in which he paid an outstanding tribute to Smith as a teacher and as a person. In describing the content and form of his lectures he used such adjectives as "excellent," "beautiful," "clear," "accurate," "correct," "perspicuous." Boswell found Smith "realy amiable," with none of "that formal stiffness and Pedantry which is too often found in Professors." Indeed, far from having such characteristics Smith "is a most polite well-bred man" and "is extremely fond of having his Students with him."[5] At this point in his career Boswell would have rated Smith very high in any appraisal of faculty personnel.

Students of Boswell and Smith can be thankful for the existence of the Boswell letter of January 11, 1760, to Johnston. But they have reason for regretting that in the voluminous Boswell journals there are not at least a few pages devoted specifically to Adam Smith and the Glasgow period. The young Boswell had started writing a diary before he entered the university but did not continue with it. There are no on-the-spot descriptions, therefore, of his student days at Glasgow and of his experiences under Smith's tutelage. But in his various writings, particularly his invaluable *Private Papers* and *Life of Johnson,* there are scattered references to views that Smith expressed in his Glasgow lectures and also to other opinions he held. In addition there are some personal references to him.

Boswell not only attended Smith's lectures in 1759-1760 but over the years, as we have already noted, he was occasionally in Smith's company: calling upon him at his home or lodgings, or at the Edinburgh Customs House where the economist became employed in 1778; meeting him at the famous Literary Club in London; or seeing him at the homes of mutual friends or elsewhere.

A rather amusing aspect of the early Smith-Boswell relationship has to do with the certificate Boswell received at the end of his attendance at Smith's lectures. On the certificate Smith stated that Boswell was "happily possessed of a facility of manners." That was an opinion Bozzy was never to forget. He mentions it—"Mr. Smith's beautiful, I shall even grant you just complaint"—in his letter of December 8, 1761, to his friend Andrew Erskine.[6] He alludes to it in his Journal entry of December 22, 1765: "That happy facility which Mr. Adam Smith allows me to possess is of vast value."[7] He speaks of it in the original copy (Isham edition) of his *Tour of the Hebrides:* "My *facility of manners,* as Adam Smith said of me, had fine play."[8] He mentions it again in his Journal for April 3, 1775: "that *facility of manners* which Adam Smith allowed me" (PP, 10, p. 181).

It is of more than passing interest to note that a few years after Smith paid his tribute to Boswell, David Hume also made an observation concerning him. He described Boswell as very good-humored and very agreeable, but also as "very mad."[9]

During his weeks of contact with Smith at the University of Glasgow, Boswell was particularly influenced by his professor's lectures on rhetoric and belles lettres—not by those on ethics and political economy. Frederick A. Pottle, the Boswellian scholar, declares that John Stevenson (the highly effective Professor of Logic at the University of Edinburgh during the long period from 1739 to 1775) may have had as great a "shaping effect" on Boswell in the long run as Smith, but at the time Stevenson's "more academic prelusions" appeared "slack in comparison with the sallies of this original and energetic mind."[10] Another student of Boswell has found traces of the influence of Smith's lectures in the former's *Corsican Journey.*[11]

As every reader of Boswell knows, our biographer had an eye—and an ear—for detail. Speaking of Samuel Johnson, Boswell declares in his *Tour to the Hebrides* that "every thing relative to so great a man is worth observing" (HP,V, p. 19). And then he goes on to mention a remark Adam Smith had made in one of his lectures at Glasgow about being "glad to know that Milton wore latchets in his shoes, instead of buckles." Is it possible that Boswell's interest in detail was at least in part attributable to Adam Smith's influence? Professor Pottle ventures the opinion that this particular Smith episode was probably the first occasion when Boswell's attention had been directed to the biographical value of "characteristic detail."[12]

In view of Boswell's association with Smith at the University of Glasgow, it is difficult to explain what appears to be a bit of personal neglect on his part. The occasion was in 1773, the year Boswell and Johnson made their celebrated tour to the Highlands of Scotland and the Hebrides. Why, it might be asked, did the two men in the accounts they render of their tour not give a little more prominence to Kirkcaldy, the birthplace and home of Adam Smith? In his account of their first day's journey from Edinburgh, Boswell skips from Kinghorn to Cupar without mentioning Kirkcaldy which lies between. He also makes no reference whatever to Smith (HP,V, p. 56). Johnson is somewhat more considerate. Both in his *Journey to the Western Islands of Scotland* and in his letter of August 25, 1773, to Mrs. Thrale, he mentions Kirkcaldy.[13] (In the letter he refers to the place as "a very long town meanly built.") But Johnson, like Boswell, does not allude to Smith. In partial though by no means complete extenuation of their oversight it should be added that Smith was in London at the time working on *The Wealth of Nations.*

Though Smith and Boswell often shared common opinions— including their liking for the poetry of Thomas Gray and William Hamilton, a liking, interestingly enough, that was not shared by Johnson—in some instances their views were in sharp conflict. For one thing Boswell strongly disagreed with Smith's criticism of Oxford, "the noblest university in the world" (HP,IV, p. 391). During the period (1740-1746) that Smith attended Balliol College at Oxford, in fact during a large part of the eighteenth century, the institution was at a low intellectual ebb. The professors, because of the basis on which they were paid and the authority under which they served, were unduly neglectful of their students. "In the university of Oxford," Smith declares in *The Wealth of Nations* (p. 718), "the greater part of the public professors have, for these many years, given up altogether even the pretence of teaching."

Smith was not the only person who was critical of Oxford. Jeremy Bentham, who at the tender age of twelve years, matriculated at Queen's College, Oxford, was especially harsh in his strictures of the university. The title of one of the lectures a professor gave, he said, was "Where is Constantinople?" It has been stated that perhaps there was never another distinguished Oxford man who so heartily disliked the institution as Bentham.[14] Edward Gibbon, however, was not far behind. Gibbon spent fourteen months at Magdalen College, months which proved to be, he said, "the most idle and unprofitable of my whole life." He declared that he acknowledged no obligation to Oxford, "and she will cheerfully renounce me as a son, as I am willing to disclaim her as a mother."[15]

Boswell felt that Smith's charges against the universities of England were "certainly not well founded" and seemed "invidious"; he declared that Smith was "ungraciously attacking his venerable *Alma Mater*" (HP,III, p. 13; IV, p. 391). It is interesting to note that earlier Thomas Warton had also come to the rescue of Oxford. Warton's sojourn at Oxford overlapped Smith's —the one attended Trinity, however, and the other Balliol. In 1749, in response to an attack that had been made on Oxford, Warton wrote his *Triumph of Isis,* including the following couplet:

> Hail, Oxford, hail! of all that's good and great,
> Of all that's fair, the guardian and the seat.

It has been said that Warton's "record" aided in correcting the views of "the ancient universities" given by Gibbon and Smith.[16] This could well be true, though Warton's case is weakened when we learn (from the *Dictionary of National Biography*) that as a tutor at Trinity he himself did not take his tutorial duties very seriously—which was one of Smith's complaints. But, we are told, Warton did encourage literary effort at the college.

Despite the testimony of Boswell and Warton, the general point made by Smith was well taken. Oxford at the time left much to be desired. The same was true of Cambridge.[17] In all fairness, however, it should be added that though Smith criticized Oxford, he expressed his gratefulness to the University of Glasgow for having made it possible for him to go there.

Another matter on which Boswell and Smith disagreed related to the latter's close and loyal friendship with David Hume, whose religious unorthodoxy offended Boswell. Here Johnson was very much on Boswell's side. In one of his letters to Johnson (June 9, 1777), Boswell, referring to a remark made by Professor Anderson of Glasgow, declared that "I agreed with him that you might knock Hume's and Smith's head together, and make vain and ostentatious infidelity exceedingly ridiculous" (HP,III, p. 119). Again, in connection with a highly eulogistic statement in Smith's tribute to Hume on the latter's death in 1776, Boswell remarked, "I could not help exclaiming with the *Psalmist,* 'Surely I have now more understanding than my teachers!'" (HP,V, pp. 31-32). On another occasion (when he visited the economist at the Edinburgh Customs House on September 14, 1779) Boswell again reacted to Smith's tribute. "I fairly told him that I did not like his having praised David Hume so much" (PP,13, pp. 286-287). Boswell then goes on to state that Smith "went off to the board huffed, yet affecting to treat my censure as foolish." However, he continues, "I did not care how he took it. Since his absurd eulogium on Hume and his ignorant, ungrateful attack on the English University education, I have had no desire to be much with him. Yet I do not forget that he was very civil to me at Glasgow." A very similar sentiment was expressed by Boswell a year later, in his Journal entry for September 29, 1780 (PP,14, pp. 126-127).

Smith and Boswell not only differed in their opinions of Oxford and Hume. We may be sure they differed on other matters too. Certainly their views on slavery were in sharp conflict. In this instance it was Smith and Johnson who were on the same side of the issue, both being strongly opposed to slavery. Boswell, on the other hand, supported it (HP,III, pp. 200-205). He advanced his "most solemn protest" against Johnson's general opinion on the slave trade, asserting that it was based on "prejudice, and imperfect or false information." He decalred that slavery was sanctioned by God; and he felt its abolition would be robbery, and also an act of extreme cruelty for the Africans themselves, some of whom would be exposed to a worse fate.

Another difference between Smith and Boswell, although in this instance Boswell may not have realized at first that there was a difference, relates to the so-called "Douglas Cause."[18] This once famous cause involved a prolonged court case, the most outsanding Scottish civil trial of the time. The case had to do with the conflicting claims of Archibald Douglas Stewart and the Duke of Hamilton to the Douglas estates. The former was allegedly the survivor of twin sons born to Lady Jane Douglas in Paris in 1748 (when she was over fifty years of age). Lady Jane had married John Stewart two years earlier. The third Marquis of Douglas (Archibald, Duke of Douglas), before his death in 1761, and responding to the arguments of Lady Jane's husband, had settled the family estates upon Archibald Douglas Stewart. This settlement was contested in the Scottish Court of Session by representatives of the Duke of Hamilton. The Hamilton claim was that Lady Jane had not given birth to twins in 1748; that the twins, indeed, were French children. By a vote of eight to seven the court in 1767 ruled in favor of the Duke. The verdict was appealed to the House of Lords and there, in 1769, the ruling was reversed.

Boswell was greatly interested in the "cause" and played an active role in it. At a later stage he became a regular counsel on the Douglas side. Among his writings about the great controversy were *Dorando,* a fictionalized description of the case, *The Essence of the Douglas Case,* and a number of anonymous articles contributed to *The London Chronicle.* In one of these articles a remarkable, and even amusing, aspect of the Douglas affair comes to light. In writing the article Boswell made it appear that the author was Adam Smith who, as a matter of fact, was a supporter of the Hamilton side in the controversy.[19] Two of the Duke of Hamilton's guardians were friends of Smith, one of them participating actively in asserting the Duke's claim to the estates. Furthermore, the Duke of Hamilton was related to the Duke of Buccleuch, for whom Smith had acted as tutor and traveling companion.

No record exists concerning Smith's reaction to the Boswell article—assuming that he must have seen it. We may be sure that he would not have approved of what his young acquaintance and former student had done; a "facility of manners" on Boswell's part was clearly lacking in this instance. There is a record, however, in the form of a letter to Lord Hailes, of Smith's strong objection to the verdict handed down by the House of Lords.

There appears to be no evidence that Smith and Boswell ever discussed the question of individual morality and behavior, with reference to Boswell himself. One can imagine, however, that the great economist and moral philosopher would not have endorsed the libertine actions of his younger countryman. In *The Wealth of Nations* (pp. 746-747) Smith draws a contrast between the two different systems of morality that he says exist in a class-developed society: the liberal or loose system and the strict or austere system. We do not know, of course, whether, among others, he had Boswell in mind when he described the former, but much of his description of the liberal or loose system would have been most applicable to him. In this system, Smith remarks, "luxury, wanton and even disorderly mirth, the pursuit of pleasure to some degree of intemperance, the breach of chastity, at least in one of the two sexes, etc. provided they are not accompanied with gross indecency, and do not lead to falsehood or injustice, are generally treated with a good deal of indulgence, and are easily excused or pardoned altogether." To no small degree Smith was a representative of the austere system, although he was not one of "the common people" with whom he links the system. In this system, he tells us, the above-mentioned excesses "are regarded with the utmost abhorrence and detestation."

During the years that intervened between his attendance at Smith's lectures in 1759-1760 and the publication of *The Wealth of Nations* in 1776, Boswell appears to have seen little of Smith. We know definitely, however, that the two men met on April 2, 1775. On that date, we learn from Boswell's Journal (PP,10, p. 175), the ex-student called on his old professor at his lodgings in Suffolk Street, London. Moreover, on April 16 of the same year the two men met at Topham Beauclerk's (PP,10, p. 219). Boswell was not at the meeting of the Literary Club on December 1, 1775, when Smith became a member of that famous group and hence did not see him there. But a few months later, in April 1776, they met, again at Beauclerk's (PP,II, p. 227).

The later meetings between the two men took place mostly in Edinburgh where Smith, from 1778 to his death in 1790, served as a commissioner of customs. According to his Journal entries, Boswell met Smith in that city once in 1779, three times in 1780, and twice in 1781.[20] On April 10, 1784, they met in Glasgow, however, on the occasion of Edmund Burke's inauguration as Lord Rector of the university, and on May 26 and June 12, they were together in London. During the latter year Smith, who was very ill, had come down to London for medical attention.

In 1775, to retrace our steps, Smith was admitted to the Literary Club of London, which included in its membership such a galaxy of celebrities as has never been matched by any similar organization. Boswell, in his letter of April 28, 1776, to his friend William Temple, makes what appears to be a slighting remark about Smith's admission to the group: "Smith, too, is now of our Club. It has lost its select merit" (HP,II, p. 430). The obvious interpretation of this statement, and the one commonly made, is that Boswell was speaking unkindly of Smith. It is to be noted, however, that Boswell once replied to a statement Johnson had made about the club losing some of its outstanding members by mentioning additions to the club, including Adam Smith and Edward Gibbon (HP,V, p. 109). It might also be pointed out that in the notable Hill-Powell edition of *Boswell's Life of Johnson* there is an index entry to the effect that Smith was elected to the club "when it had 'lost its select merit.' " This statement implies that the editors, or whoever made up the index, believed that the club had lost its select merit *before* Smith and Gibbon joined it. Thus there is some confusion on the point.

Boswell and Smith were seldom at the meetings of the club together, hence we can learn little from the famous biographer and diarist, or from anyone else, concerning what happened when Smith was in attendance. Boswell, however, does tell about an amusing episode relating to his famous countryman that occurred when the club met on March 27, 1781 (PP,14, pp. 176-177). The members who were present on the occasion, and especially Burke, were in a jovial mood and apparently had a rather hilarious time. Smith, however, was one of those absent and hence missed the fun. The episode in question had to do with a financial question: what members of the club in arrears in their contribution to the wine fund should be asked to make payment? Fox was ordered to pay; but Boswell, who was absent from London during the previous year, was excused, as were a number of other members including the Bishop of Killaloe (Dr. Thomas Barnard) who had sent a hogshead of claret to the club. Finally they came to Adam Smith. Burke and Boswell felt that he should pay the levy—"a Commissioner of the Customs, who holds a lucrative place and was absent only because he is a tax gatherer, should be taxed." And this was ordered.

Johnson, who was not at the meeting, "did not relish a repetition from me of this pleasantry," Boswell relates. Gibbon alone among those in attendance supported Smith because, Boswell further states, "he is a brother infidel." Concerning the famous author of *The Decline and Fall of the Roman Empire,* Boswell adds "He is a disagreeable dog, this Gibbon." There is no record of Smith's reaction to the levy's being placed upon him. There is good reason for believing, however, that he accepted the act with good grace.

At scattered points throughout Boswell's writings one can find still other references to Smith. His allusions to *The Wealth of*

Nations and *The Theory of Moral Sentiments* are of special significance.

In writing to William Temple early in 1767 Boswell states that "Smith, I suppose, is in London. But I do not hear that his book on jurisprudence is in any forwardness." In another letter to Temple, dated July 29, 1767, Boswell declares that "Smith is here just now. His Jurisprudence' will be out in a year and a half."[21] The implication of these statements is not clear. At the end of his *Theory of Moral Sentiments* Smith declared his intention of writing a discourse on jurisprudence (which he did not do), and Boswell may have assumed that he was nearing the end of this project. On the other hand it is possible that Boswell was thinking of *The Wealth of Nations,* on which Smith was then working. The latter possibility receives substantial support from the fact that in the early 1760s Smith not only began to concentrate his efforts on economic investigations but prepared what appears to be a preliminary draft of his great work. Boswell may not have been aware of this draft, but other friends were and they expected Smith's book to be published shortly after 1764.[22] The publication date, however, was still more than ten years away.

By 1775 Boswell gives us a very definite progress report on Smith's volume. In his Journal entry of April 2 of that year he states that he had called on Smith at his Suffolk Street lodgings in London, and that the latter had said (among other things) that "he was near finishing his Book on Commerce" (PP,10, p. 175). This, of course, was *The Wealth of Nations.*

After long effort on Smith's part his great work was finally published on March 9, 1776. It is interesting to speculate on what members of the Literary Club received complimentary copies. Did Boswell? Did Johnson? There appears to be no evidence that they did. Had Boswell been so favored it seems inevitable that he would have mentioned the fact somewhere in his journals. We know definitely that Smith presented a copy of his book to Sir Joshua Reynolds—the late Professor J. Shield Nicholson said he was "the fortunate possessor" of this particular copy—and to Edmund Burke, and it is possible that other members of the group, including Edward Gibbon, were also remembered by Smith. The likelihood of this having happened is enhanced by the fact that the author was generous in presenting complimentary copies of his works to his friends. It would seem, according to W. R. Scott, that at least one hundred copies of *The Wealth of Nations* (in its various editions) were thus distributed, less than half of which however have been located.[23]

Shortly after the publication of *The Wealth of Nations* Boswell made a number of references to the book. In a letter to Temple on April 28, 1776, he declared that "Murphy says he has read thirty pages of Smith's *Wealth* but shall read no more."[24] (What thirty pages were they? one might ask. Surely not the first thirty, which include Smith's fascinating discussion of the division of labor.) In his *Life of Johnson,* under date of May 16, 1776, Boswell states that he menutioned Smith's book to Johnson, and then he goes on to tell of the acute observation Johnson made concerning Smith's qualifications for writing the book, an observation which we shall note shortly.

Boswell's reaction to Smith's treatise was favorable. He valued "the greatest part" of it, he states in his *Tour of the Hebrides* (HP,V, p. 31). It might be added too that in one of his *Hypochondriack* essays (March 1781) he refers to Smith's famous discussion of the division of labor, applying it to "connubial copartnery."[25]

Boswell's attitude toward Smith's earlier book, *The Theory of Moral Sentiments,* was also favorable, probably more so. Whereas he said he "valued" most of *The Wealth of Nations,* he stated that he "admired" the *Theory* (HP,V, p. 31). Possibly his admiration was due in some degree to the fact that he had heard a considerable part of the substance of the book first hand, when he attended Smith's lectures in 1759-1760. (He heard too at that time some of the ideas that were later to be embodied in *The Wealth of Nations.*)

Boswell's interest in the *Theory* is suggested by the fact that he gave a copy of the book to Margaret Montgomerie, his cousin and wife-to-be. She refers to the book—"of which I remember nothing more than the name ... except one observation"—in a letter to Boswell dated October 17, 1769 (PP,8, pp. 240-241). In his tour of Holland, five years earlier, Boswell had the *Theory* along with him, or at least had it at his disposal. In his Journal entries for March 5 and March 7, 1764, he comments upon the central theme of the book: the principle of Sympathy.[26] In his letter of July 9, 1764, to Belle de Zuylen (Zélide) he remarks: "Mr. Smith, whose *Moral Sentiments* you admire so much, wrote to me some time ago, 'Your fault is acting upon system.' " Boswell then goes on to say, "What a curious reproof to a young man from a grave philosopher! It is, however, a just one, and but too well founded with respect to me."[27] In his essay "On Penuriousness & Wealth" (*The Hypochondriack,* June 1782), Boswell refers briefly to an idea from the *Theory:* that "we do not sympathise with the over-heated feelings of those who are in love"; and in his Journal entry of October 29, 1787, he also refers to the *Theory* in connection with a discussion he had with Edmund Burke (PP, 17, p. 51).

From Boswell's writings we can learn a little about Adam Smith and, indirectly, a little about Boswell himself. From Smith's writings, on the other hand, we cannot learn anything about Boswell. What a valuable literary possession it would be if the great economist, like his young acquaintance and fellow Scot, had kept a journal. (He *may* have kept a diary during his trip to Europe with the young Duke of Buccleuch, but if he did it has been lost.) In such a journal there undoubtedly would have been entries about Boswell, some highly interesting entries, especially if Smith had decided to comment on his friend's opinions and personal behavior. But unfortunately Smith was not a journal writer. As a consequence we are denied some additional sidelights on Boswell, not that we are gravely lacking in information about him, and particularly are we denied information on Smith himself, about whom much is unknown.

Adam Smith and Samuel Johnson first met in September 1761, in London. Smith was thirty-eight years of age at the time; Johnson was fifty-two. The initial contact between the two men, which took place at the home of William Strahan the publisher, was not entirely cordial. In fact, it was marked by a bitter quarrel. What words actually passed between the two celebrities when, as Johnson expressed it, they "did not take to each other" it is difficult to say, at least with absolute certainty. No direct, eyewitness record of the quarrel has come down to us.

But there does exist an account of a verbal clash between Smith and Johnson in which some of the words they used (or supposedly used) are recalled. This account, which is invariably mentioned when the great economist and great moralist are discussed, owes its popularity largely to Sir Walter Scott. Though Scott's recital of the clash is the best known, the story of the quarrel is also told by William Wilberforce's sons (who, presumably, heard it from their father), and by Francis Jeffrey who learned of it, according to his own testimony, from one who saw Smith immediately after the encounter took place.[28]

Sir Walter, who obtained his information from Professor John Millar, sets forth the famous story in his anecdotal and amusing letter of January 30, 1829, to John Wilson Crocker.[29] Crocker published it in his edition of *Boswell's Life of Samuel Johnson*, thus giving it a degree of currency it would not otherwise have had.

According to Sir Walter's account of the quarrel, Johnson and Smith met at a party in Glasgow. Johnson immediately took his new acquaintance to task about a statement he had made in a laudatory letter concerning his late friend David Hume. (Since Hume's nonreligious attitude was very distasteful to Johnson, his attack might have been expected.) After Johnson's outburst, and the retort it evoked, Smith left the party and went to another one. There the persons who were present were anxious to learn what had happened when the two men met, since they were aware that such a meeting was to take place. But now let us follow Scott directly in his telling of the story.

"Adam Smith, whose temper seemed much ruffled, answered only at first, 'He is a brute! he is a brute!' Upon closer examination it appeared that Dr. Johnson no sooner saw Smith than he brought forward a charge against him for something in his famous letter on the death of Hume. Smith said he had vindicated the truth of the statement. 'And what did the Doctor say?' was the universal query: 'Why, he said—he said—' said Smith, with the deepest impression of resentment, 'he said—*You lie!*' 'And what did you reply?' 'I said, You are a son of a *b . . . h!*' " (In the Wilberforce account the complete word is spelled out.)

Thus ends the story of the quarrel and its immediate aftermath as related by Sir Walter Scott. But Scott's concluding observation on the incident must of necessity be quoted: "On such terms did these two great moralists meet and part, and such was the classic dialogue betwixt them."

There are some gross inconsistencies in the preceding story, a fact that was long ago pointed out. Croker, whose edition of *Boswell's Life of Samuel Johnson* was so vigorously (and somewhat unfairly) criticized by his political adversary Macaulay, declared that the story "is *certainly* erroneous in the important particulars of the *time, place,* and *subject* of the alleged quarrel." Adopting what seems to be an extreme view, Crocker expressed his disbelief in the whole account.[30] John Rae, more than half a century later, also declared (pp. 157-158) that "Time, place, and subject are all alike wrong," though he does not dismiss the story in the manner that Crocker does. Another writer, whose statement suggests what a lethal weapon students of history have at their command, affirms that the place and date of Scott's story "do not bear the shrivelling rays of Historical Research."[31]

The factual inconsistencies in the Scott anecdote (and in the Wilberforce and Jeffrey versions, too) are evident from the following pieces of information. The encounter between Johnson and Smith was supposed to have occurred in Glasgow on October 29, 1773, the only occasion that Johnson was ever in the city. He and Boswell were then on the return leg of their journey to the Highlands and the Hebrides. At that time, however, Smith was not in Glasgow but in London, finishing *The Wealth of Nations.* Another glaring inconsistency in the anecdote is the fact that Hume did not die in 1773, when the clash between the two men was supposed to have taken place, but in 1776. A very good story thus turns out to be seriously at fault. However, it is still presented to the public in the general form in which Scott first told it, and without any reference to its internal inconsistencies. (One can find the story in this form in Holbrook Jackson's *Bookman's Holiday* and in Hesketh Pearson's *Sir Walter Scott.*)

Although the Scott story in its details will not stand up under analysis, many persons who have heard it undoubtedly feel like asking, with Leslie Stephen, "Should we regret or rejoice to say that it involves an obvious inaccuracy?"[32] Under any circumstances, the story is now well embedded in English literary lore and, with or without corrective explanations, will long continue to be told.

Johnson and Smith did not quarrel in Glasgow in 1773, but it nevertheless seems true that on one occasion they did have a sharp verbal encounter—what Rae (p. 157) calls "a personal altercation of an outrageous character," an altercation "at which, if not the very words reported by Scott, then words quite as strong must manifestly have passed between them." The occasion appears to have been the September 1761 meeting of the two men in London, though conceivably it could have been at another time.

A number of reasons can be given for the 1761 quarrel between Johnson and Smith and for their other and more moderate verbal skirmishes—reasons that go beyond the Great Cham's general "bearish" attitude. For one thing Smith was a Scotsman, and Johnson seemed at times to be prejudiced against the Scots. Boswell suggests why this was, or at least may have been, the case. "If he was particularly prejudiced against the Scots," he declares, "it was because they were more in his way; because he thought their success in England rather exceeded the due proportion of their real merit; and because he could not but see in them that nationality which I believe no liberal-minded Scotsman will deny" (HP,V, p. 20).

But this particular prejudice of Johnson's must not be exaggerated. It is of more than minor significance to note that not

only was Boswell a Scotsman but so were five of the six amanuenses Johnson used in compiling his *Dictionary*. Johnson's rather
frequent ribbing of the Scots (including the aspersion contained
in his celebrated definition at "oats") should therefore not be
taken too seriously, though, on the other hand, it should not be
wholly dismissed as a bit of playful vindictiveness. However, for
further observations on the issue—"Did Dr. Johnson Hate Scotland and the Scottish?"—the reader will have to look elsewhere.[33]

Johnson's early lack of enthusiasm for Smith may have been
due partly to certain remarks Smith had made in his review of
The Dictionary of the English Language. It is also possible that
there had come to Johnson's ears some of the statements Smith
had uttered in his Glasgow lectures. As we observed in the first
of our essays, he had spoken in uncomplimentary terms of *The
Rambler*. Moreover, it may be that Johnson had learned of Smith's
statement that "Of all writers antient and modern, he that keeps
the greatest distance from common sense is Dr. Samuel Johnson."[34]
Certainly, if Johnson knew of this remark he would not feel
strongly inclined to "take to" Smith. And finally, the very close
friendship that existed between Smith and David Hume did little
to endear the economist to Johnson—or to Boswell.

In the years following the 1761 quarrel the relationship between Smith and Johnson became much more amicable. On
December 1, 1775, shortly before *The Wealth of Nations* was
published, Smith became a member (No. 24, following Edward
Gibbon) of the Literary Club of London. In view of Johnson's
prominence in the club this could hardly have happened had there
existed any strong feelings of bitterness between him and Smith.
At the meetings of the club and at the homes of mutual friends the
two men occasionally met and apparently treated one another with
respect. However, they were still not averse to making strong
remarks about one another to other persons.

C. R. Fay has appropriately stated that the differences between
Johnson and Smith should not be permitted to overshadow the
admiration they felt for "each other's forte, as expressed to third

persons, however much they might snap at one another when face to face."[35] Expressions of this admiration are not difficult to find, but before examining them let us consider a few more examples of snapping. There was snapping after 1775, when Smith became a member of the famous club, as well as before, and some of it, probably most of it, was done when the two celebrities were *not* face to face.

First there is the so-called Brentford incident about which Boswell (on the basis of information from John Anderson) tells us (HP,IV, pp. 186, 615; V, p. 369). The date of this incident is not definitely known, but it could have been 1761. At whatever date it occurred, Smith, in Johnson's presence, was apparently boasting of Glasgow; he was "expatiating on the beauty" of the city. Johnson was not impressed and rebuked him with the question, "Pray, Sir have you ever seen Brentford?" Since Brentford had apparently been regarded as a very unattractive place—it was the "town of mud" in James Thomson's *Castle of Indolence*—the question was obviously a very unkind one.

Johnson had never seen Glasgow when he asked his question, a fact which makes it all the more unkind and unmerited. In 1773, however, as we noted earlier, Johnson visited the city when he and Boswell were returning from their northern tour. On that occasion (HP,V, p. 369) Boswell reminded him of the retort he had made to Smith: "I put him in mind of it today, while he expressed his admiration of the elegant buildings, and whispered him, 'Don't you feel some remorse?' " In his *Tour* Boswell does not indicate any reply to the question; but in his *Life of Johnson* (HP,IV, p. 186), where the story is somewhat amplified, he says that Johnson answered, "Why, then Sir, *You* have never seen Brentford?" Not a particularly compelling retort, one must admit.

Another episode involving a direct clash between Johnson and Smith, and here the clash is af a very minor nature, has to do with the verses of one Dr. Bentley. Again we learn from Boswell— he is our chief informant in all these matters—that Johnson praised the verses highly in Smith's presence, and recited them "with his usual energy." Smith thereupon remarked, "In his decisive professorial manner, 'Very well—Very well.' " Johnson remarked back, "Yes, they *are* very well, Sir; but you may observe in what manner they are well. They are the forcible verses of a man of strong mind, but not accustomed to write verse; for there is some uncouthness in the expression" (HP, IV, pp. 23-24).

Coming to some snapping done at a distance, there is Smith's "blockhead" statement, which seems to refer to Johnson as well as to others. In his Journal entry of February 23, 1766, Boswell tells of a conversation he had with Goldsmith, in which he referred to a story of "Johnson and Goldsmith and those Blockheads" (PP, 7, p. 83). Boswell attributed the story to Smith: "I told him 't was Smith *who said it.*" From Goldsmith's reply—"Well, by telling me it was he, you have given me a plaister for the Sore" —it would seem that he interpreted Smith's story to imply that he, Goldsmith, was a blockhead. If this is true, then it follows that Johnson too was covered by the epithet.

On April 2, 1775, Boswell called on Smith in London. Among other remarks Smith made on the occasion was one about Johnson. It was the economist's view that the latter's "roughness" was due "to a certain degree of insanity which he thought he had" (PP, 10, 176). Perhaps one should not look upon this statement as an unkind one but as an understanding, charitable remark— a remark which implied that Johnson's roughness was unintended and nonvindictive.

One can wonder whether a very mild bit of snapping on Smith's part is contained in his remark in *The Wealth of Nations* (p. 697) about the printed debates of the House of Commons as being "not always the most authentic records of truth." Johnson reported the parliamentary debates for the *Gentleman's Magazine* from July, 1741 to March, 1744 (and perhaps somewhat later), taking no small textual liberties in the process.[36]

Returning to snaps coming from Johnson, there is the one mentioned in Boswell's Journal entry for March 17, 1776. Boswell notes that Johnson had said to him the day before that "Adam Smith was a most disagreeable fellow after he had drank some wine, which, he said, 'bubbled in his mouth' " (PP, 11, p.

148). This personal remark could well have been the truth, but it was an unkind observation to make, especially by one whose own manner of eating left much to be desired.

Less than a month later, on April 13, 1776, Boswell makes another Journal entry which appears to be a statement uttered by Johnson, and one concerning Smith. One cannot be absolutely certain on the point, since Boswell removed a number of pages from his records to use as copy. His narrative, continuing on the preserved pages, has these words: ". . . said Adam Smith was as dull a dog as he had ever met with" (PP, II, p. 250). If Johnson made this statement, it should be pointed out in all justice that about the same time, as we shall see shortly, he also paid a tribute to Smith.

Two final snaps, these by Smith, may be cited. In the account of his 1780 talks with Smith, the young interviewer who wrote under the pen name of *Amicus* declares that Smith had "a very contemptuous opinion" of Johnson, and then goes on to mention a number of examples Smith had given of Johnson's peculiar behavior.[37] Again, in 1789, the year before his death, Smith made an observation to Samuel Rogers, who was visiting Edinburgh, that *may* have been an unkind reference to Johnson (who had died in 1784). Rogers inquired of Smith if he knew Mrs. Piozzi (the former Mrs. Thrale, and close friend of Johnson), who was living in Edinburgh at the time. Smith said he had not met her and then added that he thought she had been spoiled "by keeping company with odd people."[38]

The preceding examples of snapping between Smith and Johnson will serve to show that though the two celebrities became friends, their friendship was not of an intimate nature. To some extent their snappings were probably nothing more than candid expressions of opinion, but they nevertheless point to a lack of warmth in the relationship between the renowned economist and the famous moralist.

But now we must note some instances in which the two men spoke approvingly of one another. Following the sentiment expressed by Professor Fay, we must not let these instances of admiration and goodwill be overshadowed—completely overshadowed—by the critical and derogatory remarks the men made of each other.

A fine bit of testinmony in support of the contention that Smith and Johnson admired "each other's forte" is found in the tribute the former pays to the Preface in the latter's famous edition of Shakespeare, which was published in 1763. In Smith's estimation, so William Seward tells us, the Preface was "the most manly piece of criticism that was ever published in any country" (HP, I, p. 496). This tribute may sound unduly generous, but the merit of Johnson's Preface (and of his edition of Shakespeare in general), has been recognized by other critics. Indeed, one very competent modern critic refers to the Preface as "one of the most decisive documents in the entire history of criticism," and declares that the Preface remains what Smith said it was.[39]

Smith also paid a high compliment to Johnson's knowledge of books. Discussing the breadth of Johnson's reading, Boswell declares that "we may be absolutely certain, both from his writings and his conversation, that his reading was very extensive." And then he adds, "Dr. Adam Smith, than whom few were better judges on the subject, once observed to me that 'Johnson knew more books than any man alive' " (HP, I, pp. 70-71).

If on occasion Smith spoke kindly of Johnson, Johnson on the other hand sometimes spoke kindly of Smith. Smith's strong preference for verse that rhymes over blank verse struck a very responsive chord in Johnson, and his remark on the matter is often quoted. It will be recalled that when Johnson learned from Boswell of Smith's view he said (HP, I, pp. 427-428) that "had I known that he loved rhyme as much as you tell me he does, I should have HUGGED him."

A stronger expression of kindliness on Johnson's part was his defense of Smith's qualifications for writing a book like *The Wealth of Nations*. Smith's great work had just been published and Boswell mentioned it to Johnson, saying that Sir John Pringle had stated to him that "Dr. Smith who had never been in trade, could not be expected to write well on that subject any more than a lawyer upon physick." Johnson did not share Sir John's opinion. "He is mistaken, Sir: a man who has never been engaged in trade himself may undoubtedly write well upon trade, and there is nothing which requires more to be illustrated by philosophy than trade does" (HP, II, pp. 429-430).

It might be added that though Smith never engaged in trade, he had a close relationship with men who did. During the years he resided as a professor in Glasgow, "one of the most enlightened mercantile towns in this island," as Dugald Stewart (pp. 43-43) described it, and also, one might add, one of the most commercially active, Smith became acquainted with numerous business men.[40] From them he acquired a knowledge useful to him in his writing, and in turn he influenced the opinions of at least some of his informants. Before he ended his teaching career at the university he could, in Stewart's words—and on "respectable authority"—"rank some very eminent merchants in the number of his proselytes." Stewart does not tell us, however, the extent to which they were his proselytes. Did they follow Smith in favoring the more or less complete removal of trade restrictions, or just those on the importation of raw materials?[41]

In the 1780s two derogatory tracts relating to Samuel Johnson, and in which Adam Smith figured, were published. In 1782 an anonymous pamphlet, entitled *Deformities of Dr. Samuel Johnson, Selected from his Works,* appeared, first apparently in Edinburgh and then in London. Boswell refers to the author of this production as "some obscure scribbler," and George Steevens, another contemporary, describes the tract as having been written by "a Club of Caledonian Wits" (HP, IV, pp. 148, 499). Smith is mentioned a number of times in the publication, and always to his advantage and Johnson's disadvantage. The tract did not seem to bother Johnson. Steevens tells us that he laughed "at such ribaldry" and offered to give "a very ugly head of himself" to serve as its frontispiece. In 1783 a similar anonymous tract was published, with the title, *A Critical Review of the Works of Samuel Johnson.* Smith is mentioned again, although just in two minor allusions but in the same manner as in the other tract.

The authorship of these two pamphlets has posed a small mystery. Professor Jacob Viner, who tried to unravel the mystery, points to James T. Callender as the author.[42] He also refers to the question—"it may still be relevant"—as to whether Adam Smith was in any way implicated in the exaggerated attacks made by some of his hyperpatriotic countrymen on Johnson. This would appear as a very unlikely possibility.

In describing the various recorded examples of snapping and of tribute-paying on the part of Smith and Johnson we have moved too far along in our story and must now turn back to the 1750s. In 1775 Johnson's voluminous *Dictionary of the English Language* was published. The great work was reviewed the same year in the original *Edinburgh Review*. A highly interesting feature of the review is that it was written by Adam Smith.

Smith was thirty-two years of age at the time and Professor of Moral Philosophy at the University of Glasgow. With the possible exception of the brief Preface to the 1748 edition of the Poems of William Hamilton, this was the first of his writings to appear in print. Johnson was Smith's senior by fourteen years and had already written a great deal in addition to compiling the *Dictionary*. Included in his writings were the *Rambler* essays, *The Vanity of Human Wishes, Irene, The Life of Richard Savage,* and *Parliamentary Debates*. The work on the *Dictionary* itself extended over a number of years. At the same time, however, he was occupied with other writing.

What qualifications, it might be asked, did Smith have for reviewing the *Dictionary?* From the facts presented in our first essay concerning his studies at Oxford, his public lectures on rhetoric and belles lettres at Edinburgh, and the nature of the courses he gave at Glasgow it would seem that he was not unfitted for the task. Certainly a much less capable reviewer could have been selected.

Smith is not without words of praise for the *Dictionary*. "When we compare this book with other dictionaries, the merit of its author," he says, "appears very extraordinary." He feels the *Dictionary* is "highly useful, and the execution of it entitled to praise," but nevertheless he has some criticism to make of it. The chief defect he declares is in the plan of the book, "which appears to us not to be sufficiently grammatical." Though Johnson presents the different meanings of a word, these meanings, Smith affirms, "are seldom digested into general classes, or ranged under the meaning which the word principally expresses." Moreover, the reviewer feels that Johnson has not been careful enough in distinguishing words that are "apparently synonymous." Smith himself demonstrates at length how such a distinction should be made in a number of examples, including "but" and "however," and "humour" and "wit."

After setting forth Johnson's handling of "but" and "humour" and his own proposal for dealing with the two words, Smith makes a few further observations about the *Dictionary*. Among other things he points to the indebtedness that dictionary, or rather "grammar," makers will owe to Johnson and declares that the usefulness of the *Dictionary* will soon be felt in the country "as there is no standard of correct language in conversation."

Was Smith's review of the *Dictionary* favorable or unfavorable? Those who have examined his remarks have not always reached the same conclusion. James Bonar refers to it as a "gentle review"; Mildred C. Struble speaks of it as "a notable and laudatory review"; but C. R. Fay characterizes it as a "sharp review."[43] Some of Smith's detailed remarks are indeed complimentary, but a censure of the whole plan of the work places a great deal of weight on the other side of the appraisal balance, and in Johnson's mind at least the latter observation could easily have been the one that made the more forceful impression.

One or two further observations about Smith's discussion of the *Dictionary* may be noted. Included in his treatment of the word "humour" there is a verbal distinction that is open to criticism. This is the distinction that Smith makes between "wit" and "humour." "Wit," Smith declares, "expresses something that is more designed, concerted, regular, and artificial; humour, something that is more wild, loose, extravagant, and fantastical; something which comes upon a man by fits, which he can neither command nor restrain, and which is not perfectly consistent with true politeness." A few words later Smith goes on to say that "a man of wit is as much above a man of humour, as a gentleman is above a buffoon; a buffoon however will often divert more than a gentleman." (In *his* handling of the word "humour," Johnson makes no mention of "wit.")

Smith's distinction between "wit" and "humour" may have been valid according to the usage of the 1750s, but it is not valid now.[44] In fact, the meanings of the two words seem to have undergone an almost complete change, a complete reversal. Today (as one dictionary, *Funk and Wagnalls,* points out), *wit* is "keen, sudden, brief, and sometimes severe"; whereas *humor* is "deep, thoughtful, sustained, and always kindly."

As a final observation on Smith's discussion of the *Dictionary* it may be noted that the reviewer makes no mention of the word "oats." It is possible that Johnson's celebrated and playful definition escaped Smith's notice. Or perhaps he decided to pass it by with no comments—a policy that writers coming after Smith have great difficulty in following. The definition, it wil be recalled, is as follows: Oats is "A grain, which in England is generally given to horses, but in Scotland supports the people."[45]

As we have already noted, Smith and Johnson first met in September 1761. The meeting place was the home of William Strahan in London. Smith was again in London in the early part of 1764, before he and the young Duke of Buccleuch set out on their trip to the continent. His visit on this occasion was brief and apparently he did not see Johnson. Johnson may not have been in the city at the time—he could well have been with the Langton family in Lincolnshire. On his return to England with the Duke in November 1766, Smith once more stopped in London and remained there for six months, devoting some of his time to turning out a new edition of his *Theory of Moral Sentiments*. During this period the paths of the two men appear not to have crossed.[46]

In the first part of 1773 Smith journeyed to London again and spent most of the next four years there, devoting much of his time to finishing *The Wealth of Nations* and seeing it through the press. During this period he certainly came into contact with Johnson. Rae (p. 263) mentions a dinner on January 11, 1775, at which both Smith and Johnson were present. And, at the end of the year, on December 1, as we noted earlier, Smith became a member of the Literary Club, of which Johnson was the principal luminary. Johnson himself, however, was not present at the meeting at which Smith was admitted.

According to Dugald Stewart (p. 71), Smith spent the greater part of the two years following the publication of *The Wealth of Nations* (early in 1776) in London, "enjoying a society too extensive and varied to afford him any opportunity of indulging his taste for study." But, says Stewart, this time was not lost "for much of it was spent with some of the first names in English literature." Johnson, of course, would figure in that category, and he and Smith were undoubtedly together intermittently during these months.

Did they discuss Smith's great book on any of the occasions at which they met? This is a good question to ask, but it is a question to which no definite answer can be given. If they did discuss the book no record exists of what they said about it. Similarly there is no record of any correspondence between the two celebrities in which *The Wealth of Nations*—or any other matter—is discussed.

Though Rae makes no mention of the fact,[47] Smith apparently visited London again in 1782. According to the records of the Literary Club, Smith attended six of the sixteen dinners held by the group during that year.[48] Johnson was present at three. We are not told, however, whether the two men were at any of the dinners together. In 1787 Smith, now a very ill man, made his final visit to London. He met a number of famous persons during this stay in the city, including Pitt. Johnson, of course, he could not meet for the Great Cham had died in 1784.

The figures that follow, based on the records of the Literary

Club, show the frequency with which Smith and Johnson were present at the dinners of the club. The years covered, however, are only those during which Smith attended one or more of the gatherings.

Year	Number of Dinners	Times Present Smith	Johnson
1775	6	1	2
1776	15	6	3
1777	15	8	3
1782	16	6	3
1787	15	1	—

If the preceding statistics are correct, the times Smith and Johnson met at the dinners of the club could not have been more than nine (it is to be remembered that Johnson was absent when Smith joined the club in December 1775) and might well have been less. For Croker to say,[49] therefore, that the two men met "frequently" and on civil terms at the club is an exaggeration. However, Smith and Johnson also met at the homes of mutual friends. How often, one cannot say, though the likelihood is that the number of such meetings was not large. Rae's remark (p. 158) that, after 1761, they met "constantly at the table of common friends in London" would also seem to be an exaggeration.

From the preceding analysis it is clear that though Johnson and Smith were contemporaries and acquaintances, they were not close friends. In one sense of the term it might be said they were not friends at all. In any circumstances they were not very friendly friends.

Regardless of how one describes the relationship between the two men, however, a study of the contacts between them and of the attitude each assumed toward the other is of interest and value. Such a study indirectly throws a few rays of light on a truly exciting period in British intellectual history, and directly contributes to our understanding and enjoyment of two of the period's greatest figures.

NOTES

1. Professor Frederick A. Pottle speaks of the greater effect of these lectures on the development of Boswell's "powers"—presumably his powers of literary expression. See *Johnson, Boswell and Their Circle,* Essays Presented to Lawrence Fitzroy Powell (Oxford at the Clarendon Press, 1965), pp. 247-248.

2. *Economic History,* February 1938, p. 36.

3. *Boswell's Life of Johnson,* Hill-Powell, I, pp. 390-392.

4. *The Correspondence of James Boswell and John Johnston of Grange,* ed. by Ralph S. Walker (New York: McGraw-Hill, 1966), p. 7. Boswell alludes to his father's wish in the matter, but also says that his "greatest inducement" in going to Glasgow was to hear Smith lecture.

5. *Correspondence,* p. 7. This letter to Johnston is somewhat mutilated. It contains other tributes, at which the editor guesses, in addition to those mentioned above.

6. *Boswell's Correspondence with the Honourable Andrew Irskine* and *His Journal of a Tour to Corsica,* ed. by George B. Hill (London: De La Rue, 1879), p. 26.

7. *Private Papers of James Boswell from Malahide Castle,* ed. by Geoffrey Scott and Frederick A. Pottle, 18 vols. (Privately printed, 1928-1934), 7, p. 42. In the present essay all further references to and quotations from these papers will be followed by the designation "PP," accompanied by volume number and page number.

8. *Boswell's Journal of a Tour to the Hebrides with Samuel Johnson, LL.D,* ed. by Frederick A. Pottle and Charles H. Bennett (New York: Literary Guild, 1936), p. 159.

9. Quoted by J. M. Keynes in *Economic History,* February 1938, p. 39.

10. *James Boswell: The Earlier Years* (New York: McGraw-Hill, 1966), p. 42.

11. J. T. T. Brown. See *Letters of James Boswell,* ed. by Chauncey B. Tinker, 2 vols. (Oxford at the Clarendon Press, 1924), I, p. 46.

12. *James Boswell: The Earlier Years,* p. 42.

13. *The Works of Samuel Johnson LL.D.,* ed. by Alexander Chalmers, 12 vols. (London: Rivington and others, A New Edition, 1823), XII, pp. 230-231. *The Letters of Samuel Johnson,* ed. by Robert W. Chapman, 3 vols. (Oxford at the Clarendon Press, 1952), I, p. 343. References to the Chalmers edition of Johnson's *Works* will hereafter be referred to by the name of the editor.

14. *A Fragment on Government*, ed. by F. C. Montague (Oxford University Press, 1931), p. 4.

15. *The Memoirs of the Life of Edward Gibbon*, ed. by George B. Hill (New York: Putnam's, 1900), p. 50.

16. Oliver Elton, *A Survey of English Literature, 1730-1780*, 2 vols. (New York: Macmillan, 1928), II, p. 41.

17. On into the next century criticism of the two institutions continued. See *The Letters of Sydney Smith*, ed. by Nowell C. Smith, 2 vols. (Oxford at the Clarendon Press, 1953), II, pp. 535-536, 594, 693.

18. For further discussion of "the Douglas Cause," see Jacob Viner's *Guide* to John Rae's *Life of Adam Smith* (New York: Kelley, 1965), pp. 59-62; *Boswell in Search of a Wife*, ed. by Frank Brady and Frederick A. Pottle (New York: McGraw-Hill, 1956), pp. XIII-XIV, 69-70, 87-88; Lillian de la Torre, *The Heir of Douglas* (New York: Knopf, 1952).

19. The present writer has accepted the word of Lillian de la Torre (p. 214) that Boswell, "by a combination of pastiche and plagiarism," gave the impression that Smith wrote the article. Such writers as Brady and Pottle, Hill and Powell, and Smith's biographers are silent on the matter. Viner, however, who cites de la Torre, gives considerable attention to the question in his *Guide* to Rae.

20. In his Journal—PP, 14, pp. 212, 233—Boswell notes without any comment that on May 2, 3, and 29, 1781, he "called" Smith in London. Smith appears, however, not to have beeen in the city during that year. But on July 13 and 20 the two men met in Edinburgh.

21. *Letters of James Boswell*, ed. by Chauncey B. Tinker, I, pp. 103, 118.

22. William R. Scott, *Adam Smith, an Oration* (Glasgow: Jackson, 1938), p. 9. For an account of the discovery of the early draft of Smith's book and for a reprint of the draft itself, see Professor Scott's book *Adam Smith as Student and Professor*, pp. 317-356.

23. *Economic History*, February 1938, p. 50.

24. *Letters of James Boswell*, ed. by Chauncey B. Tinker, I, p. 250.

25. *The Hypochondriack*, ed. by Margery Bailey, 2 vols.(Stanford University: Stanford University Press, 1928), II, pp. 63-64.

26. *Boswell in Holland*, ed. by Frederick C. Pottle (New York: McGraw-Hill, 1952), p. 174.

27. *Boswell in Holland*, p. 308. In his *Theory of Moral Sentiments* (pp. 163-165) Smith writes of the fascination people have in seeing beautiful and grand "systems." But he declares that from "a certain spirit of system," from "a certain love of art and contrivance," we sometimes seem to attach more significance to means than to ends.

The achievement of worthy ends appears to count less with us than the attainment of fine arts and contrivances. It is possible that Smith had this attitude in mind when he made his remark to Boswell.

28. For the Wilberforce version of the story see *The Correspondence of William Wilberforce,* ed. by Robert I. and Samuel Wilberforce, 2 vols. (London: Murray, 1840), I, p. 40. The editors have Smith himself tell about the story in the spring of 1787. Rae (pp. 156-157) characterizes this way of handling the story as absurd. The Jeffrey reference to the story is contained in his review of the Wilberforce *Correspondence* in the *Edinburgh Review,* October 1840, p. 27. Jeffrey said he could "vouch for the conformity" of the Wilberforce account "in every particular," though, according to his recollection (he heard the story almost fifty years previously), "Dr. Johnson's first address was even more rude and insulting than as there represented."

29. The letter is printed in *The Croker Papers* (The Correspondence and Diaries), ed. by Louis J. Jennings, 3 vols. (London: Murray, 1884), II, pp. 28-34. It is also in *The Letters of Walter Scott,* ed. by Herbert J. C. Grierson, 12 vols. (London: Constable, Centenary Edition, 1932-1937), XI, pp. 110-120. Rae (p. 156) says that Smith himself told the anecdote to Millar the night the quarrel occurred.

30. *The Life of Samuel Johnson, LL. D. by James Boswell,* ed. by John Wilson Croker, 10 vols. (London: Bohn, 1857), V, p. 115.

31. Mrs. Clement Parsons (Florence Mary [Wilson] Parsons), *Garrick and His Circle* (New York: Putnam's, 1906), p. 231.

32. *Samuel Johnson* (London: Macmillan, 1914), p. 115.

33. An article with the above title, by Karl Brunner, will be found in *English Studies,* October 1949, pp. 184-190.

34. See Scott, *Adam Smith as Student and Professor,* p. 122. The statement concerning Johnson and common sense was included in some biographical notes on Smith, printed in the London *Times* (July 24, 1790) at the time of his death. Fay reprints the notes in *Adam Smith and the Scotland of His Day* (Cambridge at the University Press, 1956), pp. 32-35.

35. *Adam Smith and the Scotland of His Day,* p. 130.

36. According to Donald J. Greene, the consensus among students of Johnson appears to be that "what Johnson was doing was *composing* speeches, rather than *reporting* them, in the modern sense." *The Politics of Samuel Johnson* (New Haven: Yale University Press, 1960), p. 113.

37. *The Bee,* May 11, 1791, pp. 2-3.

38. W. Forbes Gray, *An Edinburgh Miscellany* (Edinburgh: Grant, 1925), pp. 40-41.

39. Walter J. Bate, *The Achievement of Samuel Johnson* (New York: Oxford, 1955) p. 41.

40. For a fuller treatment of Smith's acquaintanceship with the merchants of Glasgow and with the practical aspects of commerce, see David Murray, *Early Burgh Organization in Scotland,* 2 vols. (Glasgow: Maclehose, Jackson, 1924-32), I, pp. 443-455.

41. See Rae, pp. 92-93.

42. Viner examines the whole question in some detail in his *Guide to Rae* (pp. 62-70). He is inclined to stress somewhat more than a number of writers (including the present one) who have dealt with the issue the coldness in the relationship between Johnson and Smith. See p. 58.

43. Bonar, *The Tables Turned* (London: Macmillan, 1931), p. 43; Struble, *A Johnson Handbook* (New York: Crofts, 1933), p. 140; Fay, *Adam Smith and the Scotland of His Day,* p. 131.

44. A useful historical analysis of the meaning of the two terms will be found in *The Encyclopaedia Britannica,* under "Wit." A much longer discussion of the question, with special reference to the eighteenth and early nineteenth centuries, is presented in Stuart M. Tave, *The Amiable Humorist* (University of Chicago Press, 1960).

45. One or two further remarks on oats may be justified. The reply that Lord Elibank made to Johnson's definition, as reported by Sir Walter Scott, should be mentioned. "Very true," said this loyal and witty Scotsman, "and where will you find such *men* and such *horses?*" (Hill-Powell, I, pp. 294-295). Johnson himself was fond of oatmeal as a boy, a fact that Boswell was pleased to know since he could point out to Johnson that such a food item was not consumed by the Scottish people alone. (Hill-Powell, V, p. 308).

46. Scott, *Adam Smith as Student and Professor,* p. 122, appears to imply that Smith and Johnson did meet during this period.

47. In his account of Smith's 1787 visit to London, Rae (p. 404) indeed refers to the economist's "last" visit in 1777.

48. *Annals of The Club, 1764-1914* (Oxford: University Press, Printed for the Club, London, 1914), p. 27. This edition of the *Annals* embodies the study made by Sir Mountstuart Elphinstone Grant Duff and published in 1905. If Smith attended six dinners during the year—and one might question the accuracy of the figure—his visit in London was of long duration or else he made more than one trip to the city.

49. Hill-Powell, V, p. 370. It is also an exaggeration for Thorold Rogers to say that Smith paid "many" visits to London while he was Commissioner of Customs. Rogers modifies his statement somewhat a little later by referring to a statement made by Smith's biographer (presumably Dugald Stewart) that he made "several visits to London

while he held his office." See Preface to his edition of *The Wealth of Nations,* 2 vols. (Oxford at the Clarendon Press, Second ed., 1880), I, p. xviii. It would seem that during the period he was at the Customs House, Smith journeyed to the metropolis only in 1882 and 1887, though it is conceivable he might have made a visit or two at other times. *The Annals of The Club,* however, do not show Smith at any meeting of the group for any year during the 1778-1790 period except 1882 and 1887.

5.

Samuel Johnson's Economic Ideas—and Adam Smith

> Each of them—notably for instance, the political economist—may sometimes find Johnson mistaken; not one will ever find him dull.
>
> —John Bailey

Referring to Adam Smith's classic, *The Wealth of Nations,* George Birkbeck Hill declares (HP, II, p. 430) that "Johnson can scarcely have read Smith; if he did, it made no impression on him. His ignorance on many points as to what constitutes the wealth of a nation remained as deep as ever." It may well be that Johnson read very little of Smith's famous work—perhaps he did not read any of it, though this seems doubtful—and it is clear that he nowhere gives a well-rounded account of "what constitutes the wealth of a nation." Nevertheless, in his various writings he made pointed observations on influences that have a bearing on the economic well-being of a nation, and he also expressed opinions on numerous other, and more detailed, economic matters. And interestingly enough not a few of his views bear a close resemblance to opinions held by Adam Smith. Most of Johnson's remarks on economic matters, however, were made before 1776, the year in which *The Wealth of Nations* was published.

Johnson was much better acquainted with the "practical" aspects of economic life than Smith, though the old notion about the great economist's unbusinesslike nature is grossly exaggerated if not absolutely false. George Steevens stated that Johnson's "knowledge in manufactures was extensive, and his comprehension relative to mechanical contrivances was still more extraordinary"; and he, Steevens, referred to Richard Arkwright's opinion that Johnson was "the only person who, on a first view, understood both the principle and powers of his most complicated piece of machinery."[1] On the trip he and Boswell had to the Highlands of Scotland and the Hebrides, Johnson frequently demonstrated his knowledge of the manufacturing arts. On one occasion, for example, he described to an assembled group how coins are produced, and later how breweries are operated. (On hearing the first description one of the members of the group declared that "he thought he had been bred in the Mint," and on hearing the second, "that he had been bred a brewer.") At another point Johnson described the process of tanning and "the nature of milk and the various operations upon it, as making whey, etc." It is not surprising that Boswell was amazed at the variety of his knowledge and pleased "to find such a genius bestowing his attention on the usful arts."[2]

Johnson's knowledge of "the useful arts" was undoubtedly helpful to him in his thinking about economic matters. But he was well acquainted with the fact, sometimes lost sight of now as well as in the eighteenth century, that familiarity with the practical processes of commerce and industry—ability to "meet a payroll," in other words—is not essential to a mastery of economics. This fact is well brought out in a remark he made at the time Smith's *Wealth of Nations* was published. Boswell reported to Johnson that "Sir John Pringle had observed to me, that Dr. Smith, who had never been in trade, could not be expected to write well on that subject any more than a lawyer on Physick." Johnson thereupon replied: "He is mistaken, Sir: a man who has never been engaged in trade himself may undoubtedly write well on trade, and there is nothing which requires more to be illustrated by philosophy than trade does" (HP, II, p. 430).

Not only was Johnson acquainted with many of the practical

aspects of industry but he had a keen appreciation of the basic motivating force that governed industrial activity in the form it was then taking. "No one," it has been well said,[3] "has ever expressed in so eloquent a phrase as Johnson's the spirit of the new and insurgent capitalism"—the "phrase" being the exaggerated remark he made at the time Henry Thrale's brewery was being sold: "We are not here to sell a parcel of boilers and vats, but the potentiality of growing rich, beyond the dreams of avarice" (HP, IV, p. 87).

Though Johnson was keenly interested in economic matters, we can hardly call him an economist. It would be most improper to place him in the same category as Smith and such other, and lesser known, contemporaries as Josiah Tucker and Sir James Steuart, or to link his name with the more specialized and professional economists who first came on the scene in the nineteenth century. But using a very flexible modern expression, we can very appropriately, and in no sense derogatorily, speak of Johnson as an "amateur economist."

The evidence to support Johnson's right to notice as an amateur economist is substantial. It extends over many years of his life and is found in many of his writings, often in scattered fragments and frequently mixed with political opinions and moral dicta. Economic ideas or discussions are present in his *Dictionary of the English Language;* in *The Rambler* and *The Idler;* in such essays as "Further Thoughts on Agriculture" and "Considerations on the Corn Laws;" in his *Journey to the Western Islands of Scotland,* a book which according to Richard Jenkins had "more good sense upon trade in it, than he should hear in the House of Commons in a year, except from Burke" (HP, III, p. 137); and in a number of his other writings. Additional primary sources are *Boswell's Life of Johnson* and his *Tour to the Hebrides.*

Further evidence concerning Johnson's standing as an amateur economist can be found in a number of other places. This additional evidence we shall briefly examine before we turn to a more detailed analysis of some of the specific opinions that Johnson held.

First there is the preface he wrote for Robert Dodsley's school textbook, *The Preceptor,* which was pubished in 1748.[4] Commenting on the section of the book on trade and commerce, Johnson states that it is incumbent on every man in the country "to understand at least the general principles" of the subject. Since the well-being of every person is affected by trade and commerce everyone should know "what changes of property are advantageous, or when the balance of trade is on our side: what are the products or manufactures of other countries; and how far one nation may in any species of traffick obtain or preserve superiority over another."

Johnson further remarks that "our chief design" in this particular section of the book is to arouse interest in the question of trade and commerce. For collateral reading (as we would say today) he suggests the following authors: Thomas Mun, Sir Josiah Child, John Locke, Charles Davenant, and Joshua Gee. These writers were precursors of Adam Smith and were imbued, to varying degrees, with the economic philosophy of Mercantilism.

A short time after his *Dictionary of the English Language* was published in 1755—and, as we noted in the previous Essay, Smith reviewed the *Dictionary* in the first issue of the original *Edinburgh Review*—Johnson apparently gave some thought to compiling another dictionary. This was to be a *Dictionary of Trade and Commerce.* In his *Life of Samuel Johnson,* which was published anonymously by G. Kearsley shortly after Johnson's death, William Cooke (the presumed author) states that Johnson proposed such a volume to a number of booksellers who had convened for the purpose of considering the proposition. The proposal, we are told, was at first greeted with silence, but then "a well-known son of the trade, remarkable for the abruptness of his manners, replied, 'Why, Doctor, what the devil do you know of trade and commerce?'" In words of surprising mildness Johnson replied, "Why, sir, not much, I must confess, in the practical line; but I believe I could glean, from different authors of authority on the subject, such materials as would answer the purpose very well."[5]

Some question has been raised as to the absolute accuracy

of this story. Hill states that parts of the account are incorrect, and A. T. Hazen asserts that "Despite minor inaccuracies, there is probably a degree of truth" in the Cooke anecdote.[6] Arthur Murphy, who was a friend of Johnson's, makes a more positive statement. He speaks of Archibald Hamilton, a printer (William Strahan's manager), who remembered that Johnson "engaged in a Commercial Dictionary, and, as appears by the receipts in his possession, was paid his price for several sheets."[7] There is some reason, therefore, for believing that Johnson had given a little thought at least to producing a dictionary dealing with the subject of trade and commerce, though Cooke's amusing story may not be accurate.

Though he did not "engage" extensively in a dictionary of trade and commerce, Johnson wrote a preface to such a work. This was the dictionary compiled by "a singular character," as Johnson judged him, named Richard Rolt, and published in 1756. That Rolt was singular is suggested by the fact that he claimed acquaintanceship with Johnson, though the latter declared that he had never seen him and, what is more, had never read his dictionary. Why then, it might be inquired, did he consent to write the preface to Rolt's volume? Johnson himself answers the question in these words: "The booksellers wanted a Preface to a Dictionary of Trade and Commerce. I knew very well what such a Dictionary should be, and I wrote a Preface accordingly" (HP, I, p. 359).

Johnson's preface, which runs to approximately two thousand five hundred words, was hailed as a work of definite merit, just as the *Dictionary* itself was subject to harsh criticism. In the preface, Boswell declares, Johnson "displays such a clear and comprehensive knowledge of the subject, as might lead the reader to think that its authour had devoted all his life to it" (HP, I, p. 359). Some decades later J. R. McCulloch, himself the author of a dictionary of commerce, said with reference to Rolt's volume that "The best part of this work is its Preface, which was contributed by Dr. Johnson"; and still later McCulloch again referred to the dictionary (of which he was unduly critical) and to the

Johnson preface in these words: "A wretched compilation, without learning or talent of any kind. The only good thing in it is its preface, which was written by Dr. Johnson."[8] The preface to the *Dictionary* is indeed intelligent and interesting. It shows that Johnson had a clear and comprehensive view of "what such a Dictionary should be." It also indicates considerable economic erudition on his part.

We shall now turn to a survey of some of Johnson's economic ideas, comparing them where possible with views held by Adam Smith. Where similarities exist it is not to be inferred, however, that Smith had any particular influence on Johnson—or Johnson on Smith. Though the latter's *Theory of Moral Sentiments* was published in 1759, his great economic treatise, *The Wealth of Nations,* did not appear until 1776. Johnson was then sixty-seven years of age and, apart from the *Lives of the Poets,* his major writings had been completed. He had met Smith quite some years before but most of the personal contacts between the two celebrities, and there were not a great many such contacts, took place after Smith became a member of the famous Literary Club of London in December 1775.[9] It seems clear that Johnson's economic views, as these were expressed in his writings, could not have been appreciably influenced by the opinions of Adam Smith. On the other hand, the latter's views were little influenced, if they were influenced at all, by Johnson's writings. It is interesting to note, however, that Smith had *The Idler* and *The Rambler* essays and other works by Johnson in his personal library.[10]

If Smith did not exert any influence on Johnson's economic views, the same cannot be said of the Mercantilist writers. In his study of "Dr. Johnson and Mercantilism,"[11] John H. Middendorf examines this influence, noting however a considerable number of instances where Johnson departed from common Mercantilist tenets. In light of these departures, and in view of the rather frequent similarity that exists between the economic opinions held by Johnson and Smith, one should not overemphasize the Mercantilist element in Johnson's thinking and writing.[12]

The central theme of economics is wealth, and our author had a great deal to say about the subject. He also had much to say about poverty, about the absence or lack of wealth. Indeed, if he had written a treatise on economics before Smith's book appeared he might well have called it, not *The Wealth of Nations* but *The Poverty of Nations,* or, more accurately, *Poverty Within Nations.* Such a volume would have emphasized an aspect of economics that is today receiving an immense amount of attention. Johnson knew much about poverty from firsthand experience, and it is not surprising that he should so often return to the issue.

At a time when we have become increasingly concerned about the economic lot of the low-income receivers it is especially pertinent to note Johnson's observation, expressed in his *Journey to the Western Islands of Scotland,* that the condition of a country is not to be gauged by the position of its upper-class members. "Nor is public happiness," he maintains, "to be estimated by the assemblies of the gay, or the banquets of the rich," but by the circumstances surounding the masses. "The true state of every nation is the state of common life."[13] Adam Smith's view on the matter was much the same. "No society can surely be flourishing and happy," he says (WN, p. 79), "of which the far greater part of the members are poor and miserable." Both Johnson and Smith had a more direct and a more profound interest in the economic lot of the masses than, in general, the Mercantilists had. The two major concerns of the latter were national wealth and power. Some of the members of the group, however, including Josiah Child, were keenly interested in the condition of the poor. Along with the power-wealth type of Mercantilism, there was a "social Mercantilism" as well, a fact that has not been adequately understood and appreciated.[14]

Johnson placed poverty high on the list of human afflictions. "There is scarcely among the evils of human life," he declared in 1750 (*Rambler,* No. 53),[15] "any so generally dreaded as poverty"; and he points to a whole catalog of dire consequences that follow from poverty. In another *Rambler* essay (No. 202) he declares that "poverty may easily be endured, while associated with dignity and reputation," but he did not believe that such an association often existed. Three decades after expressing these views he again speaks of the terrible results of poverty. Writing to Boswell on March 28, 1782, he states that "Poverty, my dear friend, is so great an evil, and pregnant with so much temptation, and so much misery, that I cannot but earnestly enjoin you to avoid it." Then he goes on to tell Boswell, "Live on what you have; live if you can on less" (HP, IV, p. 149; see also p. 152). This bit of advice would have met with the enthusiastic approval of Adam Smith.

In *The Rambler* essay to which we have just referred (No. 202), Johnson makes another observation on poverty that should be noted in passing. He declares that "To be poor, in the epick language, is only not to command the wealth of nations, nor to have fleets and armies in pay." It will be observed that the abbreviated title of Smith's great treatise is embodied in Johnson's remark. In view of this fact is might be asked if that is where the Scottish economist got the title for his book. The probability is that he did not.[16]

The advice given to Boswell points to a highly important aspect of Johnson's views on poverty and wealth, namely the stress he places on frugality. He was very critical of the spendthrift. Referring to the benefits of frugality and to the miseries, "so numerous and so grievous," that result from its neglect, he states (*Rambler,* No. 57) that its practice "ought to be recommended with every variation of address, and adapted to every class of understanding." In a piling up of metaphors, he goes on to affirm that "Frugality may be termed the daughter of prudence, the sister of temperance, and the parent of liberty." And he lays down, "as a rule never to be broken," the maxim that *"a man's voluntary expense should not exceed his revenue."*

Johnson appears to have held the view that the problem of poverty could be largely solved by the practice of frugality, an unduly simple solution to be sure. It was his belief that "without frugality none can be rich, and with it very few would be poor." He declares that he was "sometimes inclined to imagine, that, casual calamities excepted, there might, by universal prudence, be procured an universal exemption from want" (*Rambler,* No. 57). However, he also emphasized voluntary idleness as a cause of poverty. In fact he refers to "multitudes repining at the want of that which nothing but idleness hinders them from enjoying" (*Rambler,* No. 134).

The advice Johnson gave to Boswell, noted a few paragraphs back, would have been endorsed by Adam Smith. Smith also believed in individual thrift. In words that modern "Keynesians" rigidly qualify, the Scottish economist remarked that "every prodigal appears to be a public enemy, and every frugal man a public benefactor" (WN, p. 324).

While both Johnson and Smith extolled the virtues of frugality, they did it for somewhat different reasons. Johnson emphasized the moral and general welfare aspects of frugality. He was not unaware of its economic advantages, however. He spoke of the piece of "mercantile wisdom" that *"A penny saved is two-pence got"* (*Rambler,* No. 57). Adam Smith felt that frugality was essential to the accumulation of capital, which in turn was highly necessary for economic growth. But he certainly would have agreed that it had great individual benefits as well.

Though Johnson preached the virtue of frugality, he was definintely aware of the dangers and the limitations of individual riches, as was Smith. In true Veblenian style he alludes to "a trivial emulation of wealth and spirit" (*Rambler,* No. 51), and he states that "we are all at full liberty to display riches by every mode of ostentation" (*Idler,* No. 73). In similar fashion Smith (WN, p. 172) declares that "With the greater part of rich people, the chief enjoyment of riches consists in the parade of riches, which, in their eye is never so complete as when they appear to possess those decisive marks of opulence which nobody can possess but themselves." Johnson and Smith, unlike Veblen, did not use the term "conspicuous consumption." As far as the relationship between wealth and welfare is concerned, the two writers were well acquainted with the fact that while wealth ordinarily contributes to welfare, it is by no means an accurate index of welfare.

Both Smith and Johnson, indeed, make statements that suggest that wealth contributes very little to welfare. Embedded in the latter's biographical sketch of Francis Drake there is this generalization: "It is, perhaps, a just observation, that, with regard to outward circumstances, happiness and misery are equally diffused through all states of human life."[17] Johnson's remark is a guarded one, but even so it seems somewhat inconsistent with his obervations on the great misery of poverty. Smith's statement, which appears in his earlier book *The Theory of Moral Sentiments* (p. 163), is more sweeping: "In ease of the body and peace of the mind, all the different ranks of life are nearly upon a level, and the beggar, who suns himself by the side of the highway, possesses that security which kings are fighting for." In light of other views that Johnson and Smith express, these remarks should not be taken at their full face value.

Johnson, as a strong supporter of frugality, believed that as long as money was not hoarded and idle it conferred benefits on society as a whole. Thus he states, "A man cannot make a bad use of his money, so far as regards Society, if he does not hoard it; for if he either spends it or lends it out, Society has the benefit" (HP, IV, p. 173). In the economic parlance of today there would be a favorable "employment effect." Smith expressed a similar view to Johnson's. It was his belief that all savings are invested. Savings and investment are in balance, and the economy normally operates under a condition of full-employment equilibrium, a view to which Keynesians again take vigorous exception.

The issue posed by Johnson, and to some extent by Smith, is intimately related to the question of luxury spending, a matter that received a great deal of attention during the Johnsonian era and before. In early economic theory, as A. L. Macfie has pointed out, the doctrine of such spending assumed an importance somewhat comparable to "investment" in current economic thinking.[18] Both promote the economic wellbeing of the nation. Johnson had a considerable amount to say on the question of luxury spending. To some degree his key observations may have been secondhand, perhaps from Bernard Mandeville's *Fable of the Bees,* with its private-vices, public-benefits argument. Some question has been raised, however, concerning Mandeville as a source.[19]

Johnson expressed doubts that luxury (which, he declared, reached very few persons) was having a degenerative effect on England. "I believe there are as many tall men in England now, as ever there were," he remarked to Goldsmith (HP, II, pp. 217-218). In contrast to such a view, however, one can cite other statements from Johnson's writings which point to his fear of luxury, certainly if it is achieved in undesirable ways.[20]

A still further aspect of the general question of wealth and poverty relates to the terms "wealth" and "money." Johnson ordinarily did not confuse the terms. In his *Journey to the Western Islands of Scotland* he points out that "Money and wealth have, by the use of commercial language, been so long confounded, that they are commonly supposed to be the same."[21] This statement could well have come from the chapter in *The Wealth of Nations* in which Smith so harshly, and somewhat unfairly, criticizes the Mercantilist philosophy. Boswell quotes another remark that Johnson once made, however, that seems to contradict the one just mentioned: "As to mere wealth, that is to say, money . . ." (HP, II, p. 430). The use of the expression "mere wealth" is misleading here, but since Johnson goes on to express support of international trade (his words, "the reciprocation of the peculiar advantages of different countries," point to an important aspect of the theory of international trade), it is evident that he did *not* believe money and wealth are synonymous.

Johnson was well aware that, over time, there may be marked differences between the nominal and the real value of money; that is, that the purchasing power of money may, and does, change. (He does not speak of "inflation" and "deflation," however, nor does Smith.) At one point in his *Journey* he refers to land tenants who, "not having yet arrived at the philosophy of commerce," look upon money as being constant in value; and at a number of other points he adverts to the value-of-money issue.[22] Adam Smith, of course, knew of the distinction involved.

Here a further terminological detail may be noted. In recent years, and largely as a result of the influence of Professor J. K. Galbraith, the word "affluence" has come into prominence. In his *Rambler* essays Johnson occasionally uses the term. In his *Journey to the Western Islands of Scotland,* however, which was published more than thirty years later, his preference is definitely for "opulence." The word "affluence" seems to be completely absent. In *The Wealth of Nations,* Adam Smith occasionally resorts to "affluence," but, as we shall see in Essay 8, he uses "opulence" much more frequently.

If Johnson looked upon poverty as a great evil, it would seem that he viewed idleness, "an anxious and Miserable State," as an even greater evil. After the practice of some of the Mercantilist writers, with their "Doctrine of the Utility of Poverty," Johnson declares that "Raising the wages of day-labourers is wrong; for it does not make them live better, but only makes them idler, and idleness is a very bad thing for human nature" (HP, IV, pp. 176-177). Adam Smith's view was different. Though he felt, in true Malthusian fashion, that "the liberal reward of labour" would, in the long run, promote population growth, it would also, on the whole, increase "the industry of the common people" (WN, p. 81; see also pp. 82-83). This statement closely resembles another, and earlier, utterance of Johnson's to the effect that luxury not only strengthens the poor but multiplies them (HP, II, p. 218). Clearly his two remarks are not entirely consistent.

Both Johnson and Smith, it is interesting to observe, indicated a disadvantage of the piece-rate method of wage payment. The former pointed to poor workmanship; the latter to the danger of overwork (HP, V, p. 263; WN, pp. 81-82). Johnson also referred to the downward stickiness of wages, as it has been more recently phrased, when he remarked that wages (of poor workers) when once they are increased are never lowered.[23]

Johnson's attitude toward idleness is also brought out in the fear he expressed about money going to the idle poor, in contrast to the industrious poor engaged in making luxuries (HP, p. 56), and in his remark that "The prosperity of the people is proportionate to the number of hands and minds usefully employed" (*Idler*, No. 22).

In making the latter remark the specific matter Johnson was dealing with was the unjust imprisonment of debtors. In this context his statement has a great deal of sense. However, as a broad generalization it is not satisfactory. The "prosperity of a people" depends not only on the number of persons in the country who are employed, and *what* these persons produce ("usefully" employed, said Johnson) but on *how much* they produce. This quantitative aspect of the issue is not mentioned by our author. Had he been directly confronted with the issue he would undoubtedly have granted the truth of our contention.

Adam Smith had a different criterion for "the prosperity of a people" than the one adopted by Johnson. He used not the size of the country's usefully employed labor force but the rate of its population increase. "The most decisive mark of the prosperity of any country," he declares (WN, p. 70), "is the increase of the number of its inhabitants." In his discussion Smith implies, however, that "the funds which are destined for the payment of wages" (known in later economic parlance as the "wage fund") increase faster than, or at least as fast as, the population increases. This means that the degree of prosperity of a country is indicated by the behavior of its material living standards. If the wage fund were "sensibly decaying" in any country, that country would indeed be in dire straits, as Smith makes clear.

There is a certain affinity between Johnson's and Smith's indexes of the prosperity of a people, but they are by no means the same. Smith's index, with the assumption that goes along with it, is the more accurate. However, it would have been better had both authors carefully discussed the effect that income distribution has on the nation's prosperity (both recognized in a general way that there is such an effect), and if they then had gone on to make an explicit distinction between economic prosperity and overall welfare (a distinction of which they were well aware).[24]

When Johnson speaks of "the number of hands and minds

usefully employed" he assumes that these hands and minds are free. In other words, freedom of contract prevails—slavery is absent. Smith also assumes the presence of free labor. To both writers slavery was a very undesirable institution, and both strongly criticized it. Johnson's denunciation is particularly sharp. In his essay "Taxation no Tyranny," he asks the rhetorical question "how is it that we hear the loudest yelps for liberty among the drivers of negroes?"[25] Of even greater point is the toast he once gave at Oxford. "Upon one occasion," Boswell relates, "when in company with some very grave men at Oxford, his toast was 'Here's to the next insurrection of the negroes in the West Indies' " (HP, III, p. 200). Smith's attitude toward slavery was perhaps not as hostile as Johnson's but the Scottish moral philosopher and economist minced no words on the matter. While both writers opposed slavery on humanitarian grounds, Smith added the argument that slavery was really economically unsound.[26]

On the question of emigration, which was very much in the forefront during the period of the tour he and Boswell had in the Hebrides, Johnson took an extreme position. He opposed emigration on the grounds that it "weakens the defence of a nation and lessens the comfort of living."[27] In economic terms, emigration (from the Hebrides) pulls down the population below "the optimum," as economists would say today, or reduces it still further below the optimum, thus diminishing per capita output and material living standards. Emigration thins out the population, whereas it is population concentration that "produces high convenience." It does this by promoting specialization, a thought suggestive of Adam Smith's declaration about the division of labor being limited by the extent of the market. Smith, however, was not opposed to emigration.

Closely connected to the question of emigration is the whole issue of the economic desirability of colonies. In general Johnson took a negative attitude toward colonies. He saw no value in establishing them in the first place, but if they had been established he felt they should serve as markets for the manufactured goods of the mother country. To this end the economies of the colonies and the mother country must be integrated and controlled.[28]

Smith had a great deal to say on colonies. He did not oppose their establishment but he was very critical of the way in which, under Mercantilist influences, the economic affairs of the colonies were conducted. He declared, with respect to the American and West Indian colonies of Britain, that "the interest of the home-consumer has been sacrificed to that of the producer with a more extravagant profusion than in all our other commercial regulations." It has not been the consumers, he argued, who have established "this whole mercantile system" but the producers, "whose interest has been so carefully attended to" (WN, p. 626). Smith's views on the rebellion of the American colonists, it might be added, were more tolerant and understanding than those of Johnson.

Johnson was of the opinion that agriculture should play an important role in the life of the nation, though he did not go to the length of the French Physiocrats. In his general economic and political philosohpy Johnson was a strong nationalist and felt that Britain should have a "balanced economy." Agriculture should not be sacrificed to the interests of commerce—commerce being, he said, "one of the daughters of Fortune, inconstant and deceitful as her mother"—nor to the interests of manufacturing. Trade and manufactures, he declared, "however profitable, must yield to the cultivation of lands in usefulness and dignity."[29] The prospect of building up a vast commercial empire had little appeal to Johnson. He was more interested in the establishment of a solid, self-sufficient state.[30]

Such a self-sufficient state did not appeal to Smith. He was interested, of course, in agriculture, greatly interested. In fact, at a number of places his views resembled those of the Physiocrats—he believed that in agriculture Nature works along with man, and that if agriculture is not the only "productive" type of employment it is the most productive. But, in developing countries, Smith placed greater emphasis than Johnson did on manufacturing (with the scope it affords to the domestic division of labor) and on international trade (with the geographical specialization it makes possible). He was not as nationalistically inclined as Johnson; though, on the other hand, he was not the cosmopolitan that some persons have made him out to be.

Indicative of Johnson's partiality toward agriculture was his strong support of the bounty on the exportation of corn (wheat) that existed in Britain at the time. He argued that the bounty resulted in the development of domestic agriculture, an increase in the consumption of wheat, and lower wheat prices.[31] Johnson's Mercantilist view on the bounty was not shared by Smith. Smith, indeed, was highly critical of the bounty. Without using the now popular term "allocation" (and "misallocation"), he maintained that "The effect of bounties, like that of all the other expedients of the mercantile system, can only be to force the trade of a country into a channel much less advantageous than that in which it would naturally run of its own accord." He also asserted that the price of corn had been adversely affected by the bounty. Moreover, he stated that the bounty was "liable" to another objection: that in reality it did *not* promote the output of wheat (WN, pp. 473, 474, 483). Two opinions could hardly be more divergent than those of Johnson and Smith on the effects of this part of the Corn Laws.

Earlier in our analysis we referred to a statement of Johnson's about international trade—"the reciprocation of the peculiar advantages of different countries." The author is here referring to the benefits of specialization on an international basis. At another point, and some years later, Johnson made a remark which seems to conflict with his earlier statement. "When all nations are traders," he says, "there is nothing to be gained by trade."[32] The answer to this discrepancy in opinion is that though strong competition may lessen, or even destroy, the private profits of trade, there are still social advantages to be received from such trade growing out of the international division of labor that it involves. Johnson's belief that trade "will stop soonest where it is brought to the greatest perfection" is indeed far-fetched. In general, he felt that trade, both domestic and international, served a useful purpose, or rather set of purposes, but it did not rank with agriculture.[33]

Johnson recognized the economic value of self-interest, which is a cardinal principle in *The Wealth of Nations*. The desire for wealth or riches is, in his opinion, a very powerful motivating factor and one of immense social and individual significance. "The whole world is put in motion by the wish for riches and the dread of poverty," he says (*Rambler*, No. 178; see also *Rambler*, No. 53 and No. 131). In another, and commonly quoted, statement he remarks that "There are few ways in which a man can be more innocently employed than in getting money" (HP, II, p. 323).

It should be observed again, however, that Johnson (and Adam Smith too) clearly recognized the limitations of riches as a source of happiness (*Rambler*, No. 58). Moreover, he bemoaned the fact that in commercial nations "money receives all the honours which are the proper right of knowledge and virtue" (*Idler*, No. 73). He also indicates that the quest for riches—"this predominant appetite"—was not always carried on "in concurrence with virtue" (*Rambler*, No. 131). Furthermore, he was of the opinion that even in economic terms the quest for riches may backfire. This can happen when almost any passion goes beyond "the bounds which nature prescribes"—thus "too much eagerness of profit hurts the credit of the trader" (*Rambler*, No. 53).

Moralist that he was, Johnson knew of the dangers and weaknesses of the quest for individual gain. But by no means did he propose as an ideal a life of asceticism and poverty. Indeed, in his statement about "getting money" he not only implies a rejection of such an ideal but suggests, somewhat faintly to be sure, his belief in the essential validity of what has been called "the Doctrine of Economic Harmonies," a doctrine that holds that each individual in seeking his own good promotes the good of everybody. This notion figured prominently in Adam Smith's thinking, though (in *The Wealth of Nations*) he recognized, as we shall see in Essay 10, that in the world as it exists, often without proper "institutional" safeguards, there is often conflict between individual interests and social interests.

Johnson, it would seem, thought the extent of this conflict, the degree of disharmony, to be greater than Smith thought. This is implied in the dictum he hands down in his discussion of advertising (to be noted shortly) that "every art ought to be exercised in due subordination to the publick good." This statement is in marked contrast to Smith's remark in his famous "invisible-hand" statement that "I have never known much good done by those who affected to trade for the public good" (WN, p. 423).

Johnson provides us with a number of excellent case studies in which there is a divergence between individual and social interests. First there is advertising, which he discusses in issue No. 40 of *The Idler*. "Promise, large promise, is the soul of an advertisement," he declares. "The trade of advertising is now so near to perfection," he maintains (and this was in 1759, long before the phenomenal growth of Madison Avenue), "that it is not easy to propose any improvement." Johnson does not discuss the effect of advertising on consumption, though in *Idler* No. 37 he speaks, in true Galbraithian fashion of "natural" and "artificial" desires, and in *Idler* No. 73, where he deals with our great quest for wealth (for "gold"), he states that "we have not been able to improve the art of using it, or to make it produce more happiness than it afforded in former times." Adam Smith, with his strong endorsement of free competition, thought that shopkeepers and tradesmen had little effect on consumer buying habits—he does not use the word "advertising." "Some of them, perhaps," he says (WN, p. 343), "may sometimes decoy a weak customer to buy what he has no occasion for." But Smith felt that the evil was too small to require public attention.

A second type of economic activity in which Johnson found a divergence between individual and social interests was the servicing and supplying of the armed forces. Our author was highly critical of what we in more recent years have referred to as war profiteers. In his essay, "Thoughts on the Late Transactions Respecting Falkland's Islands," he lashed out at such profiteers, at the "paymasters and agents, contractors and commissaries" who profit excessively from prolonged wars and "whose equipages shine like meteors, and whose palaces rise like exhalations."[34]

If present-day critics of advertising and war profiteering can obtain support from Johnson the same cannot be said of those who find strong fault with middlemen. In his *Journey to the Western Islands of Scotland, Johnson* argues in defense of middlemen, and particularly of the so-called "tacksman."[35]

Several paragraphs back wo alluded to Johnson's statement about the art of using "gold," a remark that is illustrative of his interest in the general question of the use or consumption of wealth, a question on which, as he points out, there is disagreement (*Rambler,* No. 131). Not only was Johnson interested in the individual use of funds but in the public use as well. In his *Preface to Payne's New Tables of Interest*[36] he tells "the proprietors of the publick funds" that "no motive can sanctify the accumulation of wealth, but an ardent desire to make the most honourable and virtuous use of it, by contributing to the support of good government, the increase of arts and industry, the rewards of genius and virtue, and the relief of wretchedness and want." As to the use or consumption of time, which Johnson very suggestively refers to as "property," he recommends that no particle should be let "fall useless to the ground," and that "above all other kinds of property" it should be "free from invasion" (*Rambler,* No. 108; *Idler,* No. 14).

Adam Smith, in his *Wealth of Nations,* makes a number of direct, and very general, statements about consumption. For example, he declares (p. 625) that "Consumption is the sole end and purpose of all production" (a remark that taken out of context is misleading, as we shall note in Essay 8); and he also states (p. 706) that "the cheapness of consumption and the encouragement given to production" are "precisely the two effects which it is the great business of political economy to promote." Smith also touches on the question of consumption more or less indirectly at various points. For instance his statements about "conspicuous consumption," including those in his discussion of capital accumulation, may be mentioned. However, the great Scottish economist did not delve deeply into the broad general subject of consumption, including the aspect of it relating to income distri-

bution.[37] Neither did he include in his great treatise a special
section on consumption, a pactice followed by J. B. Say and
other later economists. Smith, however, dealt with many of the
topics included in such a specialized treatment.

The eighteenth century has been described by a contemporary
economic historian as "the age of political arithmetic," an age
"when interests were directed largely to things that could be
measured and weighed and calculated."[38] As a final point in our
analysis of Johnson's economic ideas we shall note his concern
with statistical facts.

In telling of Johnson's interest in arithmetic Mrs. Piozzi relates that he once calculated that "the national debt, computing it
at one hundred and eighty millions sterling, would, if converted
into silver, serve to make a meridian of that metal, I forget how
broad, for the globe of the whole earth."[39] On another occasion
Johnson made an effort to calculate the yearly death rate in London caused by hunger (HP, III, p. 401). Again, there is the statement he once made to Boswell, a statement that could very appropriately serve as a motto for all practitioners of Quantitative
Economics: "That, Sir, is the good of counting. It brings everything to a certainty, which before floated in the mind indefinitely"
(HP, IV, p. 204).

Adam Smith was also interested in the quantitative method
and made rather extensive use of it in *The Wealth of Nations*.
But he realized its limitations, at least if not properly employed.
At one point he states that "I have no great faith in political arithmetic," and at another point he is critical of what we today would
refer to as "GNP figures."[40] In connection with the latter he speaks
of a type of output which "frequently makes no figure in those
public registers of which the records are sometimes published with
so much parade."

In his handling of economic matters Johnson did not formulate any general theory of how an economy, such as that found
in eighteenth-century Britain, operates. He was not a "system
builder," in the sense that Adam Smith was. His economic ideas

were for the most part disconnected: they were advanced under a variety of circumstances and at widely different points of time, and they were not brought together as a unified whole in any essay or treatise. (Because of this fact, any general survey of these scattered ideas does not furnish a completely adequate picture of his overall knowledge of economics.) Johnson, it should also be noted, did not formulate any original economic theory or principle. It is not surprising, therefore, that he has received little attention from professional economists.

It is true that there is an article on Johnson in Palgrave's *Dictionary of Political Economy,* first published in England in 1894-1899, and in *The Encyclopaedia of the Social Sciences,* which appeared in this country in 1930-1935. (The successor to the latter publication, the *International Encyclopaedia of the Social Sciences* [1968], does not contain a Johnson entry.) It is also true that in the *Bibliography of Economics, 1751-1775* (prepared for the British Academy by Henry Higgs, 1935) there are a number of Johnson titles. But in the more specialized economic books of today Johnson's views are rarely mentioned. An exception is the literature dealing with the economic history of eighteenth-century England and Scotland. To be sure, a considerable number of economists, including some of international repute, have quoted from Johnson. (Among economists, Johnson would seem to be as popular as a source of choice remarks as Lewis Carroll.) But in many instances the quotations from his writings are moral adages or political maxims, not pronouncements on economic matters. In the "Histories of Economic Thought," the books that trace the developments in the progress of economic ideas, Johnson is seldom if ever mentioned.

This seeming neglect is understandable. As we pointed out at the beginning of our discussion, Johnson was an amateur economist, a very observant and highly intelligent one. And most amateur economists, no matter what their other attainments may be, do not "make" the economic textbooks and studies.

But Johnson's economic views are of interest and value nevertheless. A knowledge of these views, particularly on the part of students of literature, makes for a better understanding of the Great Cham as a scholar, as a man of letters—and as a human being. And even economists, despite the growing complexity and sophistication of their discipline, can benefit from an acquaintance with Johnson's opinions. They can benefit not only because of the substance of these opinions, particularly when viewed historically, but because of the fascinating way in which the opinions are often expressed. They may, as John Bailey affirmed, "sometimes find Johnson mistaken," but "not one will ever find him dull."[41]

NOTES

1. See George B. Hill, *Johnsonian Miscellanies,* 2 vols. (Reprinted, New York: Barnes & Noble, 1966), II, p. 325.

2. *Boswell's Journal of a Tour to the Hebrides with Samuel Johnson, LL. D., 1773,* ed. by Frederick A. Pottle and Charles H. Bennett (New York: McGraw-Hill, New ed., 1961), pp. 174-175, 208. Johnsonian scholars have frequently alluded to Johnson's knowledge of "the useful arts." A good summary of this knowledge is contained in John H. Middendorf's chapter ("Johnson on Wealth and Commerce") in *Johnson, Boswell and Their Circle,* Essays Presented to Lawrence Fitzroy Powell (Oxford at the Clarendon Press, 1965), pp. 48-50. It might be added that in terms of subject matter there is considerable similarity between Middendorf's chapter and the present essay. An examination of the two studies, however, will reveal marked differences.

3. Jeffrey Hart, in *Johnsonian Studies,* ed. by Magdi Wahba (Cairo, 1962, distributed outside the U.A.R. by the Oxford University Press), p. 30.

4. The Preface to *The Preceptor* is reproduced in *The Works of Samuel Johnson, LL. D.,* ed. by Alexander Chalmers, 12 vols. (London: Rivington and others, a New Edition, 1823), X, pp. 285-304. Footnote references to the volumes in this edition will hereafter be referred to by the name of the editor. The Preface is also in Allen T. Hazen's *Samuel Johnson's Prefaces & Dedications* (New Haven: Yale University Press, 1937), pp. 171-189. Hazen presents background information concerning *The Preceptor.* Donald J. Greene discusses the Preface in *The Politics of Samuel Johnson* (New Haven: Yale University Press, 1960), pp. 280-281.

5. The Cooke account is contained in *Johnsoniana,* ed. by J. Wilson Croker (Philadelphia: Carey and Hart, 1842), p. 398.

6. *Samuel Johnson's Prefaces & Dedications,* p. 198. Hazen refers to Hill's opinion and also quotes the Cooke story.

7. Chalmers, I, p. 88.

8. *A Dictionary of Commerce and Commercial Navigation,* ed. by Henry Vethake, 2 vols. (Philadelphia: Hart, American ed., 1851), I, p. viii; *The Literature of Political Economy* (London: Longman, Brown, Green, and Longmans, 1845), p. 52 In his *Dictionary,* McCulloch declares that Rolt's volume was "for the most part abridged from Postlethwayt; but it contains some useful original articles, mixed, however, with many alien to the subject." The names of American libraries possessing copies of Rolt's volume, which is now a scarce item, are given in Hazen, p. 198. Johnson's Preface can be found in Chalmers, X.

9. On these contacts see John H. Middendorf's article "Dr. Johnson and Adam Smith," in the *Philological Quarterly,* April 1961, pp. 281-296; and the latter part of the preceding essay in the present collection.

10. Hiroshi Mizuta, *Adam Smith's Library* (Cambridge at the University Press, 1967), p. 107. According to *Amicus,* the economist was "no admirer of the Rambler or the Idler, and hinted that he had never been able to read them." *The Bee,* May 11, 1791, p. 3. The "hint" was certainly an exaggeration.

11. *Journal of the History of Ideas,* January-March 1960, pp. 66-83.

12. Professor Greene's statement—*The Politics of Samuel Johnson,* p. 281—that Johnson "was essentially in sympathy with mercantilism" seems a bit extreme.

13. Chalmers, XII, p. 252.

14. Charles Wilson discusses and reinterprets the relationship between Mercantilism and poverty in his chapter on "The Other Face of Mercantilism," in *Economic History and the Historian* (New York: Praeger, 1969).

15. All references in the text to *The Rambler* and *The Idler* will be in terms of the essay numbers. In dealing with this essay material the present writer has used the Chalmers edition of Johnson's *Works,* previously referred to. Volumes II, III, and IV contain *The Rambler* essays, and volume V *The Idler* essays.

16. The same words—"the wealth of nations" can be found in one of John Dryden's poems (Smith had a high opinion of Dryden as a poet), and very similar words were used by Sir William Petty. The likelihood seems to be that it was the Physiocrats, however, who influenced Smith in his choice of a title for his great work. The issue touched on here is discussed by Reginald F. Jones in his article "A

Conjecture About Adam Smith," in *The Dalhousie Review,* October 1938, pp. 309-314; and by William R. Scott in *Adam Smith as Student and Professor,* p. 323.

17. Chalmers, IX, p. 122. See also James Bonar, *Philosophy and Political Economy* (London: Allen & Unwin, 1927), p. 173. A somewhat similar view to the one quoted above can be found in *Rambler* No. 58.

18. *The Individual in Society* (London: Allen & Unwin, 1967), p. 61. See also Terence W. Hutchison, *A Review of Economic Doctrines, 1870-1929* (Oxford at the Clarendon Press, 1953), pp. 346-348; and John Maynard Keynes, *The General Theory of Employment, Interest, and Money* (New York: Harcourt, Brace, 1936), pp. 358-362.

19. On the affirmative side of the debate see F. B. Kaye's remarks and data in his edition of *The Fable of the Bees,* 2 vols. (Oxford at the Clarendon Press, 1924), I, pp. cxix, cxxxviii, II, p. 453; see also Hill-Powell, III, pp. 55-57 291-293. On the negative side see Earl R. Miner's article in *The Huntington Library Quarterly,* February 1958, pp. 159-166. Further discussion of the Mandeville-Johnson relationship will be found in Joan Robinson's book, *Economic Philosophy* (Chicago: Aldine, 1962), pp. 16-17; and in Keynes, pp. 359-362.

20. In an interpretative statement of Johnson's view on luxury spending, Middendorf states that the point "at which the pursuit and use of wealth becomes objectionable is not fixed, but differs from man to man, from occasion to occasion." *Johnson, Boswell and Their Circle,* p. 56.

21. Chalmers, XII, p. 426.

22. Chalmers, XII, p. 388; see also pp. 406, 425, 426.

23. *Boswell's Journal of a Tour to the Hebrides with Samuel Johnson,* p. 229.

24. Concerning Smith's view on the relationship between population size and total human happiness, see Jacob Viner's remarks in his article on Smith in the *International Encyclopedia of the Social Sciences.*

25. Chalmers, XII, p. 225.

26. A very harsh statement on slavery can be found in Smith's *Theory of Moral Sentiments,* p. 183. Pointed remarks on the economic weakness of slavery can be found in *The Wealth of Nations,* pp. 80-81, 366.

27. *Boswell's Journal of a Tour to the Hebrides with Samuel Johnson,* pp. 15, 280. For further observations of Johnson on emigration, especially from the Hebrides, see his *Journal,* Chalmers, XII, pp. 346-352, 392-393.

28. Greene discusses Johnson's attitude toward colonies at some

length in *The Politics of Samuel Johnson,* especially pp. 165-172, 284.

29. From "Further Thoughts on Agriculture," Chalmers, X, p. 396.

30. The general theme of this paragraph is discussed by Greene. See particularly pp. 237, 239, 240, 281-284 of his book. A presentation of Johnson's view on a balanced economy can be found in his essay, "Further Thoughts on Agriculture." Though Johnson stressed the importance of agriculture, he tried not to overemphasize its significance. In his "Further Thoughts" he states that "I am far from intending to persuade my countrymen to quit all other employments for that of manuring the ground." Chalmers, X, p. 400. It should be indicated that the first definition given by Johnson's *Dictionary* for the expression "to manure" is "to cultivate by manual labour."

31. From "Considerations on the Corn Laws," in Chalmers, X, pp. 406, 410. This essay was not published until 1808 though, according to Edmund Malone, it was written in 1766. Chalmers, X, p. 402.

32. *Boswell's Journal of a Tour to the Hebrides with Samuel Johnson, LL. D., 1773,* p. 193.

33. For a more detailed discussion of Johnson's general attitude toward trade, and his use of the terms "tradesman" and "merchant," see Middendorf's treatment in "Dr. Johnson and Mercantilism," *Journal of the History of Ideas,* January-March 1960, pp. 71-76.

34. Chalmers, XII, p. 144.

35. Chalmers, XII, pp. 334-337.

36. Chalmers, XI, pp. 169-170.

37. On the general point involved, see Edwin Cannan's editorial remarks on p. xxxvii of *The Wealth of Nations,* and on p. xxvii of Smith's *Lectures on Justice, Police, Revenue and Arms* (New York: Kelley & Millman, reprint, 1956). The latter book contains two brief sections (pp. 157-161) on "Natural Wants" that take one into the subject of consumption, but these sections were not included in *The Wealth of Nations.*

38. Thomas S. Ashton, *An Economic History of England: The 18th Century* (London: Methuen, 1955), p. 1.

39. *Johnsoniana,* ed. by J. Wilson Croker, p. 39.

40. *The Wealth of Nations,* pp. 501, 85. In his "GNP statement" Smith was referring not to the total Gross National Product but only to the value of manufactures that enter into exchange.

41. *Dr. Johnson and His Circle* (London: Oxford University Press, 2nd ed., revised by Lawrence F. Powell, 1944), p. 160. In speaking of "each of them," in the quotation at the beginning of the essay, Bailey refers to various persons who can profit from reading Johnson.

6.

Adam Smith, Educator

It seldom happens that a man, in any part of his
life, derives any conveniency or advantage from some
of the most laborious and troublesome parts of his
education.

—ADAM SMITH

Though Adam Smith's fame rests largely on his achievements as
an economist, he was much more than "a mere economist." As
we have already noted in our first essay, there were other areas
of knowledge in which he was actively interested. Outstanding
among these was the comprehensive subject of moral philosophy.
It was in this field that he first came into prominence. Smith was
also a keen student of literature, having very high credentials for
being linked with what he himself quaintly referred to as "that
unprosperous race of men commonly called men of letters." But
Smith's interests were still wider, extending into the area of education, both in its applied and in its more general aspects. Not
only was he a highly successful teacher but he was an expounder
of some very interesting and provocative notions concerning the
methods and purposes of education. In the present essay we shall
deal with this twofold feature of his career.

Most of Smith's formal work as educator was carried on at
the University of Glasgow. But immediately before assuming his
post at his old alma mater he had engaged in a somewhat formal

educational program in Edinburgh. Moreover, upon leaving Glasgow he continued with a type of educational work when he journeyed to the continent as the tutor of the young Duke of Buccleuch. All told, Smith's teaching career was not long, for from 1766, when he returned from the continent, until his death in 1790 he was not involved in academic activity. For the first part of this period he was engaged in extensive work, mostly at the home of his mother in Kirkcaldy, on *The Wealth of Nations,* and for the latter part of the period (from 1778 on) he served as a commissioner of Customs in Edinburgh.

Smith's own formal education began with his attendance at the grammer school in Kirkcaldy. Then, in the latter part of 1737, at the age of fourteen, he entered Glasgow University where he remained until the spring of 1740. Later in the same year he went to Balliol College, Oxford, and continued his studies there until 1746. Returning to Scotland he spent two years in Kirkcaldy. In the fall of 1748 he began a series of public lectures in Edinburgh, a city in which lectures were highly popular at the time. Smith's teaching career had now commenced. He was twenty-five years of age.

The Edinburgh lectures have been described in Essay 1, and there is no need to repeat what was said there—except for noting one thing. This is the fortunate discovery by Professor Lothian of a set of notes taken by a student of Smith's in 1762-63, and published in 1963 under the title *Lectures on Rhetoric and Belles Lettres.* These lectures, it appears safe to assume, were based on the ones Smith gave in Edinburgh.

In 1751 Smith joined the faculty at the University of Glasgow. He was appointed to the Chair of Logic, a position that included the teaching of rhetoric and belles lettres, and he also acted as a substitute for the indisposed professor of moral philosophy. The following year he received a permanent appointment to the Chair of Moral Philosophy, a post which he continued to fiill for twelve years.

The latter subject was much broader than the modern reader might imagine. It included natural philosophy, ethics, jurisprudence, and political economy. Moreover, Smith also gave lectures on belles lettres, taste, and the history of philosophy, and he injected into his discussions a great deal of literary criticism.[1]

To any college or university president of today Adam Smith would appear as an ideal faculty member. He had all the essential qualifications: he took his class work seriously; he devoted a great deal of time to research and writing (to "productive scholarship," in other words); he participated very actively in administrative work. At the University of Glasgow Smith not only served in all three of the major academic capacities, but he served in all of them with outstanding success. It might be added that he also acted as student counselor. That task, however, was possibly less onerous then than it is now.

At Glasgow the great economist built up an enviable reputation as a teacher, a reputation that extended far beyond the university campus. Many students were attracted to his classes, a number, including two Russians, coming to Glasgow from as far away as the continent. His lectures on moral philosophy aroused a great deal of interest and enthusiasm. This fact is evident from a statement made by John Millar, who was a student and then a colleague of Smith's, and who was also a great teacher himself. "Those branches of science which he taught," said Millar, "became fashionable at this place, and his opinions were the chief topics of discussion in clubs and literary societies. Even the small peculiarities of his pronunciation or manner of speaking, became frequently the objects of imitation."[2] Further evidence on the point is seen in the following statement (from the records of the university) concerning Smith, made by the Senate of the institution in 1764 shortly after he resigned his professorship: "His happy talent in illustrating abstracted subjects, and faithful assiduity in communicating useful knowledge, distinguished him as a professor, and at once afforded the greatest pleasure and the most important instruction to the youth under his care."[3]

Another piece of evidence relating to Smith's effectiveness as a teacher, and to his general influence in Glasgow, is contained in an observation made by Thomas Reid, who succeeded him in the Chair of Moral Philosophy. Writing to a friend in 1764, when he entered upon his new duties, Reid pointed to the pronounced spirit of inquiry that existed among the young people of the city. This, say Rae (p. 59), in a statement with which one must certainly agree, is "the best testimony that could be rendered of the effect of Smith's teaching."[4]

Many years after Smith finished his formal teaching career, and long after he died, another great economist declared that with the exception of Francis Hutcheson, "Adam Smith was, perhaps, the first and greatest of the teachers who have taught a modern subject in a modern way." These are the words of John Maynard Keynes.[5] It is of interest to note that Smith, as a young student at Glasgow, was privileged to study under Hutcheson. Moreover, in his letter accepting the appointment as Lord Rector of the University in 1787 he referred to his old professor as "the never-to-be-forgotten Dr. Hutcheson."[6]

What was there about Smith's manner of teaching that made him so popular and so successful? Professor Millar can give us revealing testimony on the matter. For one thing Smith did not read his lectures, a process that can be painfully dull and uninspiring. Instead, Millar declares, "he trusted almost entirely to extemporary elocution." To aid him in his lectures, however, he had written material; but this was kept very much in the background.[7] Smith departed from his general rule when he taught individual students, such as Lord Buchan. Then he apparently found it more convenient to read his lectures, pausing along the way, however, for comments and illustrations.[8]

Smith was not a silver-tongued orator. "His manner, though not graceful," observes Millar, "was plain and unaffected." But our famous moral philosopher and economist possessed one of the most desirable attributes of a teacher: he had enthusiasm for what he taught. As Millar further declares, "he seemed to be always interested in the subject" and, as a consequence, "he never failed to interest his hearers." The latter part of this statement is a little exaggerated, as is suggested by the fact that

Smith was concerned with the response on the part of the students to his lectures. He observed their reactions—on occasion the reaction of a given member of the group. Sometimes, apparently, he had to alter the content or style of his lectures to overcome listlessness.[9]

In using the extemporaneous method of presenting his ideas and material Smith was able to avoid one of the dangers involved in this particular technique of teaching. His lectures were not unduly discursive and rambling. If one may apply the picturesque metaphor of still another economist, Stephen Leacock, he did not jump on his mount and ride off in all directions. In each lecture Smith ordinarily advanced a number of clear-cut propositions, often of a paradoxical nature. These he considered one by one, attempting to prove and illustrate them. Though he dealt with his "points" systematically, Smith was quite willing to digress. In fact he seemed to enjoy digressing, particularly into the area of literary criticism. But his digressions were within limits.

Smith had some difficulty in getting his lectures under way. Rae (p. 108) says he "always stuttered and hesitated a deal for the first quarter of an hour" of his lectures. Millar is not as specific and extreme as Rae, but he declares that Smith "often appeared, at first, not to be sufficiently possessed of the subject, and spoke with some hesitation." But as he progressed with his lecture, things changed. "The matter seemed to crowd upon him," Millar continues, "his manner became warm and animated, and his expresions easy and fluent."

On controversial issues Smith used a pro-and-con type of approach, arguing with great vigor in simulated defense of positions contrary to his own. Thus those who studied under him did not hear only one side of an issue. By the generous use of illustrations he developed his subject in a way that was designed to attract the attention of his students and afford them both enjoyment and instruction as they followed the analysis. In his analysis he shifed from the simple to the complex, and back to the simple again. As Millar points out, Smith attempted to get the students to follow "the same object, through all the diversity of shades and aspects in which it was presented, and afterwards in tracing it backwards to that original proposition or general truth from which this beautiful train of speculation had proceeded."

It might seem from this remark of Millar's that Smith was highly scientific in his approach to teaching, that he directed the thoughts of his students into cold, methodical analysis. No doubt he sometimes used this method but as we just noted he embellished his lectures with numerous illustrations, and he loved to digress. Professor Lothian, as we pointed out in Essay 2, has gone so far as to affirm—on the basis of remarks by Millar and other evidence—that in his earlier years at Glasgow, and in his lectures on rhetoric, Smith used an emotional appeal to his students rather than an intellectual one; he endeavored "to stimulate their feelings and their aesthetic sense, rather than their powers of reasoning." In his classs on rhetoric and belles this could well have been the the case, though in the other areas in which he taught, including economics, Smith undoubtedly used a more "intellectual" approach. In any circumstances, the students found his lectures interesting and stimulating.

Smith was an excellent lecturer. But the lecture method (as contrasted with the discussion method) has in more recent years been subject to considerable criticism. It is possible, if one may refer to the old definition of the method, that under its use material may move from the notebook of the professor to the notebook of the student without going through the head of either. This possibility is by no means an inevitability, however. And, certainly it was not the case with Adam Smith and his students.

If the lecture method has to some extent fallen into disrepute (though in many instances, where classes are large, it is the only feasible method), it can still have much to commend it, especially if the lecturer is available to his students for consultation and discussion, as Smith was. This general point, it is interesting to note, was argued by one of America's outstanding educators, Woodrow Wilson. In his essay on "An Old Master"—the master being Smith—Wilson admits that a "paralysis of dullness" too often characterized the old lecturer, but yet he feels there is still a place for lecturing. Furthermore, he goes as far as to say that "it would seem to be a good policy to endure much indifferent lecturing—watchful trustees might reduce it to a minimum—for the sake of leaving places open for the men who have in them the inestimable force of chastened eloquence."[10]

Smith met his "public" class, which, according to Rae, never went beyond eighty or ninety students, from 7:30 A.M. to 8:30 A.M. ("eight o'clocks," now often the bane of students and professors alike, would have been a mild relief to Smith and his charges). At eleven o'clock he met this group again to test it on the lecture he had given earlier in the morning. Attendance at this second session was voluntary, however, and about a third of the students habitually came. Smith also had a "private" class of much smaller size which he taught twice a week at twelve o'clock, and in addition he apparently met occasionally with special students. He was readily available to his students for discussion; indeed, he invited the better ones to his home for that purpose.[11]

A few students also boarded with Smith and he occasionally lectured to them (and to a few others—Lord Buchan, for example) and supervised their studies. He advised students in choosing their life work and in getting equipped for it, and he took a keen interest in the health of some of his students.[12]

Smith, it is clear, was a very human and a very considerate teacher as well an intellectually competent one. He met his obligations to his students in an exemplary fashion (not like the professors at Oxford, of whom he complained). In speaking of factors that motivate professors (WN, p. 717), Smith mentions remuneration (especially if it comes directly from the students), professional reputation, and student opinion. With reference to the last of these he declares that the professor "still has some dependency upon the affection, gratitude, and favourable report of those who have attended upon his instructions; and these favourable sentiments," he continues, "he is likely to gain in no way so well as by deserving them, that is, by the abilities and diligence with which he discharges every part of his duty." This statement is an excellent word picture of Smith himself. He won from his students those "favourable sentiments" he lists in his statement, and he did it in the precise manner he indicates.

Unlike many of his colleagues of a few years ago, Smith apparently had no rebellious students in his classes. Moreover, from the interest and enthusiasm his lectures generated, it would seem that none, or very few, of the students questioned the relevancy of what he taught.

During his teaching career Smith was an active writer. In the original *Edinburgh Review,* covering the year 1755, he had a review in the first issue of Samuel Johnson's recently published *Dictionary of the English Language,* and in the second a discussion of the current state of European literature. Of greater consequence, however, was the publication in 1759 of his *Theory of Moral Sentiments.* In 1761 his essay on the Formation of Languages appeared. During the Glasgow period Smith also wrote his essay on "The History of Astronomy," and certain significant parts of *The Wealth of Nations,* which he used in connection with his lectures on moral philosophy.

Two other early pieces of Smith's writing, which we have mentioned in earlier essays, should again be noted. While he was giving his lectures in Edinburgh Smith *probably* edited and collected, and wrote a brief preface for, the poems of his friend William Hamilton of Bangour. Moreover, at the time of his installation as a faculty member at the University of Glasgow in January 1751, Smith gave an address entitled "De Origine Idearum," a portion of which was later embodied in his essay on "The History of the Ancient Logics and Metaphysics."

In present-day academic parlance, Smith was without question a productive scholar. But with his interest in writing—and in thinking, for he spent a great deal of time in quiet meditation— he did not overlook his students. He was not oblivious to the obligations he owed them.

An excellent illustration of his sense of obligation to those who attended his lectures, and also of his highly developed feeling of rectitude, is found in a dramatic and amusing account that has been given of his last class at Glasgow.[13] Since he was unable to finish his course of lectures, Smith insisted on refunding to his students the fees they had paid (though they were to have a substitute teacher). On the final day he came to his class with little paper packages, each containing the money due to the individual members of the group. The first student Smith called up to get his packages refused to take it, at the same time declaring *his* great indebtedness to Smith. A general cry of approval went up in the room. But the great teacher was determined. "You must not refuse me this satisfaction," he asserted. "Nay, by heavens, gentlemen, you shall not." Thereupon Smith seized the student who refused the refund by his coat, thrust the money package into his pocket, and pushed him away. The other students, realizing the hopelessness of their cause, accepted the refunds too.

Smith was not only a writer but a researcher. During his Glasgow days his research work was chiefly of a nonstatistical, nonquantitative type. Though he leaned heavily on the deductive method, including a "species of philosophical investigation" described by Dugald Stewart as *Theoretical* or *Conjectural History,* Smith did more than philohophize in his armchair. He resorted very extensively to original sources, as is abudantly clear in *The Wealth of Nations.* His statistical investigations, however, seem to have been made largely after he left Glasgow.

As with his writing, Smith did not permit the closely allied activity of research to interfere with his teaching. Moreover, as in all cases where teaching and research are harmoniously wedded (and today, it might be added, this happy connubial condition does not always exist) Smith's studies and investigations added luster to his lectures. It is possible, too, that his class work stimulated his own thinking and gave additional direction to his research work.

In addition to his writing and teaching, Smith was very active in administrative work at Glasgow.[14] Rae declares that during his years on the faculty Smith seems to have been more deeply involved in the business affairs of the institution than any other professor. Professor Alexander Gray even goes so far as to say that during the time Smith was at Glasgow he in fact ran the university.[15] From 1758 until his resignation early in 1764 he served as college treasurer; from 1760 to 1762 he was dean of the university faculty, and in 1762 he became its vice-rector. In addition he served on numerous committees. Because of the peculiar structural setup of the institution—there were really two separate corporate bodies, each with its own governmental arrangement, the University and the College—the administrative work that confronted Smith was both complex and difficult. In this aspect of his work, as in the other two, he acquitted himself with great success.

Smith's years at Glasgow, as teacher, as researcher-writer, and as administrator were busy and fruitful ones. They were also very happy ones. As he himself declared in 1787, when he was appointed Lord Rector of the University, the thirteen years he spent there he remembered "as by far the most useful and therefore as by far the happiest and most honourable period of my life."[16]

Adam Smith was not only an educator but an educational reformer as well, and in a particularly notable chapter in *The Wealth of Nations* (Chapter 1 in Book V) he advances a variety of suggestions aimed at educational reform. Over the years enthusiastic tributes have been paid to Smith's discussion. J. B. Say looked upon his "highly ingenious disquisition on public education" as a "magnificent digression"—"replete as it is with erudition and the soundest philosophy, at the same time that it abounds with valuable instruction."[17] A century later J. M. Keynes, expressing similar sentiments, spoke of "the magnificent first chapter of the Fifth Book" of Smith's classic.[18]

Smith held very strong opinions on school and university endowments and the accompanying policy of teacher remuneration.[19] In the field of teaching he felt there should be a very close connection between effort and reward, a goal that was absent when teachers' salaries came out of endowments or subsidies rather than directly from student fees. In other words, in the matter of faculty pay Smith favored the principle: From each according to his ability, to each according to the number of students he instructs. To put the point in a still different fashion, and this time in the words of Professor Charles F. Arrowood, the provision of education, according to Smith, "is a sort of merchandising: the teacher should offer his goods in an open market, and their quality and the demand for them would regulate the support of his work."[20] It should be added that our author was thinking here primarily of education for the well-to-do classes. He supported a somewhat different arangement for the education of the masses.

Smith (p. 717) stresses the need for diligence on the part of teachers and asserts that the attainment of that desirable quality is interfered with when faculty remuneration comes from endowments—which "have necessarily diminished more or less the necessity of application in the teachers"—and not, at least to some degree, directly from student fees.[21] This was one of the reasons why Smith felt that the teaching at Oxford was of such a low quality, where, as he declares (p. 718), "the greater part of the public professors have, for these many years, given up altogether even the pretence of teaching."[22]

When education is conducted on a private enterprise basis, with teachers paid largely or wholly out of the fees of their students, the performance of the teachers, Smith argues, is of a superior nature. "Those parts of education," he states (p. 721), "for the teaching of which there are no public institutions, are generally the best taught." Fencing or dancing schools (Smith was greatly interested in dancing) are cases in point. Somewhat the same notion is contained in Smith's remarks (p. 734) about the education of women. There are no public educational institutions for them—hence there is "nothing useless, absurd, or fantastical in the common course of their education." What they are taught is solely determined by what their parents or guardians consider "necessary and useful."

Smith emphasized the great importance of what he called domestic education. It was an essential and necessary part of the moral education of youth. Hence he was fearful of young people leaving home for their education. As he observes in his *Theory of Moral Sentiments* (p. 196), "The education of boys at distant great schools, of young men at distant colleges, of young ladies in distant nunneries and boarding-schools, seems, in the higher ranks of life, to have hurt most essentially the domestic morals, and consequently the domestic happiness, both of France and England." Children, Smith continues, may, "with propriety and advantage," attend public schools, but they should live at home. This will favorably influence the behavior of the children and "may frequently impose no useless restraint" upon the conduct of the parents. To our Scottish scholar domestic education was of nature's contrivance while public education was of man's. And, he adds (p. 197), "it is surely unnecessary to say, which is likely to be the wisest." Smith was well aware of the existence at the time of a "generation gap" (see Quotation 51 in Essay 7), and this awareness could have been a factor in his belief in the importance of domestic education. Certainly he felt the great need of parents doing their part in the general education of their children—a duty that apparently was not always recognized in the eighteenth century, and is definitely not always recognized today.

To return to the question of educational remuneration, it can be said that the payment of teachers on the basis of the number of students they have would likely encourage diligence on the part of the instructional staff, as Smith reasons; at least on the part of *some* members of the staff. But, as applied to modern institution of higher learning, ths method of reward has very obvious dangers. In colleges and universities today there are other means that can be used in disciplining or getting rid of neglectful faculty members than having their salaries wither away. Moreover, having faculty salaries based wholly or largely on student fees would mean in general either very low salaries or very high fees. Though Smith's contention in the matter of teacher remuneration is wholly impracticable, it is well to stress the general object that he had in mind, namely excellence in teaching, including up-to-dateness in approach.

As for the remuneration teachers actually receive, Smith felt that it was low compared with that found in certain other professions. The "usual reward of the eminent teacher," he says (WN, p. 132), "bears no proportion to that of the lawyer or physician." The reason is found in the supply situation in the respective groups, brought about by the differing methods used in paying for the education of the members of the groups. The teaching profession, he tells us, "is crowded with indigent people who have been brought up to it at the public expence," whereas the other two professions "are incumbered with very few who have been educated at their own." However, Smith adds, the pay of teachers would be still lower if "the competition of those yet more indigent men of letters who write for bread was not taken out of the market." Though today there is still a divergence between the financial rewards of teachers on the one hand and lawyers and doctors on the other, the amount of "indigence" among the members of the former group has greatly declined. We may yet advance to the condition of the "ancient times," of which Smith speaks, when "the rewards of eminent teachers" were quite considerable—he mentions Isocrates, Gorgias, Hippias, and a number of others as teachers who presumably were very well paid.

In his discussion of education Smith not only criticizes Oxford and other endowed educational institutions on the basis of professorial neglect but on other grounds. He feels that they do not give adequate attention to the sciences, a criticism one could hardly make of colleges and universities today. As for the subjects they take up, he declares (p. 721) that "it may, perhaps, be said" that they "are not very well taught," though he points out that such subjects would ordinarily not be taught elsewhere. He states (p. 727) that most universities have not been very forward in introducing the improvements that have been made in philosophy, and he goes on to say that "several of those learned societies have chosen to remain, for a long time, the sanctuaries in which exploded systems and obsolete prejudices found shelter and protection, after they had been hunted out of every other corner of the world." This statement has been included in a compilation of amusing utterances (Procknows' *Treasury of Humorous Quotations)* but to Smith the condition was by no means a laughing matter.

Turning to another point in Smith's remarkable chapter, we can note a different issue, and one that still arises in educational institutions, namely that of forcing students to study under certain professors, without the right, unless permission is granted, of changing sections or classes "in case of neglect, inability, or bad usage." Such compulsion not only tends strongly to destroy "all emulation among the different tutors of the same college," he maintains (pp. 719-720), "but to diminish very much in all of them the necessity of diligence and of attention to their respective pupils." The problem involved here was simpler in Smith's time, however, than it is today. Educational administrators were not then confronted with a situation in which there are 8 instructors in Sociology 1, 10 in Government 1, and 20 in English 1.

If a teacher neglects his students, and if he is "a man of sense," says Smith, it must be unpleasant for him to realize that, in his lectures, "he is either speaking or reading nonsense, or what is very little better than nonsense." When his lectures are of this nature, most of his students may stay away, or perhaps attend the lectures but "with plain enough marks of neglect, contempt, and derision." The teacher, as a consequence (and assuming he has to give a definite number of lectures), may attempt to give decent presentations. However, there are several other expedients, Smith adds, that may be resorted to and "which will effectively blunt the edge of all those incitements to diligence."

For one thing, the teacher instead of explaining to his students the subject he is supposed to be dealing with "may read some book upon it." If the book is in a foreign and dead language he may interpret it for them. Or, Smith continues delightfully, the teacher could use an even less troublesome method: he could have the students interpret the book, "and by now and then making an occasional remark upon it, he may flatter himself that he is giving a lecture."

Smith was opposed to compulsory attendance except for very young students. If a teacher does his duty, coercion can scarcely ever be necessary for persons who are older than twelve or thirteen. "No discipline," he declares (p. 720), "is ever requisite to force attendance upon lectures which are really worth attending, as is well known wherever any such lectures are given." Our author, it will be seen, supported the principle of "unlimited cuts." He was of the opinion that good teachers had nothing to fear from its application. This would generally be true also, he felt, of teachers who were not too good but who took their work seriously.

Smith's confidence in the response of students to good teachers, and in the absence of any coercive rules and regulations, is reflected in a statement he makes about the teachers—the professors, we could call them—of the later period of ancient Greece and Rome. These teachers, he tells us (p. 731), were without jurisdiction over their students; they had no authority over them except "that natural authority, which superior virtue and abilities never fail to produce from young people towards those who are entrusted with any port of their education." These teachers, obviously, would have rated very high if the students of that period had used the now-popular but sometimes disconcerting policy of rating their "profs." It should be added that in those far-off days, as Smith also tells us, the law neither compelled students to attend the lectures of the teachers nor did it provide for any reward—permission to practice a trade or profession, etc.—for having attended them. Smith himself favored rewards.

According to our author's view students should not only have the right to choose their professors but their universities. Persons who receive "scholarships, exhibitions, bursaries, etc." should be able to use them at institutions of their own choice. This right, he says (p. 719), "might perhaps contribute to excite some emulation among different colleges." The scholarships Smith had in mind are not those that colleges themselves grant, but come from "the outside." Moreover, it is obvious that he was not talking about athletic scholarships, a type that in recent years has attained to major significance in many educational institutions in the United States. These, of course, do not come from "the outside."

It is of special interest to note that Smith, who traveled on the continent for three years with the young Duke of Buccleuch (stepson of Charles Townshend, the statesman who did so much to provoke the American colonists to rebellion), was opposed to sending young men on continental tours in lieu of a university education. He recognized some of the benefits that a continental sojourn confers on the young traveler, but asserts (p. 728) that "in other respects, he commonly returns home more conceited, more unprincipled, more dissipated, and more incapable of any serious application either to study or to business, than he could well have become in so short a time, had he lived at home." Smith blames the universities, and the discredit into which they had fallen, for the repute gained by this "very absurd" practice. For the father whose son is absent in Europe there is some consolation, however. He "delivers himself, at least for some time, from so disagreeable an object as that of a son unemployed, neglected, and going to ruin before his eyes."

John Locke apparently held views on the matter of foreign travel as an educational venture that resembled those of Smith. At least in an imaginary conversation that supposedly took place in the year 1700, Richard Hurd, Bishop of Worcester, has him express such views. The Bishop's *Dialogue on the uses of Foreign Travel, considered as a Part of an English Gentleman's Education,* published in 1764, was presented as a debate between Locke and Lord Shaftesbury.[23] Interestingly enough this book was in Smith's personal library, and it is possible that Smith was influenced by Locke's—or Hurd's—opinions on the issue of foreign travel versus university attendance. Under any circumstances, the issue was one of current significance.

Though Smtih said much in support of private enterprise in education, he nevertheless recognized a place for public intervention (pp. 734-740). This intervention was for the special benefit, not of "people of some rank and fortune" but of "the common people." By setting up in each parish or district, somewhat after the fashion of the policy followed in Scotland, "a little school," in which the master would be partly paid out of public funds (not wholly, or even principally, Smith again emphasizes, because the master "would soon learn to neglect his business"), children could be taught "to read, write, and account," and without long effort. The results would be especially good if in these schools the books the youngsters use in learning to read were a bit more instructive (the criticism of textbooks is by no means a new phenomenon) and if, instead of getting a smattering of Latin, which they sometimes receive, they were given some training in elementary geometry and mechanics. This training would be advantageous in practically all trades, says Smith. To encourage the students in their work, "small premiums, and little badges of distinction" could be given for superior performance. Moreover, the government could ensure that most persons would acquire the basic educational training by requiring that they be exposed to an examination or a period of probation as a condition of freely participating in any corporation or engaging in any trade.

Smith felt that the provision of public education (in homeopathic doses," said Marx)[24] for the children of the common people would help to counteract the unfavorable results of the division of labor. At the beginning of *The Wealth of Nations* he had stressed the great importance of the division of labor as a factor in the economic development of a nation, but in his chapter on education he alludes to the unfavorable effects that are likely to follow from its use.[25] His words are almost as severe as those used by Ruskin some decades later. The worker who concentrates his efforts on the performance of a few simple operations "generally becomes as stupid and ignorant as it is possible for a human creature to become." He acquires dexterity in the trade in which he specializes but, says Smith, it appears to be "at the expence of his intellectual, social, and martial virtues." This condition relates not to a few persons but, in an advanced society, to the bulk of the people (i.e., "the labouring poor"); that is, unless the government takes corrective action. It is here that education has its part to play. It will help to develop the intellectual, social, and martial virtues and thus strengthen the body politic.

But such public education confers another benefit upon society: the people are less likely to question the authority of the government and participate in public disturbances, a point that was later emphasized by Macaulay (who made a number of references to Smith's discussion of education) in his speech in the House of Commons in defense of public education.[26] "The more they are instructed," says Smith, "the less liable they are to the delusions of enthusiasm and superstition, which, among ignorant nations, frequently occasion the most dreadful disorders." In free countries, he remarks, it is of the utmost importance that the people should not be disposed to judge the conduct of the government "rashly or capriciously."

Smith follows his discussion of education for young people with a treatment of education for people of all ages. Running to almost thirty pages his presentation takes him into a long analysis of religious instruction, including a detailed account of religious history. We shall note just one or two points in his discussion.[27]

Of special interest are the policy recommendations he makes for correcting the "unsocial or disagreeably vigorous" aspects of the austere moral systems found among the numerous little religious sects in society. The first policy relates to the study of science and philosophy. By imposing certain entry requirements—"some sort of probation," Smith states (p. 748)—to entry into the professions and elected offices of trust or profit, such a study might be rendered "almost universal among all people of middling or more than middling rank and fortune." In dealing with this point Smith declares, epigramatically, that "Science is the great antidote to the poison of enthusiasm and superstition." He feels that if "all the superior ranks of people" were protected against this poison (and such protection could be supplied by teachers operating on a private enterprise basis, not as state employees) those in the inferior groups would not be much exposed to the danger.

The second policy Smith mentions relates to public diversions. If private individuals (acting in their own self-interest, and without entering the areas of "scandal or indecency") were given the freedom "to amuse and divert the people by painting, poetry, music, dancing," and by providing "all sorts of dramatic representations and exhibitions" for them, most persons would be readily freed of "that melancholy and gloomy humour which is almost always the nurse of popular superstition and enthusiasm."

Smith did not want to have the government entrusted with the task of providing amusements and diversions for the people. Neither did he wish to have the government provide and license teachers to instruct in science and philosophy. It could insist on having a probationary period of study, but it should not provide the teachers. The people, in the middle or higher classes, "would soon find better teachers for themselves than any whom the state could provide." If there was no need for the state to provide teachers, so there was no need for it to train them. They could get this training without its help. And once they were trained, they should not form themselves into any sort of regulatory union. As E. G. West has pointed out, Smith was opposed to both the training of teachers by the state and any system of licensure that the teachers themselves would operate.[28] Smith was an exponent of competition, of fair competition it should be emphasized, not only in manufacturing and commerce but in education, and in religion as well.

In his *Theory of Moral Sentiments* Smith gave attention to a kind of education that differs greatly from the types he discusses in *The Wealth of Nations*.[29] This is a variety of self-education which involves the attribute of self-command, something, he tells us (p. 214), that is not only a great virtue in itself but from which "all the other virtues seem to derive their principal lustre." If self-command adds luster to all the other virtues, it is one of the two qualities that make up the virtue of prudence, a virtue to which Smith attached great importance: it is "of all the virtues that which is the most useful to the individual" (p. 167). The other, and first, of the two qualities he mentions, is "superior reason and understanding."

A very young child, Smith remarks (p. 126), does not possess the virtue of self-command; but later on, as it learns more about life, it "enters upon the great school of self-command" where it studies to gain increasing control of itself, and where it starts "to exercise over its own feelings a discipline which the practice of the longest life is very seldom sufficient to bring to complete perfection." The school's teachers are harsh, demanding ones: "hardships, dangers, injuries, misfortunes, are the only masters under whom we can learn the exercise of this virtue." And "these are all masters to whom nobody willingly puts himself to school" (p. 133). Smith makes it clear that self-command, important though it is, by itself is not enough. Sometimes we find, he tells us (p. 134), that persons who have the greatest amount of self-command are lacking in the sense of justice and humanity—just as we find persons of great humanity who are lacking in self-command. A person who has met all the requirements of the school of self-command need not be what we today would call a "soft" person. In our author's scheme of things, as we observed in Essay 3, there is room for the exercise of indignation, "just" or "proper" indignation he calls it (pp. 213, 216), when occasion demands such a reaction.

In concluding our discussion of some of Adam Smith's ideas concerning education, we should note that a number of the opinions he expressed might seem to brand him as a supporter of upper-class privilege. Moreover, his repeated use of the term "inferior ranks of people" and also his employment of such expressions as "the common people" and "people of some rank and fortune" might appear to justify such a conclusion. This general charge, as a matter of fact, has been leveled against him.[30] But, at least in partial extenuation of his attitude, it should be noted that Smith had great sympathy for the underdog, for the many less fortunate members of society. "His ruling passion," as Dugald Stewart declared (p. 8), was that of "contributing to the happiness and the improvement of society." Furthermore, the great economist should be judged on the basis of the political, social, and educational principles of his own day, not of ours.

Judging Smith on this basis there are grounds for believing that in some matters he was ahead of his time. For example, while he emphasized the utilitarian aspects of education, he felt at the same time that education was necessary for intellectual growth and hence for the development of the whole man. "A man without the proper use of the intellectual faculties of a man," he says in *The Wealth of Nations* (p. 740), "is, if possible, more contemptible than even a coward, and seems to be mutilated and deformed in a still more essential part of the character of human nature." Hence, he argues, even if the state derived no advantage from the education of the common people, which, as we noted before, it does, it would still be desirable to provide such education. This notion of education and the development of the whole man has led one professor of education to link Smith's name with those of Comenius, Kant, Pestalozzi, Carlyle, and Huxley.[31] On more specific matters too, matters that we have considered in the preceding pages, Smith also expressed opinions that, if not ahead of their time, point to issues that have present-day pertinence.

There is one idea of Smith's we have not mentioned in our discussion and which should be noted. This is his reference to what is now often referred to as human capital. To maintain a person during his "education, study, or apprenticeship, always costs a real expence," says Smith, and this outlay he refers to as "a capital fixed and realized, as it were, in his person" (p. 265). Smith was not the first person to advance this suggestive idea—the notion goes back at least as far as John Locke—but the idea is commonly associated with him. The concept now figures prominently in discussions of economic development, and we shall return to it in Essay 9.

At a time of immense expansion in our educational programs and institutions, of extensive discussions of educational relevance and educational policies, Smith's treatment of educational issues, particularly in his chapter on education in *The Wealth of Nations,* can be read with considerable profit and a substantial amount of delight.[32]

NOTES

1. Rae, pp. 54-56.
2. Millar's account of Smith's lectures, which we shall refer to with some frequency, was made public by Dugald Stewart in his Memoir of Smith, pp. 11-13. Much of Millar's account can also be found in Rae, pp. 54-57.
3. Stewart, p. 45.
4. Some persons in Glasgow, however, had certain qualms about Smith due to his religious unorthodoxy. See Rae, p. 60.
5. *Economic History,* February 1938, p. 36.
6. Rae, p. 411. A description of Hutcheson as a teacher is contained in William Leechman's Preface to Hutcheson's book *A System of Moral Philosophy,* 2 vols. (Glasgow: R. and A. Foulis, 1755), I.
7. Scott, in his *Adam Smith as Student and Professor,* states (p. 70) that Smith planned his individual lectures apart from this material and largely independent of it.
8. Rae, pp. 52-53.
9. Rae, p. 57.
10. *An Old Master and Other Political Essays* (New York: Scribners, 1893), pp. 3-4.
11. Rae, pp. 51-53.
12. Scott, pp. 69-70. Scott's account of Smith's classes differs somewhat from Rae's.
13. Rae, pp. 169-170.
14. A detailed discussion of Smith's administrative work can be found in Rae, Chap. VI, and Scott, pp. 71-78 and Chap. VII.
15. *Adam Smith* (London, Historical Association Publication, General Series: G 10, 1948), p. 5.
16. Rae, p. 411.
17. *A Treatise on Political Economy* (Philadelphia: Lippincott, Grambo, New American ed., 1853), p. xliv.
18. *Economic History,* February 1938, p. 36. Keynes says that Article II of this particular chapter "contains passages which ought to be pre-fixed to the Statutes of every University and College."
19. It is an interesting fact that when the one-hundredth anniversary of the publication of *The Wealth of Nations* was observed by the

Political Economy Club of London in 1876 (with Gladstone in the chair), the issue that was perhaps the most extensively discussed by the speakers was that of university endowments. The Proceedings of this meeting were published in London by Longmans, Green, Reader & Dyer in 1876.

20. *The Theory of Education in the Political Philosophy of Adam Smith,* privately printed (Texas, 1945), p. 15.

21. Smith declares at another point in *The Wealth of Nations* (p. 768) that the costs of operating institutions that provide educational and religious instruction could, without injustice, be met from the general revenue of the state. However, he is not sure that this is the best plan, for he adds that these costs "might perhaps with equal propriety, and even with some advantage, be defrayed altogether by those who receive the immediate benefit of such education and instruction, or by the voluntary contribution of those who think they have occasion for either the one or the other."

22. For further discussion on this point, a point on which Smith and James Boswell disagreed, see Essay 4.

23. See R. J. White, *The Age of George III* (London: Heinemann, 1968), p. 164.

24. *Capital,* 2 vols. (London: Dent, Everyman's ed., 1930), I, p. 384.

25. There has been some discussion as to whether Smith held two views on the effects of the division of labor or only one. See E. G. West's article in *Economica,* February 1964, pp. 23-32; and Nathan Rosenberg's analysis in the same journal, May 1965, pp. 127-139.

26. *The Complete Writings of Lord Macaulay,* 20 vols. (Boston and New York: Houghton, Mifflin, 1899-1900), XVIII, pp. 128-154. Macaulay stresses the importance of public education as a means for ensuring greater security to persons and property.

27. A more detailed treatment of this part of Smith's discussion, by Charles F. Arrowood, will be found in *The Harvard Educational Review,* January 1944, pp. 71-73.

28. *Journal of Political Economy,* October 1964, p. 467. West declares that Smith's opposition to the licensing of teachers can be inferred from his general opposition to occupational licensure. In opposition to such an arrangement in the medical profession, Smith wrote a very interesting letter to his friend Dr. William Cullen, excerpts from which West includes in his discussion.

29. The pages in *The Theory* in which Smith discusses the question of self-command furnish some of the best examples of his rhetorical and fascinating style. See Chapter III in Part III, and Section III in Part VI. The latter Part was added to the 1790 (final) revision of the author's book.

30. On this general point see David Craig, *Scottish Literature and Scottish People, 1680-1830* (London: Chatto & Windus, 1961), pp. 68-71. See also *The Story of Education* by Carroll Atkinson and Eugene T. Maleska (Philadelphia: Chilton, 1962), p. 163.

31. John W. Adamson, *English Education, 1789-1902* (Cambridge at the University Press, 1930), pp. 4-5, 114, 147-148, 317. On Smith as a pioneer educational critic, see Edward C. Mack, *Public Schools and British Opinion, 1780-1860* (New York: Columbia University Press, 1939), pp. 66, 132-133.

32. Other early economists also expressed opinions on educational matters, including the question of state support. A discussion of their views is contained in E. G. West's article "Private Versus Public Education: A Classical Economic Dispute," in *The Journal of Political Economy,* October 1964; in William L. Miller's article, "The Economics of Education in English Classical Economics," in *The Southern Economic Journal,* January 1966; and in Brian Simon's book, *Studies in the History of Education, 1780-1870* (London: Lawrence & Wishart, 1960).

7.

Thoughts from Adam Smith

The temptation to quote from the *Wealth of Nations* is very powerful, and may easily become irresistible.
—L. L. PRICE

(Along) with the theoretical doctrines of the book (*The Theory of Moral Sentiments*), there are everywhere interwoven, with singular taste and address, the purest and most elevated maxims concerning the practical conduct of life.
—DUGALD STEWART

Compilers of dictionaries of quotations are confronted with an exceedingly difficult task, a twofold task indeed. On the one hand they have an immense and unwieldy stock of adages, aphorisms, maxims, and epigrams from which to make their selections; and on the other hand they must cater to a market in which "consumer preferences" not only exhibit wide variations but change from time to time.

In view of these complex supply and demand conditions it would be expected that those who consult such dictionaries would sometimes be disappointed with what they find, and particularly with what they do not find. Reader and compiler can easily disagree on what quotations should be included and what excluded. Ordinarily this disagreement is not serious and need cause no alarm. On occasion, however, some degree of alarm is warranted.

173

Such an occasion unquestionably exists in relation to Adam Smith. In most collections of quotations less than justice is done to the great Scottish economist, moral philosopher, and man of letters. He is sadly neglected. In some collections, as a matter of fact, he is totally disregarded. Moreover, even when he is given some recognition the quotations that are used from his writings are sometimes less meaningful and provocative, at least in the world of today, than others that he can furnish.

Evidence to bear out this general conclusion is not difficult to find. In *The Oxford Dictionary of Quotations* (1953) there is only one Smith entry, namely his "shopkeeper" statement, about which we shall have more to say later. In *The Penguin Dictionary of Quotations* (1962) there is also a single quotation from Smith and it too is the shopkeeper one. In Bartlett's *Familiar Quotations* (1968) the shopkeeper statement is again the sole Smithian entry. (In the 1955 edition of Bartlett, Smith had been represented twice.)

Rudolph Flesch in his volume *The Book of Unusual Quotations* (1957) completely overlooks Smith, apparently feeling that there is nothing really unusual in any of his pithy remarks. Equally hard on Smith is *The Pocket Book of Quotations* (Cardinal edition, 1951), edited by Henry Davidoff. In this collection Alfred E., Arabella Eugenia, Langdon, Logan Pearsall, Samuel Francis, and (of course) Sydney Smith are all represented, but not Adam. Similarly, in *I Quote* (1947), "a collection of ancient and modern wisdom and inspiration," by Virginia Ely, Smith goes unhonored and unsung.

There are other compilations, however, that give him more consideration. In Stevenson's weighty tome, *The Home Book of Quotations* (1967), there are six Smith entries, including once again the one about shopkeepers. In *F.P.A.'s Book of Quotations* (1952), there are five entries. In contrast with most of the recent compilers Adams goes beyond *The Wealth of Nations* and dips into *The Theory of Moral Sentiments*. In Benham's *Book of Quotations* (1948), Smith is represented by four statements including, still once more, the one about shopkeepers.

In H. L. Mencken's *New Dictionary of Quotations* (1942), the famous economist fares better than in any of the books so far cited. Unfortunately, at least for persons probing into the treatment of Smith by compilers of dictionaries of quotations, there is no name index in the 1347-page Mencken volume, and the quotations are arranged by subject matter rather than by author. An examination of the book (lasting as long as the importance of our task warranted) revealed that there are no less than eight Smithian utterances in the collection and there could be more.

Our Scottish scholar appears to be treated best at the hands of George Seldes, at least in recent years. In this compiler's work, *The Great Quotations* (1960), he is represented fifteen times. Seldes' collection is somewhat different from most others, however. It places great emphasis on currently significant ideas, a policy that definitely favors Smith. Moreover, it goes beyond short remarks and includes fairly long statements, statements that in Smith's case run up to fifteen lines. Seldes and Mencken include, as one might expect, the shopkeeper remark.

The book that most closely resembles Seldes's in its attention to Smith is an old compilation, S. Austin Allebone's *Prose Quotations from Socrates to Macaulay* (1876). As a matter of fact, in the number of Smith entries it surpasses the Seldes volume by one, and it too includes long quotations. It also has more excerpts from *The Theory of Moral Sentiments* than from *The Wealth of Nations*. Interestingly enough, Allebone does not have the statement about shopkeepers.

Finally there are at least two books of humorous quotations in which Smith—strange as it may seem—is represented. In Evan Esar's *Dictionary of Humorous Quotations* (1949) and the Procknows' *Treasury of Humorous Quotations* (1969) there is this remark of Smith's: "Nobody ever saw a dog make a fair and deliberate exchange of one bone for another with another dog." The same quotation is also included in Lewis Copeland's *Popular Quotations for All Uses* (revised ed., 1962). The "dog" quotation is the only one from Smith in Esar and Copeland. The Procknows include another Smithian utterance, a remark about Oxford (really about "several of those learned societies"). In all these instances, it might be added, the quotations are inaccurate. As to whether the observation about dogs is humorous or not, there is room for some difference of opinion.

On the basis of the preceding analysis it would seem that our contention that less than justice has been done to Adam Smith by our dictionaries of quotations is well merited. The case is not yet completely conclusive, however; not until consideration is given to what Smith has to offer to the compilers of such dictionaries.

To that task we shall now turn. In the present essay the quotations are from *The Theory of Moral Sentiments* and a number of our author's minor writings; in the next essay they are chiefly from *The Wealth of Nations*. Some attempt has been made to bring the separate entries into coherent groups. Consequently they are not always in the order in which they appear in Smith's two books.

The quotations in our collection throw a great deal of light on our author's detailed opinions and on his economic, political, and social philosophy. It should be clear, however, that scattered verbal tidbits taken from a person's writings cannot convey any adequate impression of either his specific or general beliefs. While the quotations therefore tell us a "story" about Smith, and a very interesting one it is, they do not tell us the whole story.

Quotations have another limitation. Since it is desirable to keep the selections brief, meaningful sentences that are associated with them must sometimes be omitted. For this reason, and possibly for others, curious readers may want to examine the context in which the quotations appear. For their convenience the pages, in Smith's writings, from which the items have been taken are indicated.

Compilers of dictionaries of quotations do not usually include comments on the statements they select. In the present compilation, however, the ordinary procedure is not followed. Instead, many of the quoted remarks are accompanied by editorial observations. It is hoped that these observations will throw additional light on Smith's opinions and, in numerous instances, reveal more of their contemporary relevance.

In presenting the quotations the compiler has retained Smith's punctuation and spelling, except for the substitution of "e" for "oe" in "economy." Omitted words are indicated by three dots, and added words by the use of brackets. The source pages associated with the quotations in the present essay relate to Smith's *Essays* (which includes his *Theory of Moral Sentiments*), published in London by Alex. Murray & Son in 1869. The source pages in the next essay relate to the Modern Library edition of *The Wealth of Nations,* published in New York by Random House Inc., 1937.

The Theory of Moral Sentiments

1

> To seem not to be affected with the joy of our companions is but want of politeness; but not to wear a serious countenance when they tell us their afflictions, is real and gross inhumanity. (p. 15)

This remark, and others that follow it, point to Smith's doctrine of "Sympathy," as set forth in his *Theory of Moral Sentiments,* a book that is not only beyond the ken of most compilers of dictionaries of quotations but even of most economists. It is to be hoped that philosophers are not equally negligent, and there is evidence that they are not. For one thing, we are informed by a successor of Adam Smith's at the University of Glasgow that some contemporary philosophers are basing their psychology of morals on the notion of "sympathy," which along with "imagination" constituted the main theme of Smith's book; and A. L. Macfie, another Glasgow scholar, points to a number of other modern critics who have praised *The Theory*.[1] Moreover, Macfie himself believes, and argues, that the ethical theory embodied in Smith's neglected book, is of "considerable subtlety and balance."

2

> Hatred and anger are the greatest poisons to the happiness of a good mind. (p. 36)

3

The want of proper indignation is a most essential defect in the manly character, and, upon many occasions, renders a man incapable of protecting either himself or his friends from insult and injustice. (p. 216)

Smith himself was generally a composed man, but there were occasions when he gave expression to "proper" indignation. On one or two occasions he may even have gone beyond that limit. The matter is discussed in Essay 3.

4

Self-command is not only itself a great virtue, but from it all the other virtues seem to derive their principal lustre. (p. 214)

At a number of points in his book (pp. 126, 127) Smith speaks of "the great school of self-command." This was a highly important "institution" in his scheme of things. To Smith self-command did not involve the complete absence of indignation, however, as is clear from the preceding quotation.

5

Humanity does not desire to be great, but to be beloved. (p. 146)

6

The practice of truth, justice, and humanity is a certain and almost infallible method of acquiring what these virtues chiefly aim at, the confidence and love of those we live with. (p. 147)

7

No benevolent man ever lost altogether the fruits of his benevolence. (p. 200)

8

. . . that feeble spark of benevolence which Nature has lighted up in the human heart. (p. 120)

The first of these statements on benevolence implies this virtue is always rewarded, though in varying degrees. The second points to Smith's belief that the virtue is not one of man's outstanding characteristics. An excellent statement of the weakness of benevolence in practice is found in a celebrated remark Smith makes in *The Wealth of Nations* (p. 14) about our not expecting our dinner from the benevolence of the butcher, the brewer, or the baker but from the regard of those personages for their own interest. "We address ourselves," he adds in equally famous words, "not to their humanity but to their self-love, and never talk to them of our own necessities but of their advantages."

Despite our author's skepticism concerning the prevalence of benevolence in the world, he considered the virtue to be of the utmost significance. At one point in his *Theory* (p. 24), he declares that "the perfection of human nature" is found in restraining the selfish affections and the exercise of benevolent ones. At another point (p. 210) he finds perfect virtue in acting "according to the rules of perfect prudence, of strict justice, and of proper benevolence." Such is the nature of human passions, however, that these rules are not easy to follow. So, if one is to do his duty, he must have not only perfect knowledge of the rules but perfect self-command. In his treatment of various systems of moral philosophy Smith devotes a chapter to the system which bases virtue on benevolence. In words of glowing praise he points to his old professor, Dr. Hutcheson, as the most outstanding "patron" of the system (p. 266). See also comments to Quotations 20, 22, 24.

9

Kindness is the parent of kindness. (p. 200)

10

Whenever we cordially congratulate our friends, which, however, to the disgrace of human nature, we do but seldom, their joy literally becomes our joy; we are, for the moment, as happy as they are: our heart swells and overflows with real pleasure: joy and complacency sparkle from our eyes, and animate every feature of our countenance, and every gesture of our body. (p. 45)

11

The most sincere praise can give little pleasure when it cannot be considered as some sort of proof of praise-worthiness. (p. 103)

12

They are the most frivolous and superficial of mankind only who can be much delighted with that praise which they themselves know to be altogether unmerited. (p. 107)

13

The love of praise is the desire of obtaining the favorable sentiments of our brethren. The love of praise-worthiness is the desire of rendering ourselves the proper object of those sentiments. (p. 113)

14

The love of just fame, of true glory, even for its own sake, and independent of any advantage which he can derive from it, is not unworthy even of a wise man. (p. 105)

15

We frequently see the respectful attentions of the world more strongly directed towards the rich and the great, than towards the wise and the virtuous. (p. 57)

In the brief last chapter of Part I of his *Theory of Moral Sentiments* Smith has a fascinating discussion of how our moral sentiments are corrupted by our disposition "to admire the Rich and the Great, and to despise or neglect Persons of poor and mean Condition." Though he felt that the admiration of the former was of value in society, indeed necessary—"both to establish and to maintain the distinction of ranks and the order of society"—he regretted the way in which it distorted our moral judgments; he lamented the lack of consideration given to "the wise and virtuous," who presumably were persons whose condition was poor and mean. Among his remarks on the rich and the great are a number with Veblenian overtones. In his discussion as a whole one can see some of his favorite stylistic practices: his use of triplicates, his resort to contrasting, balancing statements, his use of figurative language, his employment of historical illustrations.

16

The candidates for fortune too frequently abandon the paths of virtue; for unhappily, the road which leads to the one, and that which leads to the other, lie sometimes in very opposite directions. (p. 59)

17

To a real wise man the judicious and well-weighed approbation of a single wise man, gives more heartfelt satisfaction than all the noisy applauses of ten thousand ignorant though enthusiastic admirers. (p. 225)

Smith was dubious about the merit of public applause. At another point in his discussion (p. 57) he speaks of how "the great mob of mankind" admires and worships wealth and greatness, and not wisdom and virtue. Shortly after the publication of *The Theory of Moral Sentiments,* David Hume wrote a very whimsical letter to Smith (printed in Stewart, pp. 38-41) in which he expressed a view similar to the one that has been quoted above. "A wise man's kingdom is his own breast; or, if he ever looks farther, it will only be the judgment of a select few, who are free from prejudices, and capable of examining his work. Nothing indeed can be a stronger presumption of falsehood that the approbation of the multitude; and Phocion, you know, always suspected himself of some blunder, when he was attended with the applauses of the populace." Hume goes on to tell his good friend Smith, humorously, "the melancholy news, that your book has been very unfortunate, for the public seem disposed to applaud it extremely."

18

A wise man never complains of the destiny of Providence, nor thinks the universe in confusion when he is out of order. (p. 244)

19

> We may often fulfil all the rules of justice by siting still and
> doing nothing. (p. 75)

The point Smith makes here is that usually "mere justice" is a
negative virtue—all it involves is our abstaining from hurting our
neighbor. Justice of this sort, since it involves no positive actions,
"is entitled," he says, "to very little gratitude." Smith believed,
and demonstrated in his personal life, that justice should also involve positive features. This he considered desirable not only in
individual behavior but, to a considerable extent, in governmental
behavior. Smith uses the expression "sit still" in another connection (p. 131). Speaking of unsuccessful efforts to get ahead
in life, he remarks that in most cases the misfortunes of those
persons who failed were due to the fact that they did not know
"when they were well, when it was proper for them to sit still and
to be contented."

20

> The most sublime speculation of the contemplative philosopher
> can scarce compensate the neglect of the smallest active duty.
> (p. 210)

Adam Smith himself was a "contemplative philosopher," with
remarkable powers of mental concentration. But to him the *summum bonum* of man's existence was not just the life of contemplation. It was rather the active pursuit both of his own interests
(which were usually, but by no means wholly, in harmony with
those of society) and the interests of others. To man is entrusted
not the running of "the great system of the universe," but the
task, "a much humbler department," of taking care "of his own
happiness, of that of his family, his friends, his country." We must
avoid being the object of any such charge, he tells us, as that
which Avidius Cassius is purported to have leveled, maybe unjustly, against Marcus Antonius, namely that while he (Antonius)
was engaged in "philosophical speculations, and contemplated the

prosperity of the universe" (the administration of which, Smith says a few lines back, is God's business, not man's) he neglected the prosperity of the Roman Empire. Now comes our main quotation.[2]

Smith makes another observation (p. 97) that is closely related to the present quotation. After pointing out that "man was made for action," he goes on to declare that one must not be content with what he refers to as "indolent benevolence," nor must he "fancy himself the friend of mankind, because in his heart he wishes well to the prosperity of the world."

21

To what purpose should we trouble ourselves about the world in the moon? (p. 122)

Since the era of the astronauts, and particularly since the achievement of Armstrong, Aldrin, and Collins, this remark, as a detached observation, has lost much of its significance. But the point Smith had in mind is still of interest. He was opposed to the shedding of idle tears for those who are in misery but whom we do not know, with whose miseries we are not acquainted, and for whom we could do nothing anyway. (The number of persons in misery in the world he greatly underestimated.) Smith belabors "those whining and melancholy moralists" who reproach us for being happy while so many persons are miserable. He was interested, of course, in aiding those whom it was possible to help. But why be concerned, he asks, with those whom we are in no position to help, with "the world in the moon." Smith was opposed to the "artificial commiseration" that this particular set of philosophers advocated. One's concern may be very wide; indeed, as we learn from the comment accompanying the previous quotation, it may be at least as wide as "the Roman Empire." But the moon is clearly out of the orbit of one's worries. These worries should be about one's self, one's family, one's friends, one's country. These constitute, to Smith's way of thinking, what we might describe as our "controllable universe."[3]

22

> Wise and judicious conduct, when directed to greater and nobler
> purposes than the care of the health, the fortune, the rank and
> reputation of the individual, is frequently and very properly
> called prudence. (p. 191)

Smith's description of the prudent man, which is in many respects
a self-portrait, is one of the finest character sketches in his *Theory*.
Though personal security, widely conceived, is the primary and
chief aim of such a man—an aim that "does not seem entitled to
any very ardent love or admiration"—he may also seek more
worthy goals, as our quotation suggests. Conduct of this sort is
more than ordinary prudence, however. Smith refers to it as "superior prudence." The latter, "when carried to the highest degree
of perfection," he defines as "the best head joined to the best
heart," as "the most perfect wisdom combined with the most perfect virtue." Some pages later (p. 210) our author states a somewhat different view, and one with a reverse relationship. The
perfectly virtuous man, he says, is one "who acts according to the
rules of perfect prudence, of strict justice, and of proper benevolence." This statement would seem to imply, in contradiction to
what Smith said earlier, that "perfect prudence" does not include
such "greater and nobler" purposes as justice and benevolence.
But enough of verbal quibbling. It should be added, however, that
most of Smith's discussion of prudence relates to what we have
called the "ordinary" type, though "other virtues" (as well as im-
prudence and "other vices") figure in it.

Smith uses the "head-heart" combination in *The Wealth of
Nations* as well as in his *Theory*. In the former (p. 727) he declares that certain educational changes the universities of Europe
had introduced did not make "the ancient course of philosophy"
more likely "either to improve the understanding, or to mend the
heart." One of the greatest tributes paid to Smith himself involves
the same verbal combination. Reversing the sequence, and thus
emphasizing the characteristic of generosity, Edmund Burke remarked that Smith's heart was as good as his head.[4]

The great economist has recently been hailed for the emphasis he placed on the head-heart notion (and the principle of self-command). Smith, R. F. Brissenden declares, made "one of the clearest statements of a theme that was to be sounded with growing force and clarity, especially in fiction, in the latter half of the eighteenth century." This was "the theme of sense and sensibility, of the necessity to preserve a proper balance between the head and the heart, the reason and the feelings."[5]

23

The most intrepid valour may be employed in the cause of the greatest injustice. (p. 214)

24

Society may subsist, though not in the most comfortable state, without beneficence; but the prevalence of injustice must utterly destroy it. (p. 79)

Following the above statement Smith makes a number of interesting observations about beneficence and justice. The former, which Nature exhorts man to engage in, but for the neglect of which she provides no "terrors of merited punishment," he calls "the ornament which embellishes" ("not the foundation which supports") life's building; the latter he refers to as "the main pillar that upholds the whole edifice." Continuing, he says that if justice is removed "the great, the immense fabric of human society . . . must in a moment crumble into atoms." Smith attached very great importance to justice in human society. Benevolence is also of significance, but he not only puts it in a secondary position but he was pessimistic concerning the extent to which man would as a matter of fact engage in it. This does not mean, of course, that Smith himself was opposed to beneficence; far from it, indeed, as is clear from our comments on a number of our previous quotations.

Smith identifies two main types of justice: commutative and distributive (p. 240). The first consists in not claiming as one's own what rightfully belongs to another (and which, consequently, does not call for any positive action) and in voluntarily performing those acts which we might with propriety be compelled to do. The emphasis here is negative; it involves abstaining from "violating either the person or the estate, or the reputation" of one's neighbors (p. 75). On p. 77 he adds "personal rights, or what is due to him from the promises of others." The rules of this kind of justice, the end of which he again says is "to hinder us from hurting our neighbour," are like the rules of grammar: they are "precise, accurate, and indispensable" (p. 155).

The second type of justice that Smith identifies is wholly positive in nature and has to do with the notion of sharing. This is distributive justice, and it consists "in proper beneficence, in the becoming use of what is our own"—in suitable acts of charity or generosity.

Our author points to still another, and more comprehensive, use of the concept of justice, a use that has a close kinship to distributive justice. The general meaning involved here is suggested by an illustration Smith introduces: "We are said to do injustice, to a poem or a picture, when we do not admire them enough, and we are said to do them more than justice when we admire them too much."

When Smith uses the word "justice" in his writings he ordinarily means commutative justice.[6] This dose not mean, however, that he completely sets aside distributive justice. This latter type of justice has a close relationship to benevolence. Smith links it to "proper beneficence." In his *Theory,* though not in *The Wealth of Nations,* our author has a great deal to say about benevolence, and we have already noted a number of his remarks on the theme.

25

The peace and order of society, is more of importance than even the relief of the miserable. (p. 200)

Smith here alludes to an issue that in recent years has taken a somewhat different form, namely "law-and-order versus justice." The problem involved is a complex one, raising the difficult question of whether unpeaceful conduct in seeking highly desirable social ends can ever be justified. Smith links up peace and order with what he calls "the distinction of ranks," a distinction, he tells us, which Nature in its wisdom has based upon "the plain and palpable difference of birth and fortune"—not upon "the invisible and often uncertain difference of wisdom and virtue." Whatever merit the underlying philosophy of this class-conscious opinion may have had in the eighteenth century, it does not meet with much approval today. It should be added, however, that after making the main statement quoted above, Smith says that "accordingly"—as a result of the priority given to peace and order—the respect we have for the great "is most apt to offend by its excess; our fellow-feeling for the miserable, by its defect." Whatever class feelings he may have harbored, Smith had great sympathy for the less fortunate members of society.

26

> He is not a citizen who is not disposed to respect the laws and to obey the civil magistrate; and he is certainly not a good citizen who does not wish to promote, by every means in his power, the welfare of the whole society of his fellow citizens. (p. 205)

This remark is in the same general category as the preceding one. It suggests a highly difficult problem that faces the citizens of a state: the class between their desire for a stable government on the one hand, and their wish for needed reforms—"to render the condition of our fellow citizens as safe, respectable, and happy as we can"—on the other. In times of peace and quiet, there is ordinarily no conflict, says Smith. However, "in times of public discontent, faction, and disorder" the situation may be different. Under such circumstances "even a wise man" may feel that some constitutional or structural changes in the government are desirable. "In such cases, however, it often requires, perhaps, the highest effort of political wisdom to determine when a real patriot ought to support and endeavour to re-establish the authority of the old system, and when we ought to give way to the more daring, but often dangerous, spirit of innovation." Today the "civil faction" that exists is probably not as simple and as sharp as the type Smith had in mind. Much of it, however, takes the same general form that he describes. There are those who are strong law-and-order citizens and there are those who frequently, and at times rebelliously, strive for innovations. Certainly, "the highest effort of political wisdom" would seem to be needed if "the patriot" is to make the proper adjustment, in his own mind, between the often conflicting goals of political stability and desirable social change.

27

The flirting levity of youth, and the immovable insensibility of old age, are equally disagreeable. (p. 178)

28

We are charmed with the gaiety of youth, and even with the playfulness of childhood: but we soon grow weary of the flat and tasteless gravity which too frequently accompanies old age. (p. 218)

29

And thus, place, that great object which divides the wives of aldermen, is the end of half of the labours of human life; and is the cause of all the tumult and bustle, all the rapine and injustice, which avarice and ambition have introduced into this world. (p. 55)

Long before Vance Packard, Adam Smith had something to say about "status seekers." One should not assume from this remark of Smith's that he was unalterably opposed to all attempts to gratify one's vanity by achieving "place." When to vanity there is united a desire to win the esteem of one's fellows—to place oneself "most in the view of general sympathy and attention"—the result is, or certainly can be, socially good.[7]

30

The frequent, and often wonderful, success of the most ignorant quacks and impostors, both civil and religious, sufficiently demonstrate how easily the multitude are imposed upon by the most extravagant and groundless pretensions. (p. 222)

31

The animosity of hostile factions, whether civil or ecclesiastical, is often still more furious than that of hostile nations; and their conduct towards one another is often still more atrocious. (p. 136)

32

He is a bold surgeon, they say, whose hand does not tremble when he performs an operation upon his own person; and he is often equally bold who does not hesitate to pull off the mysterious veil of self-delusion, which covers from his view the deformities of his own conduct. (p. 138)

33

If we saw ourselves in the light in which others see us, or in which they would see us if they knew all, a reformation would generally be unavoidable. (p. 139)

Smith is here referring to what he called "the impartial spectator." This personage, whom the author alludes to under various terms, occupies a key role in his theory of morality. Professor Macfie surmises, and it seems quite correctly, that this statement of Smith's must have inspired what are probably Robert Burns's two most familiar lines, a point we noted in Essay 2.

34

A man of sensibility is apt to be more humiliated by just censure than he is ever elevated by just applause. (p. 109)

35

Nothing is more graceful than habitual cheerfulness, which is always founded upon a peculiar relish for all the little pleasures which common occurrences afford. (p. 40)

Smith stressed the great importance of small enjoyments in human life. These enjoyments—the basis of our "real happiness"—he tells us at another point (p. 131), are nearly always close at hand

and within our power of attainment. Except for "the frivolous pleasures of vanity and superiority," the person in the most humble station in life can, if personal liberty prevails, have all the other pleasures "which the most exalted can afford." Moreover, the "frivolous pleasures" just referred to, "are seldom consistent," he says, "with perfect tranquility, the principle and foundation of all real and satisfactory enjoyment." Preceding our selected quotation Smith lists some of these readily available pleasures, including "all those frivolous nothings which fill up the void of human life." The statements we have just noted, and the one that comes next, point to a paradox in Smith's social philosophy: man struggles for power and possessions, and it is proper, in the interests of economic progress, that he should do so; but, in terms of personal happiness, power and possessions are of small avail. It is of interest to note that Samuel Johnson shared Smith's view on the great importance of "little pleasures." "It is by studying little things," he told Boswell (HP, I, p. 433), "that we attain the great art of having as little misery and as much hapiness as possible," a general view that was also held by Benjamin Franklin (p. 434).

36

> In ease of the body and peace of the mind, all the different ranks of life are nearly upon a level, and the beggar, who suns himself by the side of the highway, possesses that security which kings are fighting for. (p. 163)

This is one of Smith's most famous utterances. It is found in his fascinating discussion of the relationship between wealth and greatness on the one hand and happiness on the other. This discussion includes the author's graphic character sketch of the Poor Man's Son—"whom Heaven in its anger has visited with ambition"; his treatment of the "deception" idea, touched on in Essay 10; and his allusion to the "invisible hand," a figure of speech that has been much discussed by economists and which is also examined in Essay 10.

37

What can be added to the happiness of the man who is in health, who is out of debt, and has a clear conscience? (p. 43)

38

We suffer more . . . when we fall from a better to a worse situation, than we ever enjoy when we rise from a worse to a better. (p. 188)

39

We are not ready to suspect any person of being defective in selfishness. (p. 269)

40

When two nations are at variance, the citizen of each pays little regard to the sentiments which foreign nations may entertain concerning his conduct. (p. 135)

41

What institution of government could tend so much to promote the happiness of mankind as the general prevalence of wisdom and virtue? (p. 165)

42

A well-written poem may last as long as the world. (p. 172)

43

There is no greater tormentor of the human breast than violent resentment which cannot be gratified. (p. 107)

44

Society and conversation, therefore, are the most powerful remedies for restoring the mind to its tranquility, if, at any time, it has unfortunately lost it. (p. 22)

45

The great pleasure of conversation and society, besides, arises from a certain correspondence of sentiments and opinions, from a certain harmony of minds, which like so many musical instruments coincide and keep time with one another. (p. 300)

Some idea of the nature of the kind of conversation Adam Smith preferred can be gathered from certain remarks he makes in his vivid portrayal of the Prudent Man in his *Theory of Moral Sentiments*. This imaginary person does not try to impose upon others "by the cunning devices of an artful impostor, nor by the arrogant airs of an assuming pedant, nor by the confident assertions of a superficial and impudent pretender" (p. 188). The conversation of the prudent man—who is opposed "to all the quackish arts by which other people so frequently thrust themselves into public notice and reputation"—is, we are told, "simple and modest." The prudent man, we are further informed (p. 189), is "an exact observer of decency" in his conduct and his conversation; he "respects with an almost religious scrupulosity, all the established decorums and ceremonials of society."

Smith himself was not a great conversationalist; he was not in the same class as Burke and Johnson. But David Garick's remark about Smith's talk being "flabby" is not an accurate generalization. Boswell tells us in his *Life of Johnson* (HP, IV, p. 24) that Garrick, after listening to Smith, slyly whispered this observation to a friend.

The famous economist did not intrude himself into the discussions of others. Indeed, he was inclined to listen rather than speak; so much so as a matter of fact that his friends often devised "little schemes," as Dugald Stewart tells us (pp. 77-79), "in order to engage him in the discussions most likely to interest him." To some extent Smith's silence was undoubtedly due to his habit of engaging in deep thought, even when with his friends. A good example of this practice is found in a walk he had with his close friend Dr. Hutton. Smith often strode along in silence despite efforts made by his companion to engage him in conversation. As William Smellie states,[8] "though the cheerful Doctor, in order to arouse Mr. Smith's attention, talked to him frequently, he seldom uttered a word, but walked on moving his lips, and talking to himself." Similar testimony is given by Alexander Carlyle.[9] Smith, says Carlyle, was the most absentminded man he had ever seen in company, "moving his lips, and talking to himself, and smiling."

But, Carlyle continues, if one aroused Smith from his reverie and directed his thoughts to the matter being discussed, "he immediately began a harangue, and never stopped till he told you all he knew about it, with the utmost philosophical ingenuity."

Possibly as a result of his work as a teacher, Smith sometimes "lectured" in his conversation, as Carlyle intimates and Stewart affirms. On such occasions he was probably carried away mentally with his preoccupation with the question before him. Certainly it would be unjust to charge such an arch-foe of monopoly with conscious monopolization of conversation.

Smith not only showed a reluctance to begin a conversation but he showed a hesitancy to introduce new topics into a discussion. However, he appeared to be ready to discuss any topics raised by others, and even on occasion (as Dugald Stewart informs us) to discuss topics with which he was not too conversant.

Stewart adds another interesting point about Smith as a conversationalist: "When perfectly at ease, and when warmed with conversation, his gestures were animated and not ungraceful; and, in the society of those he loved, his features were often brightened with a smile of inexpressible benignity."

Smith's conversation was not always sweetness and light, however. This we know from his altercation with Samuel Johnson and from a number of other episodes.

If David Garick described Smith's talk as flabby, Henry Mackenzie thought it "was solid beyond that of any man."[10] As Mackenzie had often said to Smith, after chatting with him for half an hour, "Sir, you have said enough to make a book."

46

The man of system . . . seems to imagine that he can arrange the different members of a great society with as much ease as the hand arranges the different pieces upon a chess-board. He does not consider that the pieces upon the chess-board have no other principle of motion besides that which the hand impresses upon them; but that, in the great chess-board of human society, every single piece has a principle of motion of its own, altogether different from that which the legislature might choose to impress upon it. (p. 207)

The man of system in this statement might be compared with the authoritarian planners of today, who feel that "the market," about which Smith wrote so enthusiastically, cannot satisfactorily arrange the pieces "in the great chess-board of human society."

47

It is often more mortifying to appear in public under small disasters, than under great misfortunes. (p. 55)

48

Domestic education is the institution of nature; public education, the contrivance of man. It is surely unnecessary to say, which is likely to be the wisest. (p. 197)

49

The great secret of education is to direct vanity to proper objects. (p. 230)

Smith's use of the word "vanity" should not be misunderstood. To him it was not a completely derogatory word, indicating human frailty. Indeed, the attribute of vanity, if it was accompanied by a desire to win the esteem of one's fellows, serves a worthy social purpose.[11]

50

It is acquired wisdom and experience only that teach incredulity, and they very seldom teach it enough. (p. 299)

51

Nature, for the wisest purposes, has rendered, in most men, perhaps in all men, parental tenderness a much stronger affection than filial piety. (p. 123)

Filial piety was not one of the characteristic affections of the latter 1960s, not with the existence of the so-called "generation gap." Such a gap, however, in various widths has long existed, and back in the eighteenth century Smith was well aware of its presence.

The following statement of his (p. 81) is most timely today, more than two hundred years after it was written: "We frequently hear the young and the licentious ridiculing the most sacred rules of morality, and professing, sometimes from the corruption, but more frequently from the vanity of their hearts, the most abominable maxims of conduct." It should be added, however, that many of the younger "rebels" of today derive their "abominable maxims" from the existence of what they consider to be injustices in modern society. They would agree with Smith in "the necessity of justice to the existence of society" (p. 82), but they would not always agree with him on the virtue of "law and order." Other references by Smith to the parent-son relationship can be found on pp. 74 and 152 of his *Theory*. In *The Wealth of Nations* (p. 582) Smith pointed to the possibility that the kind of "parental affection" and "filial respect" that once existed between the colonies of ancient Greece and "the mother city from which they descended" might be established between Great Britain and her American colonies (if there was a voluntary, friendly separation between them, something he considered most unlikely).

Other Sources

52

It would be a strange picture which required an inscription at the foot to tell us, not only what particular person it meant to represent, but whether it meant to represent a man or a horse, or whether it meant to be a picture at all, and to represent any thing.

Smith, it would seem, would not have appreciated some of the avant-garde productions of the present day. He appears to have been a staunch realist in paintings, though his powers of imagination in other matters was vast. The quotation is from his essay "The Imitative Arts" (p. 423). Rae, who feels that the essay is "one of the most finished pieces of work" Smith ever did, states (p. 214) that had the author lived it was his intention to write a whole book on the subject. The great economist had long been interested in the theme of the essay, as is evidenced by a letter of John Millar's.[12] In the early part of the 1780s Smith must have returned to his work on the theme,[13] but his essay was not published until after the author's death.

53

> The sentiments and passions which Music can best imitate are those which unite and bind men together in society.

In this statement, which is also from the essay "The Imitative Arts" (p. 419), Smith points to a type of "harmony of interests" that differs from the kind ordinarily associated with his name. After pointing out the particular passions he has in mind, the author declares (p. 420) that the passions which separate man, "the unsocial, the hateful, the indecent, the vicious passions, cannot easily be imitated by Music." Moreover, he declares, the music that "does imitate them is not the most agreeable"—these same words are found in *The Theory of Moral Sentiments* (p. 36) where the general theme of our main quotation is also discussed. Further observations on Smith and music can be found in Essay 1.

54

> Wonder, therefore, and not any expectation of advantage from its discoveries, is the first principle which prompts mankind to the study of Philosophy.

This statement is from Smith's essay "The History of Astronomy" (p. 340) which, as we noted in Essay 1, was written quite early in the author's career.

55

> The philosophers who have taken so much pains to prove that there is no heat in the fire, meaning that the sensation or feeling of heat is not in the fire, have laboured long to refute an opinion which the most ignorant of mankind never entertained.

The above quotation, from Smith's essay "The External Senses" (p. 444), suggests the virtue of common sense—a human attribute

that Smith sometimes mentions in his *Theory of Moral Sentiments*
and, as various commentators have pointed out, a feature that
marked his own mental processes.

NOTES

1. See D. D. Raphael's discussion in *The Listener,* March 5,
1959, pp. 407-408; and Macfie, *The Individual in Society,* Essay 3
and pp. 70-71. Another modern scholar, R. F. Brissenden, in commenting on *The Theory of Moral Sentiments,* refers to the work as
"this extremely significant book." *Texas Studies in Literature and
Language,* Summer 1969, p. 945.

2. For a more detailed treatment of the general theme of the
above comment and the one that follows it, see Joseph Cropsey's discussion in *Polity and Economy* (The Hague: Nijhoff, 1957), pp. 7-11.

3. Observations that Smith makes on the issue covered in our
comment can be found in his *Theory,* pp. 121-123, 204, 210. Jacob
Viner, who points to the dual aspect of Smith's use of "distance"—
spatial and what one might call, for want of a better term, human—
indicates the author's use of the notion in his thoughts about many
of the transactions in the market. Here, because of the anonymity
that exists, there is not much scope for the operation of any of the
moral sentiments apart from justice. See *International Encyclopedia
of the Social Sciences,* article on Adam Smith.

4. Robert Bisset, *The Life of Edmund Burke,* 2 vols. (London:
Cawthorn, British Library, 2nd ed., 1800), II, p. 429.

5. *Texas Studies in Literature and Language,* Summer 1969, p.
957.

6. Jacob Viner says Smith "always used the word to mean sub-
stantially" commutative justice, in the sense that Aristotle and the
Schoolmen used the term. *International Encyclopedia of the Social
Sciences,* article on Adam Smith.

7. On this point see A. L. Macfie's remarks in *The Individual in
Society,* pp. 72-73.

8. *Literary and Characteristical Lives of John Gregory, M.D.,
Henry Home, Lord Kames, David Hume, Esq., and Adam Smith,
L.L.D.* (Edinburgh: A. Smellie, 1800), p. 292.

9. *Autobiography of the Rev. Dr. Alexander Carlyle* (Boston:
Ticknor and Fields, 1861), p. 227.

10. Quoted by Rae, p. 269, from Peter W. Clayden's *Early Life
of Samuel Rogers.*

11. For further observations on Smith's use of "vanity" and of "pride" see A. L. Macfie's discussion in *The Individual in Society*, pp. 72-73.

12. Scott, *Adam Smith as Student and Professor*, pp. 311-313.

13. The evidence is contained in a letter written by Sir Joshua Reynolds to Bennet Langton. See Essay 1 for a discussion of Smith and Reynolds in relation to the subject of "imitation."

8.

More Thoughts from Adam Smith

His book accordingly is like the Proverbs of Solomon
. . . and its sayings would furnish a quite pleasant
anthology.

—JAMES BONAR

The Wealth of Nations

1

It is the great multiplication of the productions of all the different arts, in consequence of the division of labour, which occasions,
in a well-governed society, that universal opulence which extends
itself to the lowest ranks of the people. (p. 11)

Smith's discussion of the division of labor, found principally in the
first three chapters of *The Wealth of Nations,* is famous. It will
be noted that the author here employs the word "opulence," not
"affluence." Though, like Professor Galbraith, he makes use of the
latter term, particularly in his chapter on "The Wages of Labour,"
he clearly prefers the former. W. R. Scott has made the point that
as the years went by Smith set aside "opulence" in his writings and
used "wealth." Where the former word occurs in *The Wealth of
Nations,* we are told, it is in sections that the author wrote early
in his career.[1] In a broad, general sense Professor Scott is undoubtedly correct. A number of observations on the point should

be made, however. The word "opulence" is used rather widely in Smith's classic; indeed it can be found in all five books of the work. In at least seven chapters both "wealth" and "opulence" are present. Though "opulence" is by all odds the favorite term in Smith's early *Lectures on Justice, Police, Revenue, and Arms* (1763), the words "wealth" and "riches" are also found. Scott's statement that "wealth" is "rarely" used in these lectures is a little exaggerated—it appears at least fifteen times. It is also pertinent to note that in his *Lectures on Rhetoric and Belles Lettres* (1762-63), Smith also uses "wealth," though not often. The word can also be found, and with greater frequency, in his *Theory of Moral Sentiments* (1759) although always in relation to individuals, not nations. (In *The Wealth of Nations* both "wealth" and "opulence" usually, though not always, relate to nations or other geographical units.) In the *Theory* "opulence" seems to be entirely absent.

2

Nobody ever saw a dog make a fair and deliberate exchange of one bone for another with another dog. (p. 13)

Our author declares that the division of labor was not based originally on human wisdom but on man's "propensity to truck, barter, and exchange one thing for another"—hardly a convincing explanation. C. R. Fay, in a "bizarre" illustration, furnishes us with a list of almost all the instances in which dogs are mentioned in *The Wealth of Nations*.[2] In his *Theory of Moral Sentiments* Smith draws another interesting contrast between the human and the nonhuman "animal," this time with reference to the faculty of speech and the desire of man to influence others. "No other animal possesses this faculty, and we cannot discover in any other animal any desire to lead and direct the judgment and conduct of its fellows" (p. 299). In discussing differences between prose and poetry, in his *Lectures on Rhetoric and Belles Lettres* (p. 132), Smith has a remark that sounds a little like the first part of the "dog" statement: "No one ever made a bargain in verse."

3

By nature a philosopher is not in genius and disposition half so different from a street porter, as a mastiff is from a greyhound, or a greyhound from a spaniel, or this last from a shepherd's dog. (p. 16)

In contrast to Plato's assumption that the division of labor is based on original diversities in human nature, Smith believed that human beings at birth are essentially similar. The mind of each is a *tabula rasa,* to use an expression Locke brought into prominence, upon which "experience" does the writing.

4

The man whose whole life is spent in performing a few simple operations . . . generally becomes as stupid and ignorant as it is possible for a human creature to become. (p. 734)

Though Smith speaks highly of the beneficial results of task specialization, he—like Marx, Ruskin, Kropotkin, and Morris—was well aware of its possible unfavorable consequences. Does this mean that there was a certain dichotomy in Smith's treatment of the principle? This question is touched on in Essay 9.

5

It is not from the benevolence of the butcher, the brewer, or the baker, that we expect our dinner, but from their regard to their own interest. We address ourselves, not to their humanity but to their self-love, and never talk to them of our own necessities but of their advantages. (p. 14)

This is one of the best-known statements in *The Wealth of Nations.* Economists like to quote it in indicating the great importance that self-interest plays in Smith's economic and political philosophy. In this conection it should be emphasized that our author's doctrine of self-interest, or self-love, is not to be made synonymous with selfishness as that term is now ordinarily understood. Self-love when operating under the proper conditions, and in a way that would be approved of by an "impartial spectator," is not only compatible with the general good but actually promotes it. As Professor Macfie points out,[3] to Smith and other eighteenth-century philosophers, true self-love was not an undesirable quality but an admirable one. Two further observations should be made. First, a nice problem that has long engaged the attention of students of Smith, is the extent to which there is a difference in the underlying philosophy of his two books. Macfie argues strongly (and convincingly) that on this matter the books are in harmony. Secondly, however one interprets Smith's self-interest, self-love doctrine, it must be recognized that in his personal life the great economist and moral philosopher was a very benevolent person.

6

The uniform, constant, and uninterrupted effort of every man to better his condition, the principle from which public and national as well as private opulence is originally derived, is frequently powerful enough to maintain the national progress of things toward improvement, in spite both of the extravagance of government, and of the greatest errors of administration. (p. 326)

Another statement suggesting the ability of self-interest to promote the economic welfare of society in spite of governmental obstacles, is found on p. 508 of *The Wealth of Nations*. There Smith speaks of the surmounting of "a hundred impertinent obstructions with which the folly of human laws too often encumbers" the operation of the self-interest principle.

7

He (the individual investor) generally, indeed, neither intends to promote the public interest, nor knows how much he is promoting it. By preferring the support of domestic to that of foreign industry, he intends only his own security; and by directing that industry in such a manner as its produce may be of the greatest value, he intends only his own gain, and he is in this, as in many other cases, led by an invisible hand to promote an end which was no part of his intention. Nor is it always the worse for the society that it was no part of it. (p. 423)

Here we have Smith's famous remark about the invisible hand, the agency that brings individual self-seeking and the public good into harmony. Some economists point to this figure of speech and the harmony it involves as "the fundamental thesis," "the basic thesis," "the fundamental proposition" of *The Wealth of Nations*.[4] This is a point on which opinions differ. But what, specifically, is "the invisible hand?" What did Smith have in mind when he used the metaphor? On that point, as we shall see in Essay 9, there have been various opinions. In that essay, too, we shall note that Smith recognized, in his *Wealth of Nations,* numerous exceptions to the harmony idea, more exceptions than one might expect after reading the sweeping statement he makes a few pages before his invisible-hand remark, and which is our next quotation. It is interesting to observe that the expression "invisible hand" occurs only once in *The Wealth of Nations,* and once in *The Theory of Moral Sentiments*. The term is also used by Smith in his essay "The History of Astronomy," but here he speaks of "the invisible hand of Jupiter."

8

Every individual is continually exerting himself to find out the most advantageous employment for whatever capital he can command. It is his own advantage, indeed, and not that of the society, which he has in view. But the study of his own advantage naturally, or rather necessarily leads him to prefer that employment which is most advantageous to the society. (p. 421)

9

I have never known much good done by those who affected to trade for the public good. (p. 423)

10

It is the highest impertinence and presumption, therefore, in kings and ministers, to pretend to watch over the economy of private people, and to restrain their expence, either by sumptuary laws, or by prohibiting the importation of foreign luxuries. They are themselves always, and without any exception, the greatest spendthrifts in the society. Let them look well after their own expence, and they may safely trust private people with theirs. If their own extravagance does not ruin the state, that of their subjects never will. (p. 329)

11

There is no art which one government sooner learns of another, than that of draining money from the pockets of the people. (p. 813)

12

Taxes upon the necessaries of life have nearly the same effect upon the circumstances of the people as a poor soil and a bad climate. (p. 433)

13

For though management and persuasion are always the easiest and safest instruments of government, as force and violence are the worst and the most dangerous, yet such, it seems, is the natural insolence of man, that he almost always disdains to use the good instrument, except when he cannot or dare not use the bad one. (p. 751)

14

Fear is in almost all cases a wretched instrument of government, and ought in particular never to be employed against any order of men who have the smallest pretensions to independency. (p. 750)

Jeremy Bentham contended, in his *Rationale of Reward,* that Smith was in error in his view—due to his "mistaken notions of humanity." Bentham admitted the frequent abuse of fear, but maintained that it is "a necessary instrument, and the only one applicable to the ordinary purposes of society." To support his argument he uses an amusing illustration about a king who substituted rewards for goodness instead of punishment for badness.[5]

15

The good temper and moderation of contending factions seems to be the most essential circumstance in the public morals of a free people. (p. 729)

16

All systems either of preference or of restraint, therefore, being thus completely taken away, the obvious and simple system of natural liberty establishes itself of its own accord. (p. 651)

17

The servants of the most careless private person are, perhaps, more under the eye of their master than those of the most careful prince. (p. 790)

18

War and the preparation for war, are the two circumstances which in modern times occasion the greater part of the necessary expense of all great states. (p. 773)

A study of the governmental budgets of modern nations would suggest that not much progress has been made in this particular aspect of governmental finance since Smith's time. The great economist makes a number of observations on the war "theme." Though he speaks approvingly of the martial spirit (p. 738), and refers to war as "the noblest of all arts" (p. 658), Smith was nevertheless a man of peace. As is abundantly clear from *The Wealth of Nations,* he endeavored to promote international cooperation.[6] It is especially interesting to note a statement Smith made back in 1780, long before the Atomic Age. A young interviewer, who wrote under the pen name of *Amicus,* tells us that Samuel Johnson's political pamphlets, and especially one of them, aroused Smith's admiration: "But, above all, he was charmed with that respecting Falkland's Islands, as it displayed, in such forcible language, the madness of modern wars."[7]

19

Defence . . . is of much more importance than opulence. (p. 431)

20

All for ourselves, and nothing for other people, seems, in every age of the world, to have been the vile maxim of the masters of mankind. (pp. 388-389)

21

Monopoly, besides, is a great enemy to good management, which can never be universally established but in consequence of that free and universal competition which forces everybody to have recourse to it for the sake of self-defence. (p. 147)

Smith was highly critical of monopolies—commercial monopolies. He felt they led to improper allocation of the factors of production, raised prices, retarded economic growth, and exerted undue influence on the government. Some of his harshest statements are directed against monopolistic enterprises.

22

The price of monopoly is upon every occasion the highest which can be got. (p. 61)

This statement is extreme and misleading; it is also inaccurate. Smith contrasts monopoly price with natural price ("the price of free competition") in general terms. He does not, of course, make use of the sophisticated modern analysis of the problem, with its graphs and its marginal concepts.

23

People of the same trade seldom meet together, even for merriment and diversion, but the conversation ends in a conspiracy against the public, or in some contrivance to raise prices. (p. 128)

24

This monopoly has so much increased the number of some particular tribes of them, that, like an overgrown standing army, they have become formidable to the government, and upon many occasions intimidate the legislature. (p. 438)

Smith greatly emphasized the effect that monopolies, through their lobbies, had on governmental policies. Indeed, his whole attitude toward the general question of governmental intervention was sharply colored by his views on the political activities and powers of the monopolists. As we shall see in Essay 10, however, it is quite possible, if not probable, that he overstressed their influence.

25

> To be merely useless, indeed, is perhaps the highest eulogy which can ever justly be bestowed upon a regulated company; and all the three companies above mentioned seem, in their present state, to deserve this eulogy. (p. 693)

26

> To found a great empire for the sole purpose of raising up a people of customers, may at first sight appear a project fit only for a nation of shopkeepers. It is, however, a project altogether unfit for a nation of shopkeepers; but extremely fit for a nation whose government is influenced by shopkeepers.

This frequently quoted statement is from Smith's famous chapter, "Of Colonies," which includes his provocative proposal for a United Parliament for the British Empire—"a courageous Utopia," as E. A. Benians has described it.[8] Smith, with his anti-Mercantilist opinions, was strongly opposed to the monopolistic trading companies and criticized them very harshly. Benians (p. 255) applies the expression "sharpest sarcasm" to this particular statement of Smith's.

Though Smith's name is commonly associated with the shopkeeper remark, the term, or at least variations of it, had been used earlier. The Oxford *New English Dictionary on Historical Principles* (which points out that the expression "A Nation of Shop-keepers" is "applied disparagingly to a nation whose chief interest and concern lies in commerce—now often, to England") gives a number of examples. In 1766 the words "shop-keeping nation" were used by Josiah Tucker. Moreover, in 1769 Benjamin Franklin referred to a "shopkeeping state." In his *Dictionary of Historical Allusions* (1903), Harbottle says that the expression was first applied to England by Samuel Adams, in 1776. And according to Brewer's *Historic Notebook* (1891), Louis XIV of France called Holland "a nation of shopkeepers."

Smith could well have found the term in the writings of Tucker or elsewhere, and hence it may not have been original with him. But it was Smith who popularized the term, and it will long be associated with his name. Our dictionaries of quotations will see that it is.

27

Country gentlemen and farmers are, to their great honour, of all people, the least subject to the wretched spirit of monopoly. (p. 428)

28

Our merchants and master-manufacturers complain much of the bad effects of high wages in raising the price, and thereby lessening the sales of their goods both at home and abroad. They say nothing concerning the bad effects of high profits. (p. 98)

In view of our current concern with the problem of inflation, and in the light of official appeals for wage and price restraint, this utterance of Smith's is very timely. The statement has an obvious bearing on the debate that has been going on for quite some years over the question of "cost-push" and "demand-pull" inflation. Certainly, our union leaders are in keen sympathy with Smith's remark. Another statement similar to the one quoted can be found on p. 565.

29

We rarely hear, it has been said, of the combinations of masters, though frequently of those of workmen. But whoever imagines, upon this account, that masters rarely combine, is as ignorant of the world as of the subject. (p. 66)

This statement and a number of the ones that immediately follow in our compilation suggest Smith's sympathy toward wage earners and his general concern with the economic lot of the masses. But Smith was a strong supporter of free competition, of a "market economy," and was opposed to the monopolistic practices of unions as well as of employers.

30

Masters are always and every where in a sort of tacit, but constant and uniform combination, not to raise the wages of labour above their actual rate. (pp. 66-67)

31

The workmen desire to get as much, the masters to give as little as possible. The former are disposed to combine in order to raise, the latter in order to lower the wages of labour. (p. 66)

32

The liberal reward of labour, therefore, as it is the necessary effect, so it is the natural symptom of increasing national wealth. (p. 73)

Smith speaks of "the liberal reward of labour" a number of times. A few pages after he makes the above statement he declares that "The liberal reward of labour, as it increases the propagation, so it increases the industry of the common people." The payment of "good" wages is a sign of economic growth, but also promotes growth. The latter quotation, though it to some extent follows Malthusian logic, also serves as a denial of "The Doctrine of the Utility of Poverty," which had sometimes been propounded during the Mercantilist period.[9] Smith's remark points to the opposite notion, namely "The Economy of High Wages"—not "The Economy of Low Wages."

33

The patrimony of a poor man lies in the strength and dexterity of his hands. (p. 122)

This statement is made in connection with Smith's criticism of long apprenticeships. The author speaks of the worker having a "property" right in his labor—a right that is "the most sacred and inviolable"—and to hinder him from using it as he deems proper, without injuring others, "is a plain violation of this most sacred property." In a somewhat related manner, and largely as a result of the insecurity caused by automation, increasing use has recently been made of the notion that a worker has a property right in his job. Smith speaks of "the patrimony of the poor" in a much different fashion in an historical allusion on pp. 755-756.

34

With the greatest part of rich people, the chief enjoyment of riches consists in the parade of riches, which in their eye is never so complete as when they appear to possess these decisive marks of opulence which nobody can possess but themselves. (p. 172)

35

Capitals are increased by parsimony, and diminished by prodigality and misconduct. (p. 321)

Smith attached great importance to capital accumulation as an element in promoting the wealth of a nation, and quite correctly. The same factor is strongly emphasized in present-day Growth Economics. The road to capital accumulation in Smith's view was personal thrift, and he thus had harsh words to say of those who squandered their money. Today we still recognize the need for, and the virtue of, thrift but—largely under the influence of Keynesian analysis—we also recognize that there are times when the frugal man may, in a sense, be a "public enemy" and not a "public benefactor." The present quotation and the two that immediately follow should be considered in the light of our longer discussion of capital accumulation in Essay 9.

36

Every prodigal appears to be a public enemy, and every frugal man a public benefactor. (p. 324)

37

What is prudence in the conduct of every private family, can scarce be folly in that of a great kingdom. (p. 424)

38

The cheapness of consumption and the encouragement given to production, (are) precisely the two effects which it is the great business of political economy to promote. (p. 706)

At another point (p. 352) Smith speaks of "riches and power" as being the great object of national political economy; and, again (p. 643), he equates political economy with "the nature and causes of the wealth of nations."

39

Consumption is the sole end and purpose of all production. (p. 625)

As it stands, in isolation, this statement is misleading in that it suggests productive effort is wholly a means to an end, and in no sense an end in itself. This is a point of view that John Ruskin, William Morris (with his "freedom in work" and "freedom from work" contrast), L. P. Jacks, and other social critics have strongly opposed. In justice to Smith, however, it should be noted that this particular statement is part of his indictment of the Mercantilist system, under which he feels consumer interests were sacrificed to producer interests. He was not dealing with the *process* of production.

40

No society can surely be flourishing and happy, of which the far greater part of the members are poor and miserable. (p. 79)

The problem of economic growth, to which we shall give some consideration in Essay 9, is an issue that is now commanding widespread attention throughout the world. In fact a new branch of economics covering this area of study has sprung up, and a great deal is being said and written about economic growth in the developed and underdeveloped areas of the world. Smith can contribute a number of *bon mots* to this new, and yet old, field of economic investigation. *The Wealth of Nations* as a whole represents a notable contribution to the subject. To the statement we have just quoted, Smith adds the further observation that in the interests of equity those who "feed, cloath and lodge" the nation should themselves be "tolerably well fed, cloathed and lodged."

41

The progressive state is in reality the cheerful and the hearty state to all the different orders of the society. The stationary is dull; the declining melancholy. (p. 81)

42

As a rich man is likely to be a better customer to the industrious people in his neighborhood, than a poor, so is likewise a rich nation. (p. 461)

Almost two decades before *The Wealth of Nations* was published, David Hume's essay, "Of the Jealousy of Trade," appeared.[10] In this short essay Smith's friend developed the general theme suggested by our quotation, and gave expression to an even more striking utterance. "I shall therefore venture to acknowledge," said Hume at the end of his discussion, "that, not only as a man, but as a British subject, I pray for the flourishing commerce of Germany, Spain, Italy, and even France itself." Just a year after the appearance of Hume's essay, Smith's *Theory of Moral Sentiments* was published, and in it (p. 203) there is a much more general statement of the theme of our quotation, with special reference to France and England. The same argument, with mention of the same two countries, was used by Josiah Tucker in his *Cui Bono?* —published in 1781.[11]

43

A nation that would enrich itself by foreign trade, is certainly moᵗt likely to do so when its neighbors are all rich, industrious, and commercial nations. (p. 462)

44

After all that has been said of the levity and inconstancy of human nature, it appears evidently from experience that a man is of all sorts of luggage the most difficult to be transported. (p. 75)

Smith's statement suggests one of the reasons why persons who are displaced as a result of technological innovations, or who are unemployed for other reasons, often have difficulty getting into new jobs: they are geographically (and frequently occupationally) immobile. With the invention of the locomotive, the steamboat, and the airplane we have made phenomenal progress since Smith's time in providing means for transportation. But because of home ties, and for other reasons, man is still a type of "luggage" that cannot easily be transported, transported to new jobs. Adequate labor mobility is a desirable feature in any economy. It is not necessary nor desirable, however, that all workers be mobile— that, in Francis A. Walker's words, they all be "organized like a Tartar tribe, packed and saddled ready for flight."[12]

45

The desire of food is limited in every man by the narrow capacity of the human stomach; but the desire of the conveniencies and ornaments of building, dress, equipage, and household furniture, seems to have no limit or certain boundary. (p. 164)

Until comparatively recently one of the outstanding economic issues in the United States, and in Canada as well, was the so-called "farm problem." It was a problem of surpluses. There were several reasons why such surpluses existed, one of which is strikingly suggested by Smith's remark. In the parlance of economics, the demand for food under ordinary conditions tends to be *inelastic,* with no large change in quantity wanted with given small changes in its price. Bread is a good example. In contrast to food there are "the conveniencies and ornaments of buildings," etc., of which Smith speaks. The demand for such things is more elastic.

Though compilers of dictionaries of quotations may neglect this statement of Smith's, the great economist's remark, or at least the truth it contains, was put to good use by the Agricultural Commission and the Economic Policy Commission of the American Banker's Association. In their pamphlet on *The Farm Problem,* published some years ago, the ABA commissions, without mentioning Smith by name, refer to "the limited stretch in the human stomach." Moreover, they include a factual detail of which the Scottish economist was probably ignorant. "Food is destined for a container," they state, "which has an average capacity of 40 fluid ounces—the human stomach."

The interrelationship between the size of this container and the old American farm problem was much more involved, however, than one might gather from Smith's remark.[13]

In his *Theory of Moral Sentiments* Smith makes a number of "stomach" references, one of which has an affinity with the first part of our quotation. In the paragraph that includes his invisible-hand statement (pp. 162-163), he says, with reference to the landlord, that "The capacity of his stomach bears no proportion to the immensity of his desires, and will receive no more than that of the meanest peasant."

46

I have no great faith in political arithmetic. (p. 501)

The term "political arithmetic" owes its early popularity, if not its origin, to Sir William Petty. Petty's policy of making use of the statistical method was followed by other seventeenth- and eighteenth-century writers, such as Gregory King, Charles Davenant, and Arthur Young,[14] and even Adam Smith makes rather extensive use of statistics in his *Wealth of Nations*. With some justification one might give the term "political arithmetic" a new meaning, applying it to the statistics sometimes used by politicians and even national governments for nonscientific purposes. In such instances we may certainly resort to Smith's remark.

47

In ancient times the opulent and civilized found it difficult to defend themselves against the poor and barbarous nations. In modern times the poor and barbarous find it difficult to defend themselves against the opulent and civilized. (p. 669)

48

It is not because one man keeps a coach while his neighbor walks a-foot, that the one is rich and the other poor; but because the one is rich he keeps a coach, and because the other is poor he walks a-foot. (p. 76)

The difficulty of distinguishing cause and effect in the great number of instances in which the issue arises is, unfortunately, not always as easy as in Smith's example. He uses the example to illustrate the error that had frequently been made concerning the relationship between wage differences and differencs in subsistence standards between the people of England and Scotland. Today the relationship between wages and living standards is not always as "one-sided," as it was (or may have been) in eighteenth-century Britain.

Smith has another illustration (p. 343) in which the cause-and-effect relationship may not have been quite as simple as he assumes. This one has to do with "a general disposition to drunkenness among the common people" on the one hand, and "the multitude of ale-houses" on the other. Smith recognized, of course, that a given element or factor may be *both* cause and effect. Thus he tells us (p. 81), that the liberal reward of labor is "the necessary effect and cause of the greatest public prosperity." More specifically, it is the effect of increasing national wealth, and the cause of population growth (presumably with no decline in living standards). It should be added, finally, that cause-and-effect relationships may proceed in a vast, unfolding series; like Tennyson's brook, they may go on forever.

49

The pride of man makes him love to domineer, and nothing mortifies him so much as to be obliged to condescend to persuade his inferiors. (p. 365)

This statement is from some remarks Smith makes in *The Wealth of Nations* on slave labor. He was strongly opposed to such labor, arguing that it "is in the end the dearest of any." "A person who can acquire no property"—indeed, one might add, that the slave is property himself, a piece of animated property as Aristotle long ago pointed out—"can have no other interest but to eat as much, and to labour as little as possible." In words equally as harsh as some of those used in a similar connection by his celebrated contemporary and acquaintance, Samual Johnson, Smith, in speaking of the natives of Africa, declares in his *Theory of Moral Sentiments* (p. 183) that "Fortune never exerted more cruelly her empire over mankind, than when she subjected those nations of heroes to the refuse of the jails of Europe, to wretches who possess the virtues neither of the countries which they come from, nor of those which they go to, and whose levity, brutality, and baseness, expose them to the contempt of the vanquished."

50

In public, as well as in private expences, great wealth may, perhaps, frequently be admitted as an apology for great folly. (p. 489)

51

A shepherd has a great deal of leisure; a husbandman, in the rude state of husbandry, has some; an artificer or manufacturer has none at all. (p. 659)

A manufacturer used to be a person who made things *(facere)* by hand *(manus)*. That is the way Smith uses the term here. But what a change has taken place in word content. As Andrew Ure pointed out more than a century ago, "Manufacture is a word, which, in the vicissitude of language, has come to signify the reverse of its instrinsic meaning, for it now denotes every extensive product of art, which is made by machinery, with little or no aid of the human hand; so that the most perfect manufacture is that which dispenses entirely with manual labour."[15] Despite the use of the more accurate word "machinofacture" by Eden and Cedar Paul (in their translation of *Das Kapital*) and Eric Gill's employment of "machine-facture" (in his *Last Essays*), the inaccurate word "manufacture" still prevails. Unlike many of the human victims of technological progress, it refuses to be displaced. Today, however, in contrast to Smith's time, the "manufacturer" usually has a great deal of leisure.

52

Upstart greatness is everywhere less respected than ancient greatness. (p. 672)

53

A man educated at the expence of much labour and time to any of those employments which require extraordinary dexterity and skill, may be compared to one of those expensive machines. (p. 101)

Smith's use of the notion of "human capital," a notion that is given a great deal of attention in current discussions of economic development, is noticed in Essay 9.

54

No discipline is ever requisite to force attendance upon lectures which are really worth the attending. (p. 720)

55

Science is the great antidote to the poison of enthusiasm and superstition. (p. 748)

This statement is a popular one among the compilers of dictionaries of quotations. The word "enthusiasm" as it is used here has a different meaning than the one we ordinarily associate with it. In general sense it relates to religious fanaticism. A broader definition is "the reliance on emotional conviction as a basis of truth."[16] John Locke, reflecting on the history of his country, saw two especially outstanding causes of human error: indiscriminate following of tradition and enthusiasm. Smith himself looked upon "faction and fanaticism" as the greatest corrupters of moral sentiments (TMS, p. 136).

56

The over-weening conceit which the greater part of men have of their own abilities, is an ancient evil remarked by the philosophers and moralists of all ages. (p. 107)

57

Age is a plain and palpable quality which admits of no dispute.
(p. 671)

Other Sources

58

They whom we call politicians are not the most remarkable men
in the world for probity and punctuality. Ambassadors from different nations are less so.

The above statement is from Smith's *Lectures on Justice, Police,
Revenue and Arms,* Reported by a Student in 1763.[17] Though the
famous economist counted among his friends a number of outstanding political leaders (Edmund Burke and William Pitt the
Younger were the most notable), his opinion of the mill-run of
politicians was not high, as the above quotation and a number
of earlier ones in the present essay suggest. Concerning the
remark about ambassadors, one wonders whether Smith had
Sir Henry Wotton's choice remark in mind when he made his
statement: "An Ambassador is a man of virtue sent to lie abroad
for his country."

59

Little else is requisite to carry a State to the highest degree of
opulence from the lowest barbarism, but peace, easy taxes, and
a tolerable administration of justice.

This observation was contained in a paper Smith presented to
a group in 1755, a paper that Dugald Stewart tells us (p. 68)
was in his possession when he wrote his biographical sketch of
Smith, but which later disappeared. The remark will be discussed
in Essay 9, hence there is no need to comment on it here beyond
saying that, despite the substantial amount of truth it contains,

it does not meet the requirements of modern nations, particularly the so-called underdeveloped ones.

60

Be assured, my young friend, that there is a great deal of *ruin* in a nation.

This remark is not found in Smith's writings but is quoted by Sir John Sinclair.[18] Sinclair relates that he had been lamenting to "the Doctor" the misfortunes Britain had been experiencing in the American war. Rae (p. 343) says that Sinclair was apprising Smith of the surender of General Burgoyne at the battle of Saratoga. Sinclair exclaimed, "If we go on at this rate, the nation *must be ruined."* Smith did not seem unduly disturbed, and gave the reply we have quoted. James Bonar, putting his own words in Smith's mouth, speaks in one of his pleasant fantasies about "my Saratoga joke," which "I am told has been taken literally."[19] Whether Smith meant it literally or not may be debatable, but the truth of the statement in terms of modern nations at least seems patent. The experience of World War II and its aftermath, especially in Western Germany, would seem to bear out the truth of Smith's observation.

NOTES

1. *Adam Smith as Student and Professor,* pp. 114, 322-323.

2. *Adam Smith and the Scotland of His Day* (Cambridge at the University Press, 1956), p. 75.

3. *The Individual in Society,* p. 80. Macfie also declares (p. 78), however, that Smith's self-love theory "does not imply an unduly high estimate of man's moral quality."

4. Elie Halévy, *The Growth of Philosophical Radicalism* (New York: Macmillan, 1928), p. 89; W. Stark, *The History of Economics in its Relation to Social Development* (London: Kegan Paul, Trench, Trubner, 1944), p. 23; Eduard Heimann, *History of Economic Doctrines* (New York: Oxford University Press, 1945), pp. 64-65.

5. See *The Works of Jeremy Bentham,* ed. by John Bowring, 5 vols. (New York: Russell and Russell, reproduced, 1962), 2, p. 208.

6. Further observations on this point will be found in W. R. Scott, *Adam Smith, an Oration* (Glasgow: Jackson, 1938), p. 8.

7. *The Bee,* May 11, 1791, p. 3.

8. *The Cambridge Historical Journal,* 1925 (Vol. I, No. 3), p. 249.

9. Edgar S. Furniss, *The Position of the Laborer in a System of Nationalism* (Boston: Houghton Mifflin, 1920), Chap. VI.

10. The essay is included in David Hume, *Writings on Economics,* ed. by Eugene Rotwein (Madison: University of Wisconsin Press, 1955), pp. 78-82.

11. *Josiah Tucker,* A Selection from His Economic and Political Writings, with an Introduction by Robert L. Schuyler (New York: Columbia University Press, 1931), p. 32.

12. *The Wages Question* (New York: Holt, 1876), p. 180.

13. An extensive discussion of the question can be found in Joseph S. Davis's article "Adam Smith and the Human Stomach," in *The Quarterly Journal of Economics,* May 1954.

14. See Palgrave's *Dictionary of Political Economy,* articles on "Arithmetic, Political."

15. *The Philosophy of Manufactures* (London: Knight, 1835), p. 1.

16. The definition, and the accompanying observation about Locke, are from Maurice Cranston, *John Locke* (New York: Macmillan, 1957), p. 40. Further discussion of "enthusiasm" can be found in Kenneth MacLean, *John Locke and English Literature of the Eighteenth Century* (New Haven: Yale University Press, 1936) pp. 154-160; and Essay VII by J. E. V. Crofts in *Eighteenth Century Literature: An Oxford Miscellany* (Freeport, New York: Books For Libraries Press, Inc., Essay Index Reprint Service, 1966).

17. Ed. by Edwin Cannan (New York: Kelley & Millman, Reprint, 1956), p. 254.

18. *The Correspondence of Sir John Sinclair,* 2 vols. (London: Colburn and Bentley, 1831), I, pp. 390-391.

19. *The Tables Turned* (London: King, 1926), p. 31.

9.

The Wealth of Nations—Yesterday and Today

> It is not in truth a book for one country or one age,
> but for all countries and all ages.
> —J. R. McCulloch

In May 1767 Adam Smith returned to the home of his mother in Kirkcaldy after a sojourn of almost three years on the continent as tutor to the young Duke of Buccleuch, followed by a stay of six months in London. At Kirkcaldy he began a long period of intensive work—the latter part of it in London—on his *Wealth of Nations,* which was finally published in March 1776.

Smith's great treatise was a product of more than ten years of work, however. While he was at the University of Glasgow Smith probably envisaged, at least in many of its essential characteristics, such a book as he was later to produce. Indeed, he actually wrote parts of *The Wealth of Nations* during these years. This is evident from his *Lectures on Justice, Police, Revenue and Arms,* a book that embodies the rewritten notes taken by one of his students in the early 1760s, and from an early draft of his masterpiece which dates to the same time.[1] But the beginning of *The Wealth of Nations* goes back even beyond these years, probably by a decade and a half. Professor Cannan believed that the composition of the book was started by at least 1749.[2] This was before Smith's appointment, at the age of twenty-seven, to the faculty of the University of Glasgow, but during the time he was giving a series of public lectures in Edinburgh.

The Wealth of Nations was thus long in preparation. Apart from the fact that during the early years there were other matters that occupied the author's attention, particularly his teaching and administrative duties at the University of Glasgow and the writing of his *Theory of Moral Sentiments,* there were still other influences that slowed up the writing process.

First there was the scope of the undertaking Smith set before himself. During the eighteenth century there was much less intellectual specialization than there is today, and in writing his book Smith moved into many areas of human knowledge, including economics, politics, sociology, education, psychology, and history. In his famous treatise (p. 10) the author speaks of philosophers as men "whose trade it is not to do any thing, but to observe every thing." This description, in a less sweeping form, fits Smith himself. *The Wealth of Nations* gives every evidence that the author's observations were wide and his interests extensive. The task of writing such a comprehensive work was an immense one, and naturally (to use the author's favorite word) took a long time. One wonders about the techniques Smith employed in amassing his materials. He may not have used three-by-five, or four-by-six, cards, as many modern scholars do; but he must have employed some comparable method.

The burden Smith labored under in writing *The Wealth of Nations* was not increased "by the virtues of his immediate predecessors."[3] As a matter of fact, with one or two exceptions, including Sir James Steuart,[4] no writer had attempted to produce a book that came near Smith's treatise in its scope and learning. If Smith did not labor under the disadvantages imposed by the merits of earlier writers, he labored under the hardships accompanying the absence of examples to follow. This fact undoubtedly helped to account for the slowness with which he carried on his undertaking. In contrast to John Stuart Mill, who had helpful precedents to follow, Smith could not "dash off" his great book. This does not mean, of course, that he was not aided by earlier writers. He was helped by their wisdom, as in the case of Hume, and by their faults (as he saw them) in the case of the Mercantilists. In general it can be said that if Smith had had good examples to follow, his *Wealth of Nations* would not have been the epoch-making work that it turned out to be.

Smith was a slow, fastidious writer, as we noted in Essay 3. This characteristic was with him throughout his career, as we can gather from a remark he made, shortly before his death, to Dugald Stewart. He told Stewart that despite all his practice he wrote as slowly and with as much difficulty as he did originally. Much of *The Wealth of Nations* was dictated to an amanuensis. This practice may have speeded up the process of composition, making the date of publication less late than it otherwise would have been. But, from the nature of the treatise, one can easily see why progress was slow even with the services of an amanuensis.

After years of diligent effort Smith finally completed his vast undertaking, and the book was published in two quarto volumes by Strahan and Cadell of London on March 9, 1776. The belated appearance of *The Wealth of Nations*—its publication had been expected for quite some years previous to its actual appearance—was one of a number of events that made 1776 notable both in intellectual history and in economic and political affairs. In addition to Smith's book the year saw the publication of the first volume of Edward Gibbon's *The Decline and Fall of the Roman Empire,* and of Jeremy Bentham's *Fragment of Government.* And, it need hardly be added, it also witnessed the Declaration of Independence.

One of the first persons to express an opinion on Smith's book was the author's friend Edward Gibbon. In his letter of April 1, 1776, to Adam Ferguson, Gibbon wrote: "What an excellent work is that which our common friend, Mr. Adam Smith, has enriched the public!—an extensive science in a single book, and the most profound ideas expressed in the most perspicuous language." Near the end of the next year, in a letter to Smith himself, Gibbon referred to his fellow author as "a Philosopher who for his own glory and for the benefit of mankind had enlightened the world by the most profound and systematic treatise on the great objects of trade and revenue which had ever been published in any age or in any country."[5]

Over the years high tributes continued to be paid to *The Wealth of Nations*. There were numerous criticisms of specific parts of the book, to be sure, and even the author himself was subject to some censure and even abuse. But the overall verdict among those best qualified to judge was most favorable. It was generally recognized, and it is still generally recognized, that in writing his treatise Smith made an outsanding contribution to scholarship, to the development of human thought. While this contribution was particularly great in the realm of economics, it also found expression in such fields of knowledge as political science, history, sociology, and education. Looking at Smith's book in historical perspective, one can still regard it as the greatest work in general economics that has ever been produced.

In addition to having an immense influence on the development of human knowledge, *The Wealth of Nations* had a great influence, especially during the nineteenth century, on the course of human affairs. This has been due to the fact that the treatise relates not only to theory but to policy, not only to description and analysis but to prescription as well.

More than a century after Gibbon made his remarks about Smith's work, James Bonar neatly summed up the author's achievement when he said that the book "has probably secured its author as near an approach to immortality as can fall to any economic writer."[6]

What characteristics does *The Wealth of Nations* possess that have made it a classic, a book for the ages? A number of features readily suggest themselves. First, there is the scope of the work. Smith was not an economic specialist who devoted his major efforts to one part of the field of economic inquiry. He was a general practitioner, and in a very meaningful sense of that term. Not only did he carefully examine the body politic, but on the basis of his examination he told how to cure its ills. But Smith, after the fashion of Bacon (who made all knowledge his province), ventured into other areas of human knowledge in addition to political economy. As a consequence *The Wealth of Nations* is a vast panorama of human society in many of its most important aspects. Indeed, because of the immense amount of historical material it contains, the book may be compared to a moving picture of society.

It was Thomas De Quincey's view that in the matter of "total architecture" no book on political economy could approach Smith's in "philosophic beauty."[7] In order to construct a verbal edifice of such large architectural proportions and beauty, Smith obviously had to be a very learned man. And this he was, as were such other contemporaries of his as Edmund Burke, Samuel Johnson, and Thomas Gray. Nassau Senior, an economist of considerable intellectual virtuosity himself, thought that in the scope and accuracy of his knowledge Smith was perhaps unequaled since Aristotle.[8]

Many parts or features of *The Wealth of Nations* have contributed to its great reputation among economists. Two in particular deserve attention at this point. First there is the author's extensive, but scattered, treatment of the subject of economic growth. Particularly noteworthy in this connection is his famous chapter on capital accumulation, with its provocative subtitle, "Of Productive and Unproductive Labour." Some scholars— Malthus many years ago, and J. R. Hicks more recently—have looked upon this chapter as the very core of the book. The subject of economic growth, which was rediscovered after World War II and which has since occupied a predominant place in economics, was of great concern to Smith. This is obvious from the title of his treatise. As we shall see shortly, Smith dealt with the subject in a very comprehensive fashion. Even though the production of literature in this branch of economics in recent years has been overpowering, Smith's analysis, despite its nonmathematical and nongraphical nature, is still highly regarded, at least by some observers. One authority on the subject has gone so far as to say that "It is significant that no single work on development has yet appeared that is markedly superior in its insights to Adam Smith's *Wealth of Nations*."[9]

The second notable feature of Smith's book is the picture it presents of how a highly competitive economy functions, or tends to function; how it performs the very complex task of ordering and carrying out the diverse activities of the economy. Though Smith, somewhat like Monsieur Jourdain, was not aware of the verbal fact, he created what we now refer to as a "model." In our discussion of "The Invisible Hand" in our next essay, we shall discuss this model and various related matters at length. Here all we can do it to point to the general nature of his achievement. Smith was a system builder, a model constructor. This of itself is sufficient basis for recognition. But when one is a pioneer in the field, the degree of recognition must of necessity be exceptionally high.

Smith's model was of a market economy, an economy in which the unfettered forces of supply and demand regulate, systematize, and coordinate the varied economic activities carried on. Smith's portrayal of how all this is done has been hailed as a notable accomplishment. Commenting on the insight of the classical economists in general in their dealing with the division of labor and the spontaneously operating market, involving the adjustment of production to pecuniary demands, Professor Lionel Robbins remarks that "the working out of this theory is pre-eminently the achievement of Adam Smith."[10]

In recent decades a considerable number of market economies have been replaced by other economic systems, as in Soviet Russia; and where market economies are still operative they have undergone varying dgrees of modification. Despite all these changes, however, Smith's model is still of interest and significance.

As was implied a few paragraphs back, Smith was more than a model builder. To him economics was not only a science (a "positive" science) but an art (a "normative" science); it had to do not only with "what is" but with "what ought to be." And not with what ought to be as a matter of contemplation, but with the best means for actually achieving what ought to be. In other words, Smith was policy-minded, even if the policy was often none other than that of no-policy.

There is a nice question as to how far, if at all, economics as a science and economics as an art, can safely coexist. Regardless of the verdict eached in abstract discussions of the issue, most economists, in their total economic interests, *make* them coexist. They do what Adam Smith did in *The Wealth of Nations*. The interest that Smith had in the policy aspect of economics should not be overemphasized, however. While it is fair enough to view his book as a manifesto as well as a treatise, it is extreme to describe it "principally as a polemic."[11]

Another feature that contributed to the influence of Smith's classic was its timeliness, both as a work of economic analysis and as a manifesto calling for action, action of both a negative and a positive type. More than twenty years before Smith's great treatise was published, Joshia Tucker had thought of writing a comprehensive work on political economy, but he did not complete his project.[12] Sir James Steuart had written a large, monumental book, but the Mercantilist spirit that it partly expresses did not represent the spirit of the emerging age. (Interestingly enough, Steuart's works is more in keeping with the spirit of the present age, with its more favorable attitude toward governmental intervention.) In the second half of the eighteenth century there was special need for a comprehensive treatment of economics, a treatment that would bring together ideas and material from widely scattered sources and mold them, along with new insights, into a more or less unified whole. This is what Smith did in *The Wealth of Nations.*

Smith's policy recommendations were also very timely. After years of Mercantilist interventionism (some of which, it is now recognized, was definitely beneficial to society) there was a widespread yearning for greater economic freedom. Just as new times demand new measures and new men, so they call for new books. And Smith's great work answered the call. As Thomas S. Ashton has declared, *"The Wealth of Nations* gave matchless expression to the thoughts that had been raised in men's minds by the march of events."[13]

One further factor contributing to the great acclaim accorded to *The Wealth of Nations* may be noted. This is the style in which the book is written. As we observed in Essay 3, high compliments have been paid to Smith on this score. With a few exceptions—including those instances in which the author, in trying to be perspicuous, becomes monotonous—Smith's treatise is well written. Today, in contrast to the more slowly moving past, the book sometimes calls for a certain amount of patience and concentration on the part of the reader. However, it was one of Smith's achievements that he did not blur or conceal the intellectual merits of his masterpiece by an awkward style.

So outstanding was Adam Smith's contribution to the development of economics (or political economy, to use the older term) that he has frequently been referred to as "The Father of Political Economy." It is true that other persons have been suggested as worthy claimants for this honor. Karl Marx thought Sir William Petty (whose great grandson, interestingly enough, the Hon. Thomas Fitzmaurice, was a student of Smith's) should have been chosen.[14] Some scholars would point to the very high credentials of François Quesnay, the famous Physiocrat (and, had he lived, the man to whom Smith had intended dedicating his book). Still other persons might be suggested, if not as top claimants to the title, as least as writers deserving of honorable mention. Cantillon, Boisguillebert, and Sir James Steuart have been mentioned as worthy of consideration. But Smith's right to the title of "Father of Political Economy" has been so widely recognized, and for so long, that there appears to be little danger of his ever losing it.

The title has been frequently modified, however. "The Father of Modern Political Economy," "The Father of Economics," "The Father of Modern Economics," "The Founder of Systematic Political Economy," "The Founder of Modern Economics," "The Father of Bourgeois Economics"—these are other titles that have been applied to Smith. A number of other descriptive labels have also been attached to him, including "the Great Founder," "the Master Builder," "the doyen of political economists," "the patron saint of economics."

Smith's great achievement has sometimes been linked up with those of other famous figures of the past. Thorold Rogers referred to the Scottish scholar, with his extensive use of facts, as "the practical Bacon of Economical science";[15] and J. R. McCulloch, another editor of Smith's classic, declared that *The Wealth of Nations* did for political economy what Hugo Grotius's *Treatise on the Law of War and Peace* did for public law. McCulloch also refers to an observation made by Sir James Macintosh that the works "which have most directly influenced the general opinion of Europe during the two last centuries" were Grotius's treatise, Locke's *Essay on the Human Understanding,* Montesquieu's *Spirit of Laws,* and Smith's *Wealth of Nations.*[16]

If Smith's book had an immense effect on the development of economic thought, it also had a profound influence on the practical affairs of Great Britain and of the world in general, especially during the last century. The author's doctrine of economic freedom, his espousal of a market type of economy in which governmental intervention would be limited and individual initiative given wide scope, his extensive and excellent discussion of the factors that promote economic growth—these and other parts of his analysis undoubtedly had a great effect on the economic policies of Britain and other countries. These effects were both direct and indirect, the latter being transmitted through the works of other writers who had been influenced by Smith.

It is impossible to say with any degree of precision, however, how extensive the effects of *The Wealth of Nations* has been. Perhaps as time goes on the "new economic history," with its stress on quantification, will be able to throw more revealing light on this highly complex question. In the meantime one will have to rely on conjecture, on general opinions that have been expressed on the matter. And such opinions have not been lacking.

Possibly no tribute to Smith's book and the influence it exerted was loftier in tone than the one uttered by Henry Thomas Buckle. In terms of its "ultimate results," Buckle stated that *The Wealth of Nations* was "probably the most important book that has ever been written." It was his opinion that "this solitary Scotchman" had, "by the publication of one single work, contributed more towards the happiness of man, than has been effected by the united abilities of all the statesmen and legislators of whom history has preserved an authentic account."[17]

Other writers have also made far-reaching claims concerning the anticipated or actual influence of Smith's classic on human affairs. In 1796 a German professor, C. J. Kraus, declared that "no book since the New Testament was likely to produce more beneficial results than *The Wealth of Nations.*"[18] Writing in the 1880s, and looking back on the preceding decades, Stanley Jevons remarked that the wealth and prosperity of the United Kingdom was due, "in as great a degree as to any other circumstance," to Smith's book.[19] Arnold Toynbee, the young economist and social reformer, expressed the view that the two persons who were most responsible for the Industrial Revolution were Adam Smith and James Watt.[20] An indirect tribute to the Scottish economist's influence was paid by J. B. Bury when he stated, in reference to the Roman Empire, that "If an Adam Smith had arisen, the Empire might have been rescued from decline."[21]

In addition to the general tributes that have been paid to *The Wealth of Nations* as a whole, there have been numerous words of praise for specific parts of the book. Two of the most important of these parts have already been noted: Smith's description and support of a market economy, and his treatment of economic growth. Both of these matters deserve further discussion. In the next essay we shall consider at length the first one, and in the next few pages of the present essay we shall deal, in briefer compass, with the second. In the present essay too we shall give attention to other notable parts and features of our author's great work.

Though Smith's discussion of the various factors that have a bearing on economic growth is widely scattered in his book, attempts have been made in recent years to set forth his "theory" of growth—along with that of other classical economists—in algebraic and graphical form. Benjamin H. Higgins, for example, constructs the classical growth model as follows: $O = f(L,K,Q,T)$. In this equation O, the total output, is a function of the size of the labor force, the volume of capital, the extent of the "land," and the level of technique.[22] Presentations of this sort have the great merit of simplicity and precision, but in the present discussion we shall use a more general approach, dealing with a number of the influences covered in the above equation but also considering some highly important influences that the equation assumes as "given."

In 1755, more than twenty years before *The Wealth of Nations* was published, Smith made an interesting pronouncement on the question of economic growth. "Little else is requisite," he declared, "to carry a State to the highest degree of opulence from the lowest barbarism, but peace, easy taxes, and a tolerable administration of justice; all the rest being brought about by the natural course of things." This early observation of Smith's, recorded by Dugald Stewart (p. 68), understates the author's more mature views on the relationship between governmental action and economic growth. As we shall see in the next essay, Smith was willing to grant a considerable range of functions to the government, especially if the processes of government were carried on efficiently and freely.

There was as least one function of government of which our author approved that has a direct bearing on economic growth and which deserves mention at this point. This was the task of "erecting and maintaining certain public works and certain public institutions" (WN, pp. 651, 681ff), projects which no individual or group of individuals would find it profitable to undertake. Among these projects was the construction and maintenance of good roads, bridges, canals, and harbors. Earlier in his treatise (p. 147), Smith mentions good roads, canals, and navigable rivers as "the greatest of all improvements," since they link more closely together country and town.

After making due allowance for the governmental interference that Smith would allow, the fact remains that for the most part our author felt that economic growth would be best promoted by a policy of governmental hands-off. Growth would be most rapid if, in general, it were left to "the natural course of things," which, in Smith's mind, included the pursuit of self-interest and the presence of a freely competitive type of economy.

Today opinion varies a great deal on the specific extent to which government should be engaged in the process of economic development, extending from advocacy of overall planning on the one hand to support of an essentially free market-economy on the other. But even those who support the latter arrangement would agree that on the matter of economic growth there is a stronger case for governmental interference today than there was two hundred years ago. They would even be willing to depart, especially on certain occasions, from Smith's principle of "easy taxes."

Algebraic equations of Smith's growth model do not include "a tolerable administration of justice," a matter to which the author attached great significance. "Commerce and manufactures," he declares in *The Wealth of Nations* (p. 862), "can seldom flourish long in any state which does not enjoy a regular administration of justice"—where property is not secure, contracts not legally enforeceable, and the payment of debts (on the part of those able to pay them) not compulsory.[23] Today the close relationship between the administration of justice and economic growth is widely granted. However, there are wide differences of opinion from country to country as to what "justice" really means, and in any given country the principles of justice, regardless of how the term is defined, are often neglected.

The relationship between peace and economic development, a relationship that Smith felt was very close, is a complex one. As a general proposition it can be said, however, that peace—continuing peace—is a strong and necessary foundation for such development. No country can experience rapid economic growth if it is constantly engaged in wars. But peace itself does not guarantee growth, of course. More dynamic influences must be present.

Among these dynamic influences, Smith attached immense importance to the division of labor. "The greatest improvement in the productive powers of labour," he says in *The Wealth of*

Nations (p. 3), "and the greater part of the skill, dexterity, and judgement with which it is any where directed, or applied, seem to have been the effects of the division of labour." In his book our author gives considerable attention to what later came to be called the "territorial" division of labor. His advocacy of free trade necessarily involved this kind of specialization. Such specialization obviously is conducive to economic growth. But Smith's notable treatment of the division of labor, found largely in the first three chapters of his treatise, relates to "trade" specialization. The author uses this term in the sense that we employ it today, but he also applies it to specific tasks within trades. Thus the developed process (trade) of pin-making "is divided into a number of branches, of which the greater part are likewise peculiar trades" (p. 4). It is this latter type of specialization, which is so highly conducive to increased labor productivity, that Smith emphasizes. And interestingly enough, he finds it operative not only in industry but in philosophy as well. The latter is "subdivided into a great number of different branches, each of which affords occupation to a peculiar tribe or class of philosophers" (p. 10). But the employment to which, for illustrative purposes, he directs his major attention is pin-making, with its distinct operations, "about eighteen" in number. He also refers to the process of nail-making, a process that in its totality is sometimes specialized but which does not involve a subdivision of operations. In the college textbooks, which almost invariably refer to Smith's celebrated discussion of the division of labor, it is pin-making, not nail-making, that is mentioned.

There is little that is original in our author's discussion. It has been found that most of what he said had been said before. Even his famous pin illustration came to him secondhand. But his systematic and fascinating handling of the theme, and the importance he attached to it, have attracted wide attention and have made this part of his classic particularly well-known.

In his discussion of the division of labor, Smith takes up three specific "circumstances" why this technique of production increases productivity; next he deals with the "principle" that gives rise to the division of labor; and finally he tells why the division of labor is limited by the extent of the market. All three of these main aspects of his handling of the subject have been either amplified or criticized. These amplifications and criticisms cannot all be noted here, but there is one that is especially significant and which deserves some attention. This is the addition made to the discussion by Allyn A. Young in a famous article published in 1928.

Professor Young thought that Smith's "theorem" relating to the size of the market was "one of the most illuminating and fruitful generalizations which can be found anywhere in the whole literature of economics." He grants Smith's contention, but declares that, in reverse fashion, "the extent of the market also depends upon the division of labour." Young attached great significance to this fact: herein "lies the possibility of economic progress, apart from the progress which comes as a result of the new knowledge which men are able to gain."[24] The possibility involved the economic phenomenon of "increasing returns."

At a time when the social costs of economic progress are becoming increasingly matters of public concern, it is not surprising that Smith's remarks concerning the adverse effects of the division of labor should now be coming into prominence. These remarks, which we noted in Essay 8, bear a close resemblance to those subsequently made on the subject by Karl Marx and John Ruskin. More recently they have been included in discussions involving "alienation"—to use the current popular term. Perhaps Smith exaggerated the evil consequences of the minute division of labor, though it appears to be far-fetched to say that in historical perspective this part of his discussion "is largely golden-age romancing."[25] In any circumstances, the statements Smith makes about the division of labor in the latter part of his book should not be forgotten when one reads the treatment of the subject in the early chapters. Whether or not these two sets of statements represents a clash or inconsistency in the author's thinking about the division of labor is a matter that has recently been debated.[26] In general, Smith's remarks about the adverse consequences of the division of labor clearly indicate that he was well aware of the fact that influences that bring beneficial results, such as a higher GNP, can also bring results that are definitely harmful.

In recent discussions of economic development, increasing attention has been given to the quality of the labor force. Smith did not enter upon any detailed discussion of this highly important growth factor, but he nevertheless made a number of acute observations on the issue. In *The Wealth of Nations* (p. 265) he refers to the capital that is invested in the individual human being—"a capital fixed and realized, as it were, in his person." This very suggestive idea was not original with Smith, however; it goes back at least as far as Sir William Petty.[27] Carrying his figurative language still further our author states (p. 266) that "The improved dexterity of a workman," consequent upon the use of funds for training purposes, "may be considered in the same light as a machine or instrument of trade which facilitates and abridges labour, and which, though it costs a certain expence, repays that expence with a profit." As a factor in economic development this so-called human capital is so highly regarded today that one commentator, Daniel Bell, has declared that the fundamental influence restricting the growth of society is not financial capital limitations but human capital limitations.[28] Adam Smith did not go that far in his argument. Indeed, Smith, and the classical economists in general, did not develop in any detail the notion that education could be used intentionally as an instrument for economic growth.[29] Our author wrote long before the development of "the economics of educational planning."

Capital accumulation occupies a highly important place in Adam Smith's theory of economic growth, an importance that has been borne out both in "theory and practice" since his time. There cannot be much of an increase in the number of productive workers, he declares (p. 326), unless there is an increase in capital. Nor can there be much of an increase in the productivity of the present workers "but in consequence either of some addition and improvement to those machines and instruments which facilitate and abridge labour; or of a more proper division and distribution of employment." Smith is here referring to both "circulating" or "working" capital and to "fixed" capital, though in his treatise, and especially in his growth-model, he stresses the former.[30]

Much of what our author has to say about capital accumulation is contained in Chapter III of Book II of *The Wealth of Nations*. This chapter is entitled "Of the Accumulation of Capital, or of Productive and Unproductive Labour," and it is one of the most remarkable chapters in the whole book. It is remarkable for its striking pronouncement of the self-interest doctrine, and for its excellent epigrammatical statements. But above all, it is remarkable for the distinction the author makes between "productive" and "unproductive" labor. This distinction, with its accompanying examples or illustrations, can be superficially discussed with considerable amusement. But in actuality the distinction, along with its paean to the virtue of frugality, is of the greatest importance in Smith's discussion of the nature and cause of the wealth of nations. Malthus thought the distinction was "the corner stone of Adam Smith's work, and the foundation on which the main body of his reasonings rests."[31] In somewhat similar fashion, J. R. Hicks has expressed the feeling that there can be little doubt that Smith himself looked upon Chapter III of Book II as "the centre-piece of his whole work."[32]

The long debates over the productive-labor and unproductive-labor concepts cannot be discussed here. But the central point Smith had in mind, namely the accumulation of capital, must be further considered. Though capital is still looked upon as a key factor in economic development, some new notions concerning the process of capital growth—and which involve departures from Smith's analysis—have arisen.

Smith looked upon individual thrift as the means for accumulating capital. To him "parsimony, and not industry, is the immediate cause of the increase of capital" (p. 321); and he declares (p. 324) that "every prodigal appears to be a public enemy, and every frugal man a public benefactor." It is now recognized—and the point is emphasized by modern "Keynesians"—that when there is a condition of less than full employment there may be too much saving, with a definite possibility of a worsening of economic conditions as a consequence. Under such circumstances the frugal man instead of being a public benefactor may be a public enemy; unless, of course, the government steps in and increases the amount of spending.

The solution to what appears to be an error on Smith's part rests on the assumption he makes concerning expenditures. He argues that what is saved is always spent, for investment or non-investment purposes; spent with little delay though by "a different set of people" (p. 321). Whatever validity this assumption had in Smith's day, it cannot be granted today. There are times when savings are not put to use, and we can then have a type of disharmony of interests that our author does not mention.

Smith's assumption concerning the inseparable relationship between savings and investment ruled out any recognition of a possibility of general deficiencies in "effective demand." The notion that such deficiencies might exist had been clearly recognized by other writers of the period, and a variety of suggestions, including the support of luxury spending and a volatile money supply, had been offered for coping with such a situation. But Smith's optimistic theory prevailed.[33] And it continued to prevail, despite scattered voices to the contrary, until the 1930s. Then, under the influence of a number of writers, particularly J. M. Keynes, the notion that in free societies the economy tends to operate at a full-employment equilibrium was discarded by most economists.

Speaking of the Classical economists in general, with their emphasis on saving, Karl Marx exclaimed "Accumulate! Accumulate! That is Moses and all the prophets!"[34] The emphasis that Smith and his successors placed on accumulation was indeed great, and on the whole justifiably so. To promote economic growth, however, the accumulated savings must be invested, and it is here that difficulties arise. It was Keynes's contention that there has always been a tendency for "the propensity to save" to be more powerful than "the propensity to invest," a condition which, according to Keynes, has always been "the key to the economic problem." In the past few decades, in contrast to Smithian times, a great deals of attention has been given to this "key." The great weakness of Smith's approach, and of the Classical approach in general, a weakness well recognized by Malthus, was the assumption of a balance between savings and investment.

Today the process of saving is more complex than it was in Smith's day. As we have noted, our author looked upon individual thrift as the essence of the process. Such thrift involves a voluntary abstention from consumption. Today a great deal of saving is only semivoluntary. Or, to state the matter differently, it is semiforced. This is the case with the portion of the net earnings that corporations retain for internal financing. Some of the saving that is used for capital purposes is completely forced. This is true of a portion of our taxes. It is also true of the savings accumulated by price increases, including those imposed by monopolistic business firms. Higher taxes and higher prices are effective means for forcing people to abstain from consumption (if their money incomes do not increase proportionately), thus making larger sums (more resources) available for investment purposes. There is the situation previously referred to, however, in which savings may outrun investments, with a resulting contraction of economic activity. Under such circumstances consumer spending may stimulate the economy, resulting in greater production, and the possibility of an actual increase in savings. This is a condition under which less aggregate saving (and more spending) results ultimately in greater aggregate saving. Needless to say this happy, general situation may not be experienced by every individual in the economy.

In his discussion of accumulation, Adam Smith was referring to saving in market economies. In the highly planned economics of today, accumulation is given immense stress, and the rate of savings is ordinarily greater than in the nonplanned economies. Little reliance is placed on individual thrift, however, as a means of capital accumulation. Most saving is forced, and effective means are close at hand to carry out the process. In Soviet Russia, for example, much of the monetary purchasing power in the hands of the people is taken away from them through taxation, particularly by the turnover tax. But a second and much more effective and significant way of forcing people to abstain from consumption (which is the key feature of saving) is by directly limiting the producton of consumer goods in the first place. Under authoritative planning this is a simple process, though it is not without some limitations. Adam Smith, with all the importance he attached to accumulation, did not advocate such a method. Obviously, he could not have done this and at the same time support a free market economy.

Smith's discussion of economic development, some parts of which we have just examined, is of outstanding importance. But, it may be asked, was he more interested in the general question of growth than he was in the problem of effective resource use? Professor Hla Myint gives an affirmative answer to this question; he argues that the "growth" interpretation of *The Wealth of Nations* (and of Classical economics in general) is more meaningful and correct than the "allocation" interpretation.[35] This view seems well founded. It should be pointed out, however, that Smith attached great signifiance to resource allocation, and numerous references can be found in his treatise relating to the matter. But he did not use the word "allocation," and what is of greater moment he provided no exact formula or detailed explanation of the concept of "ideal" or "optimal" allocation.

Had Smith (much ahead of his time) become intellectually involved in the logical and mathematical niceties of optimal allocation, it is possible that his discussion of economic development would have suffered. There is a conflict between "allocation" and "growth," not only as objects of national policy but as matters of intellectual concern.[36] At least this is the case if the problems of allocation receive exclusive or predominant attention. This does not mean, however, than an economist cannot be interested, in a balanced fashion, in *both* the static problem of resource allocation and the dynamic problem of economic growth. Adam Smith had this dual interest.

Among other important features of *The Wealth of Nations* is the large amount of historical material contained in the book, a characteristic that has been alluded to in Essay 3. Some of

Smith's contributions to history have been very highly praised. To George Unwin, Book III of the treatise, entitled "Of the different Progress of Opulence in different Nations," seemed "the best piece of economic history that has yet been written," a sentiment that comes close to being shared by W. H. B. Court, a contemporary economic historian.[37] On a more restricted plane, another present-day historian declares that our author's book "is still perhaps the major text for anyone interested in the industrial revolution in Scotland."[38]

In his role as historian and interpreter of history, Smith has not entirely escaped criticism. In a gentle manner, Stewart (pp. 83, 84) wondered whether our author, in his two books, "allowed his partiality to the Ancients to blind him a little too much to the merits of his contemporaries." In a much sharper observation, Charles Wilson, a strong critic of Smith's treatment of the Mercantilists, remarks that "It is enough to say that, like so many economic writers of the eighteenth century, Adam Smith was little bothered by any real sense of historical change."[39]

Despite such criticism—and in both instances cited there are grounds for the criticism—*The Wealth of Nations* remains an important historical work. In his book Smith goes far beyond political and economic history, however. He enters into such adjacent and, in varying degrees, related areas as military history, social history, educational history, and even religious history as well. Walter Bagehot's remark that Smith's treatise is "a very amusing book about old times," is exaggerated of course; particularly the first part of the remark. But there is indeed a great deal in *The Wealth of Nations* about old times.

Some of the material in Smith's book relates to *very* old times. In his analysis the author quite often refers to "that early and rude state of society" (preceding "the accumulation of stock and the appropriation of land"), "that rude state of society," "that original state of things." His information for such distant periods is sparse if not nonexistent, and as a consequence he is forced to resort to a type of approach that Dugald Stewart described as *Theoretical or Conjectural history.*[40] This "species of philosophical investigation," as Stewart called it, was based on "the known principles of human nature" and it was rather extensively used at the time.

The Wealth of Nations contains a vast quantity of historical facts. Smith was not interested in presenting antiquarian tidbits, however. He used facts for specific purposes. In his use of facts he made a contribution both to history itself and to the methodology of history. In these accomplishments, however, Smith was not alone. He was one of a group of Scottish scholars who in the latter half of the eighteenth century undertook to write history in an empirical, philosophical, and systematic manner.[41] That these objectives were not always achieved is evident from what has already been said.

Closely related to his extensive treatment of history, indeed to some extent an important part of it, is Smith's discussion of colonies—colonies in general and those of Great Britain in particular. *The Wealth of Nations,* it will be recalled, was published in the same year in which the Declaration of Independence was signed, a coincidence that suggests the great timeliness of Smith's enlightened and provocative discussion. Lecky, the historian, felt that no section of Smith's book was more remarkable than that in which the author deals with colonies; and to a more recent historian, Smith's chapter on colonies is "a landmark in the history of the British Empire."[42] Looking at our author's analysis from another point of view, a contemporary writer declares that "Nothing, perhaps, so well illustrates the qualities of Smith's mind as the chapter on colonies." The same wrtier goes on to indicate these qualities.[43]

In Essay 6 we discussed at length that part of *The Wealth of Nations* that relates to education. There is no need to repeat here what was observed in that essay, except to say that while some of Smith's ideas on education are out of date, there are others that have a particular relevance to contemporary society and to the difficult and even embattled condition in which it finds itself.

While tributes have long been paid to *The Wealth of Nations,* criticisms of the great treatise have by no means been lacking. And these too date back to the time when Smith's classic was first published. Some of the criticisms of the book and its author have been very general in nature. In Essay 4 we noted the observation Sir John Pringle made concerning Smith's lack of qualifications for writing such a treatise. Much later John Ruskin, in a truly outstanding example of misinterpretation, a misinterpretation we shall examine in the next essay, contended that the Scottish scholar taught the virtue of selfishness—he taught "the deliberate blasphemy" that "Thou shalt hate the Lord thy God, damn His laws, and covet thy neighbor's goods." Some of the criticism of *The Wealth of Nations* centers around the political philosophy that is not only described but advocated in the book, the philosophy of free enterprise. Socialistic critics have found Smith highly vulnerable on this point, though paradoxical as it may seem, and as we shall discuss in the following essay, *The Wealth of Nations* has been regarded as a positive source of support for socialism.

In addition to the more or less general criticisms that have been made of Smith's book, there have been many criticisms of specific parts or features of the treatise. Some of these may be noted.

A puzzling feature of *The Wealth of Nations* is the author's neglect of the technological developments that were occurring during the time he was writing his masterpiece, and also during the years of its periodic revisions. Smith was undoubtedly aware of these developments, yet he failed to give them the attention they deserved, a fact that was early pointed out by the Earl of Lauderdale in his *Inquiry into the Nature and Origin of Public Wealth*. A number of reasons might be given for this neglect, including Smith's preoccupation with "circulating" capital rather than with "fixed" capital and his rather restricted view of the work of the intrepreneur. It is quite possible, as R. Koebner has asserted, that Smith did not look upon a discussion of current technological developments as being essential to his argument.[44]

Having given inadequate attention to the technological innovations of his day, it is not surprising that Smith should say little about the employment impact of mechanization—about "technological unemployment," to use a more recent term.[45] To be sure, one can find numerous uses of the term "abridge labour" in *The Wealth of Nations,* but Smith does not delve into the problem posed by the replacement of men by machines. Arthur Young, Josiah Tucker, and Sir James Steuart were well aware of the problem, and said something about it. And interestingly enough, Smith had *Political Arithmetic, Instructions for Travellers,* and *Principles of Political Economy* in his personal library. The fact that the author generally assumed "fixed coefficients of production," "the absence of substitution relationships,"[46] does not absolve him completely from this particular sin of omission.

Some criticism has been directed at Smith for his failure to develop adequately the functions of the entrepreneur, a task that was well done some decades later by J. B. Say, who introduced the term into economics. In his remarks about this highly important functionary, Smith uses other expressions. On occasion he speaks of the "projector," and of the "undertaker." But his favorite term appears to be the very suggestive word "adventurer." There has been some feeling, however, that the great economist's adventurer was not venturesome enough. "Smith's undertaker," it has been said, "strikes one as a prudent, cautious, not overly imaginative fellow, who adjusts to circumstances rather than bring about their modification."[47]

It would seem that Smith's entrepreneur was overly concerned with economic security. In his discussion, in *The Theory of Moral Sentiments,* of prudence and "the prudent man," a personage possessing attributes that one can easily associate with entrepreneurs, our author declares (p. 188) that security is "the first and principal object of prudence." Security, he tells us, "is rather cautious than enterprising, and more anxious to preserve the advantages which we already possess, than forward to prompt us to the acquisition of still greater advantages." The prudent man plays it safe, as we would say today, and in so doing he may fail to take chances that would greatly contribute to his own and society's gain.

It has been argued that Smith did not give due attention to

the intermediate organizations between the individual citizen and the government, namely the business coporation and the labor union.[48] Both of these organizational types are dealt with in *The Wealth of Nations* but not in any comprehensive fashion. As for labor unions, Smith was perhaps in a quandary. He had great sympathy for the workers, as is evident from some of his statements about "masters and men," but the actual or potential power of unions to interfere with the free functioning of the labor market undoubtedly disturbed him. At any rate he could have said more about labor organizations. As for corporate enterprise and its future place in the economy, his view was very limited.

For a business to operate successfully as a joint stock company, and without the possession of an exclusive privilege from the government, three conditions, according to Smith, were necessary. Especially essential is the requirement of routine operations in the business. But the business should also be of high social utility, and its capital requirements should be of such a magnitude as cannot easily be amassed by "a private copartnery" (pp. 713, 714). The author felt that there were only four types of businesses that lent themselves to the corporate form of organization: banking, fire insurance and insurance for "sea risk and capture in time of war," the construction and maintenance of "a navigable cut or canal," and the trade of "bringing water for the supply of a great city." In light of the vast expansion in the uset of the joint-stock-principle, Smith was indeed a poor prophet.

A considerable number of writers have pointed to Smith's failure to appreciate the dynamic effect money has in an economy experiencing less than full employment.[49] For one who presupposes that there is a constant tendency in the economy toward a full-employment equilibrium, such an oversight does not seem altogether unnatural. Under any circumstances, the more up-to-date analysis of Smith's friend, David Hume, is sometimes mentioned, as is the more enlightened attitude of the Mercantilists concerning money.

Smith's belief that budgets should be balanced annually seems quaint today.[50] With the development of "The New Economics" back in the 1930s such a policy came to be widely looked upon as economic sacrilege. Our author's contention, however, about the effect of governmental borrowing in redirecting funds from useful industrial and commercial venture is not without merit. It at least points to a danger that must be carefully considered, especially in attempts to rearrange our "national priorities." One might even find some plausibility in Smith's contention that if nations followed a pay-as-you-go policy (as we would say today) "wars would in general be more speedily concluded, and less wantonly undertaken" (p. 878).

It has long been claimed that in *The Wealth of Nations* Smith was unduly harsh in his handling of the Mercantilists. In more recent years, however, this criticism has received fresh emphasis.[51] Mercantilist doctrines, especially those relating to the Navigation Acts, and Mercantilist political and economic policies and practices have been reappraised. And they have *not* been found wanting to the extent that Smith depicted them. Indeed, considered in their historical stting they have in some cases been justified. The general result has been an increase in the intellectual stature of the Mercantilists and a decrease in that of Adam Smith.

Numerous other criticisms of *The Wealth of Nations* could be mentioned, but only two or three further ones will be noted. Smith's emphasis on the factors promoting the production of wealth has been highly praised, and correctly so. He could have given greater attention, however, to the distribution of wealth. While it would probably be inaccurate to say that Smith was uninterested in "distributive justice," nevertheless his chief concern was with "commutative justice," involving the protection of individual rights. Stating the issue in more modern terminology, and in a somewhat different fashion, it can be said that our author gave his attention to "Production Welfare Economics," not to "Distribution Welfare Economics."[52]

Smith has been criticized for shifting interest away from the Physiocrats, particularly from Quesnay with his remarkable Economic Table. This table bears a striking kinship to modern input-output analysis, a type of economic analysis that has gained great importance in recent years. Because of this kinship, and for other reasons, the prestige of the Physiocrats among economists has been definitely increasing.[53]

Finally, Smith has been taken to task for his slight attention to women. This is not a result, however, of the Women's Revolt of the 1970s. This criticism, indeed, goes back at least to the last century. In the 1880s Cliffe Leslie pointed to the neglect of women in *The Wealth of Nations*.[54] They figure, he said, in only one passage, namely the author's discussion of education. Without attempting to excuse Smith—if he really needs to be excused— one should point out that this observation is not correct. Women are mentioned at a number of other points in Smith's book (pp. 79, 85, 110, 362, 822, 871). W. H. Hutt, possibly following Cliffe Leslie, also speaks of our author's single reference to women. Hutt cites this reference as perhaps the best example of "the tyranny of contemporary ideas upon the Classical economists."[55] It must be confessed that in his *Wealth of Nations* Smith gave only limited attention to women. How serious a weakness this is, how- ever, is a question on which opinions may differ. It need hardly be added that in any comparable treatise written today women would occupy a much more prominent place. In further defense of Smith it should be pointed out that women are given more consideration in his *Theory of Moral Sentiments*.

During the first part of the nineteenth century there was a widespread notion that most of the basic work in economics had been completed, or was near completion. James Mill, J. B. Say, Robert Torrens, Thomas De Quincey, and (later) Robert Lowe were among observers who expressed optimistic views on the theme. Much of the credit for this remarkable achievement was given, at least by some writers, to Adam Smith. Thus, in one of his Letters to Malthus, J. B. Say declared, with reference to Smith, that "The most vague and obscure of all the sciences, will, thanks to his researches, soon become the most precise, and leave fewer facts unexplained than any of the others."[56] In similar vein, Lord Mahon (Philip H. Stanhope) stated some years later that

"But not merely did Adam Smith found the science of Political Economy; we might almost say of him that he completed it, leaving, at least as some have thought, to his successors, not so much any new discoveries to make, or any further principles to prove, but far rather conjectures to hazard and consequences to pursue."[57]

As we look back at the developments in economics since the time of Adam Smith, including the highly important developments of the last four decades, we are amused at the optimism of these early writers. Little did they realize the scope of the future changes that would occur in the economic life of the nations, and in the formal study of economics. Economics has been transformed. Today economists ordinarily do not venture, at least with confidence and competency, into the numerous fields of knowledge into which Smith moved. Though one can point to a number of books—by such authors as Alfred Marshall and Joseph Schumpeter—that are very wide in scope, treatises such as *The Wealth of Nations* are no longer written. And, one might say, this has been true since 1776. The field of economics has been more clearly and more narrowly defined, with a consequent exclusion of much of the subject matter that Smith considered appropriate for his great book.

At the same time that economics (*qua* economics) has been divorced from the other social sciences, all of which have become specialized studies in their own right, it has experienced a vast increase in the specific matters with which it deals within its own area. The basic economic problems that Smith discussed or touched on in *The Wealth of Nations,* problems such as value determination, distribution theory, economic growth, resource allocation, remain basic today. But other highly important issues have arisen, issues to which Smith gave little or no attention. Many of these issues bear names with which Smith was unfamiliar. The terminology of economics has been greatly enlarged, especially since the 1920s. Oligopoly, monopsony, input-output analysis, indifference curves, national income accounting, the multiplier, externalities, expectations, production functions—these are a few of the contemporary economic terms not found in *The Wealth of Nations.*

With this large increase in the subject matter and also in the complexity of economics it is no longer possible for a person to teach himself the subject simply by reading Smith's book, as was done by that soldier who was "on a distant tour of duty" and by the stockbroker as he casually visited Bath.[58]

Since the Smithian era, and particularly during the present century, the division-of-labor principle has been extensively applied in economics. Like the field of philosophy, which by the time *The Wealth of Nations* was published had been broken down into "branches," economics has become highly specialized, each division of the subject affording "occupation to a peculiar tribe or class" of economists. The most outstanding of the "tribes" is the one that concentrates on economic theory. Lesser tribes are the labor economists, the public utility economists, the public finance economists. The latter groups do not (or at least should not) neglect economic theory, but they use it in a limited sense and devote much of their attention to the descriptive characteristics of particular segments of the economy.

The economics of the 1970s differs in innumerable ways from the economics (the political economy) of 1776, as well as from the economics of 1876 and of 1926. *The Wealth of Nations* cannot be looked upon, therefore, as an up-to-date treatise, presenting us with an adequate analysis of how price-guided economies operate and satisfactory explanations of, and solutions to, the many economic problems that arise in such economies. After almost two hundred years one would not expect any such miracle. Indeed, *The Wealth of Nations* as a general treatise or textbook on economics became inadequate many years ago. Back in 1848 John Stuart Mill declared that the book was "in many parts obsolete, and in all, imperfect."[59] If this was the case a century and a quarter ago, it is more the case today.

And yet one should not dismiss Smith's great work as of no current significance, a danger that in this age of impatience with the past is all too common. There are many parts of Smith's book that are relevant to the present, and written in a form that has a contemporary ring. As a matter of fact, one capable observer has gone so far as to declare that "Almost 200 years after publication," *The Wealth of Nations* "reads like a modern treatise."[60] This is exaggerated, to be sure, even for one who seems to possess a marked sense of "filial devotion." But there is much in Smith's book that is timely. Particularly is this true in the descriptive and analytical parts of the work. It is less true of the prescriptive parts. If the latter sections of his treatise are not useful as policy guides, and here some economists would maintain otherwise, even on such a question as governmental intervention, they at least have the merit of being provocative, of raising highly important issues.

There are several more or less abstract features of *The Wealth of Nations* that contribute greatly to its timeliness. Among these is the spirit that is manifest in the book, the spirit of curiosity, of diligent effort, of thoroughness. Another feature, one that has been noted more than once by commentators, is the high degree of common sense that is given expression in the work. Smith would certainly have agreed with his admirer, Alfred Marshall, that "In all social questions we must supplement the use of the economic organon by unorganized common sense."[61]

The chief claim of *The Wealth of Nations* to fame, however, is historical in nature. It is the outstanding contribution the treatise has made to the development of economic thought and policy. With changing times and circumstances, and changing intellectual interests and social philosophies, other earlier writers have in recent years gained in popularity. This is true of such men as Sir William Petty, François Quesnay, Sir James Steuart, and Thomas Robert Malthus. But Smith remains "The Father of Political Economy," and his *Wealth of Nations* still stands as the greatest landmark in the history of economic thought.

NOTES

1. The *Lectures* were edited by Edwin Cannan (New York: Kelley & Millman, Reprint, 1956): the draft of Smith's book is contained in William R. Scott's *Adam Smith as Student and Professor,* pp. 317-356.

2. *The Wealth of Nations*, p. lv.

3. The words are Pliny's and were uttered with reference to princes and government. Pliny's remark was quoted by Samuel Johnson who applied it to writers. Thence it was used by W. J. Bate, in *Aspects of the Eighteenth Century*, ed. by Earl R. Wasserman (Baltimore: Johns Hopkins University Press, 1965), p. 245.

4. Smith's failure to mention in his book Sir James Steuart's *Inquiry into the Principles of Political Economy*, which was publshed in 1770, has sometimes given rise to comment. A. J. Youngson has declared that "By cutting Steuart out of *The Wealth of Nations*, Adam Smith cut him out from serious consideration by almost all subsequent writers." *The Scottish Historical Review*, October 1967, p. 171. If, in the light of the economic and political conditions prevailing in the century and a half after 1770, Steuart's work had great merit, Smith's neglect would hardly have prevented it from being seriously considered by most subsequent writers. This does not justify Smith's treatment of the work of his fellow Scot, however. With greatly altered economic and political conditions, Steuart's treatise is now receiving considerable attention from economists.

5. *The Letters of Edward Gibbon*, ed. by J. E. Norton, 3 vols. (London: Cassell, 1956), 2, pp. 101, 166.

6. Palgrave's *Dictionary of Political Economy*, article on Adam Smith.

7. *The Collected Writings of Thomas De Qunicey*, ed. by David Masson, 14 vols. (London: Black, 1896-1897), IX, pp. 115, 116.

8. *Selected Writings on Economics* (New York: Kelley, Reprints of Economic Classics, 1966), "Four Introductory Lectures on Political Economy," p. 5. Stanley Jevons alluded approvingly to a remark someone had made that "Adam Smith had some of the many-sidedness at which all have wondered in Shakespeare." *The Principles of Economics* (London: Macmillan, 1905), p. 192.

9. Stephen Enke, in *The Journal of Economic Literature*, December 1969, p. 1127.

10. *Robert Torrens and the Evolution of Classical Economics* (London: Macmillan, 1958), pp. 234-235. Frank H. Knight expresses a similar view. See *On the History and Method of Economics* (University of Chicago Press, 1956), p. 9.

11. Duncan Forbes, *The Cambridge Journal*, August 1954, p. 648; and Frank Petrella, in *The Southern Economic Journal*, January 1968, pp. 365, 373.

12. See *Josiah Tucker*, A Selection from His Economic and Political Writings, with an Introduction by Robert L. Schuyler (New York: Columbia University Press 1931), pp. 11-12.

13. *The Industrial Revolution* (London and New York: Oxford University Press, 1961), pp. 138, 139.

14. *Capital*, 2 vols. (London: Dent, Everyman's Library ed., 1930), I, p. 277. One becomes enmeshed in metaphorical complexities when he reads that Hume's *Political Discourses*, published in 1752, "are in truth the cradle of political economy." *Life and Correspondence of David Hume*, ed. by John Hill Burton, 2 vols. (Edinburgh: Tait, 1846), I, p. 354.

15. *Revised Report of Proceedings*, Dinner of the Political Economy Club in Celebration of the Hundredth Year of the Publication of the *Wealth of Nations* (London: Longmans, Green, Reader & Dyer, 1876), p. 33. Rogers contrasts the "speculative Bacon" with the "practical Bacon," Smith being compared with the latter, not the former.

16. See McCulloch's "Introductory Discourse" to his edition of *The Wealth of Nations* (Edinburgh: Black, New ed., 1870) p. xlv, and his "Sketch of the Life and Writings of Adam Smith," in the same volume, pp. xi-xii. A. L. Macfie remarks that Book I of Smith's treatise "is now a part of world thought, as is the *Origin of Species*, or *Principia Mathematica*." *The Individual in Society*, p. 21.

17. *History of Civilization in England*, 2 vols. (New York and London: Appleton, from 2nd London ed., 1920), I, pp. 154-156.

18. The words quoted are those of Thomas Seccombe, in his book *The Age of Johnson* (London: Bell, Sixth ed., revised, 1926), p. 91.

19. *The Principles of Economics*, p. 187.

20. *Lectures on the Industrial Revolution* (London: Longmans, Green, 1908), p. 204.

21. *Selected Essays of J. B. Bury*, ed. by Harold W. V. Temperley (Cambridge at the University Press, 1930), p. 238.

22. *Economic Development* (New York: Norton, revised ed., 1968), p. 57. Another presentation, largely in algebraic and graphical terms, of the classical growth model, including Smith's, can be found in Leif Johansen's contribution to *Socialism, Capitalism and Economic Growth*, Essays Presented to Maurice Dobb, ed. by C. H. Feinstein (Cambridge at the University Press, 1967), pp. 13-29.

23. At another place in *The Wealth of Nations* Smith makes a statement suggesting the existence of a reciprocal relationship between economic growth and justice. "Commerce and manufactures," he declares (p. 385) in speaking of the effect of urban on rural development, "gradually introduced order and good government, and with them, the liberty and security of individuals, among the inhabitants of the country." Smith refers to Hume as the only writer he knows of who has taken notice of this point—of what has been "by far the most important" effect of commerce and manufactures.

24. *The Economic Journal*, December 1928, pp. 529, 539-540.

25. Frank H. Knight, in *Ethics,* July 1953, p. 285.

26. See footnote 25 in Essay 6.

27. Burton A. Weisbrod, in *The Journal of Human Resources,* Summer 1966, p. 6.

28. *Technology and Social Change,* ed. by Eli Ginsberg (New York: Columbia University Press, 1964), p. 49.

29. See Samuel Bowles, *Planning Educational Systems for Economic Growth* (Cambridge: Harvard University Press, 1969), pp. 2, 3.

30. Smith's pure model of economic growth, says J. R. Hicks, "is consistently carried through on the assumption that the only form of capital (or the only form that matters) is circulating capital." *Capital and Growth* (New York: Oxford University Press, 1965), p. 36.

31. *Principles of Political Economy* (London: Pickering, 1836), p. 44

32. *Capital and Growth,* p. 36.

33. See T. W. Hutchison, *A Review of Economic Doctrines, 1870-1929* (Oxford at the Clarendon Press, 1953), pp. 347-348. Hutchison refers to Smith's "unconditional eulogy of the beneficence of saving, supplemented by his dictum that no one holds money for its own sake," and to a number of nineteenth-century writers and ideas. All these contributed to drive "almost completely underground," in England at least, the fruitful notions that had been advanced earlier.

34. *Capital,* 2, p. 654.

35. *Theories of Welfare Economics* (Cambridge: Harvard University Press, 1948), pp. 57-58, 78, 85, 94-95.

36. On the latter type of conflict see Joan Robinson's statement about the chief concern of Neoclassical economics with allocation, in *The Teaching of Development Economics,* ed. by Kurt Martin and John Knapp (London: Cass, 1967), p. 149. On the clash of the two approaches in terms of public policy, see Peter Wiles's article on "Growth Versus Choice," in *The Economic Journal,* June 1956, pp. 244-255. Further discussion of the issue by Kurt Klappholz and Mr. Wiles will be found in *The Economic Journal,* June 1957, pp. 341-347.

37. *Studies in Economic History: The Collected Papers of George Unwin,* ed. by Richard H. Tawney (London: Macmillan, 1927), p. 23. "Perhaps the first great piece of economic history writing in English was the third chapter of Adam Smith's *Wealth of Nations,*" says W. H. B. Court. See *Approaches to History,* ed. by H. P. R. Finberg (London: Routledge & Kegan Paul, 1962) p. 19. Court undoubtedly means Book III rather than Chapter III.

38. R. H. Campbell, in *The Scottish Historical Review,* April 1967, p. 39.

39. *Economic History and the Historian* (New York: Praeger,

1969), p. 64. Wilson goes on to mention specifically Smith's entire neglect, in his section on Mercantilism, of money and credit and of the structure of the trading system of Britain ("which he describes so vividly elsewhere"). The author, he adds, scarcely examines the possibility that the bullion doctrine of the Mercantilists "might have rational historical roots."

40. Stewart, p. 34. E. G. West points out that the method of conjectural history would be referred to today as "sociological evolutionism." *Economica,* February 1964, p. 26. For a general discussion of conjectural history, see J. W. Burrows' book, *Evolution and Society* (Cambridge at the University Press, 1966), especially pp. 10-23, 48-64.

41. For an extensive discussion of this theme, see Andrew S. Skinner's article "Natural History in the Age of Adam Smith," in *Political Studies,* February 1967, pp. 32-48. See also Professor Skinner's article "Adam Smith: Philosophy and Science," in the *Scottish Journal of Political Economy,* November 1972, pp. 307-319.

42. William E. H. Lecky, *A History of England in the Eighteenth Century,* 7 vols. (New York: Appleton, new ed., 1903), IV, p. 156; and E. A. Benians, in *The Cambridge Historical Journal,* 1925 (Vol. I, No. 3), p. 249.

43. Donald Winch, *Classical Political Economy and Colonies* (Cambridge: Harvard University Press, 1965) p. 7.

44. Professor Koebner discusses the general problem in his article "Adam Smith and the Industrial Revolution," in *The Economic History Review,* Second Series, XI, 1959, pp. 381-391.

45. This term was coined a century and a half after *The Wealth of Nations* was published, by Sumner H. Slichter. See his article on "The Price of Industrial Progress," in *The New Republic,* February 8, 1928, pp. 316-318.

46. Samuel Hollander, "Some Technological Relationships in *The Wealth of Nations* and Ricardo's *Principles,*" in *The Canadian Journal of Economics and Political Science,* May 1966, pp. 186, 190, 192.

47. Joseph J. Spengler, in *The Southern Economic Journal,* July 1959, p. 8.

48. On Smith and the business corporation, see Emmette S. Redford, *American Government and the Economy* (New York: Macmillan, 1965), pp. 70, 595.

49. Eduard Heimann, *History of Economic Doctrines* (New York: Oxford University Press, 1945), p. 30; and J. M. Low, in *The Manchester School of Economic and Social Studies,* September 1952, p. 329.

50. For a longer discussion of Smith's opinions on balancing the

budget, see Jesse Burkhead's article "The Balanced Budget," in *The Quarterly Journal of Economics,* May 1954, pp. 192-194, 212.

51. See, for example, Charles Wilsons *England's Apprenticeship, 1603-1763* (London: Longmans, 1965), pp. 184, 374-375; and his *Economic History and the Historian* (New York: Praeger, 1969).

52. Hla Myint, *Theories of Welfare Economics,* p. 26. Smith's neglect (and also that of "his earlier successors") of the distribution of wealth is pointed out by Henry Sidgwick, in *The Principles of Political Economy* (London: Macmillan, 1883), pp. 25, 402.

53. See *Economic Thought,* ed. by James A. Gherity (New York: Random House, 1965), p. viii, and contributions therein by Ronald L. Meek and Almarin Phillips.

54. Thomas Edward Cliffe Leslie, *Essays in Political Economy* (Dublin: Hodges, Figgis, 2nd ed., 1888), pp. 39-40.

55. *Eonomists and the Public* (London: Cape, 1936), p. 316.

56. *Letters to Mr. Malthus* (London: Sherwood, Neely, and Jones, 1821), p. 21.

57. *History of England, 1713-1783,* 7 vols. (Boston: Little, Brown, 3rd ed. revised, 1853-1854), VII, p. 336.

58. Referred to by Lionel Robbins, *Robert Torrens and the Evolution of Classical Economics,* p. 9.

59. *Principles of Political Economy,* ed. by W. J. Ashley (London: Longmans, New ed., 1926), p. xxviii.

60. Lloyd G. Reynolds, *Economics* (Homewood, Ill.: Irwin, 3rd ed., 1969), p. 699. Reynolds points to specific matters in Smith's book that he considers timely.

61. The words quoted are those of Henry Higgs, *The Economic Journal,* December 1926, p. 614. A fine statement concerning common sense and economics can be found in Marshall's *Principles of Economics* (London: Macmillan, 8th ed., 1925), p. 38.

10.

Another Look at the Invisible Hand

> Every individual is continually exerting himself to
> find out the most advantageous employment for
> whatever capital he can command. It is his own
> advantage, indeed, and not that of the society, which
> he has in view. But the study of his own advantage
> naturally, or rather necessarily leads him to prefer
> that employment which is most advantageous to the
> society.
>
> —ADAM SMITH

No terms or notion in *The Wealth of Nations* is better known than
"the invisible hand." Not only is the expression very familiar to
academicians, but it has a certain popularity among other persons
as well, especially editorial writers. Over the years economists
have given no small amount of attention to the invisible hand and
its accompanying principle of economic harmony, but despite all
the attention the theme has received there is still room for a few
more words. Particularly is this true if, as in the present essay,
an attempt is made not only to study the general theme, as dealt
with by Smith, in its various aspects, but to discuss the present-day
applicability of the theme. The "various aspects" of the invisible-
hand notion include Smith's extensive, though scattered, discussion of free competition, his analysis of the prime driving force in
economic life, his treatment of the highly important question of
resource allocation, and his view on the proper scope of governmental intervention. To these related aspects of the invisible hand,
and to the "hand" itself, we shall now direct our attention.

255

In his *Wealth of Nations* Smith gives a great deal of attention to how a freely competitive economy operates, or tends to operate. Using a common and indispensable contemporary term, he assumes in his analysis a "model"—a competitive model. This model presupposes the existence of a market economy, an economy in which the forces of supply and demand, both with respect to products and the factors of production, are permitted to operate in an unfettered fashion.

The interactions of these forces, in the Smithian analysis, are constantly tending to establish positions of balance; they are constantly working not only in the direction of specific types of equilibrium, but toward a general kind of equilibrium as well. A century after the publication of *The Wealth of Nations* another great economist, Léon Walras, constructed a picture of general equilibrium which (with the modifications added by later writers) has been described as "the most intellectually satisfying, the most generally inclusive, efficient, incisive and beautiful construction which economics has ever produced."[1] Smith's pioneer model was very far removed from the sophisticated Walrasian model, which itself has now been found wanting. Indeed, his model does not match in analytical precision and structural beauty the Tableau Économique that François Quesnay produced almost twenty years before Smith's book was published.[2] And yet despite its mathematical indefiniteness and its general descriptive limitations, our author's model has great merit and significance. Possibly Professor Boulding permits his admiration for his famous countryman to carry him a little too far, but it is his belief that Smith "set up an internally consistent framework of equilibrium theory, especially in regard to relative prices, which all subsequent work has modified only in detail rather than in essence."[3]

In this general connection it might be added that Smith, with his great preoccupation with systems, including particularly the freely competitive system, has been hailed for still another achievement. He has been described as "one of the greatest exponents of systems analysis of all time."[4] And interestingly enough, as such an exponent he has helped to promote interest in economic planning, something we do not ordinarily associate with his name.

The notion of "natural" prices plays a key role in Smith's competitive model. Such prices would prevail throughout the economy if the forces of supply and demand could operate freely and work themselves out to a condition of equilibrium. But in the world as it is, actual prices (or market prices, as Smith calls them) are often above the normal prices, and sometimes they are below. But there is a tendency for the two sets of prices to be equivalent. The more competitive the situation, the more closely can a condition of equivalence be achieved. And the better will be the social consequences. As Smith himself says (p. 313), "In general, if any branch of trade, or any division of labour, be advantageous to the public, the freer and more general the competition, it will always be the more so."

With his strong belief in the beneficent effects of free competition, Smith was naturally opposed to monopolies. Some of his harshest words are reserved for his criticism of them. The monopolies that he had in mind were chiefly commercial monopolies, fostered by the government, not the industrial monopolies that are a common feature of today's economics and which may develop without any particular government aid. Had he been confronted with the issue, Smith would probably have granted that the latter may bring certain technological advantages, but he would have been gravely concerned with their market power—with their ability to keep market prices above natural prices. "The monopolists," he tells us (p. 61), "by keeping the market under-stocked . . . sell their commodities much above the natural price, and raise their emoluments, whether they consist in wages or profit, greatly above their natural rate."

Smith's competitive model rests upon the supposition that competition would not only be free but fair. An excellent statement of his position on this point is found in his earlier book, *The Theory of Moral Sentiments*. The self-seeking individual, he declares (p. 76), must "humble the arrogance of his self-love, and bring it down to something which other men can go along with." "In the race for wealth, for honours, and preferments," he further states, "he may run as hard as he can, and strain every nerve and every muscle, in order to outstrip all his competitors. But if he should justle, or throw down any of them, the indulgence of the spectators is entirely at an end." Unbridled competition, devil-take-the-hindmost competition, was not the kind Smith supported.

Our author recognized that the results of competition are not always and necessarily the best. In competitive selling some of the sellers, he declares in *The Wealth of Nations* (p. 343), "perhaps may sometimes decoy a weak customer to buy what he has no occasion for." To Smith this very familiar twentieth-century evil was not of much importance, nor would it necessarily be done away with by limiting the number of sellers. Apparently the customers could look after the situations themselves. "It is not the multitude of ale-houses . . . that occasions a general disposition to drunkenness among the common people; but that disposition arising from other causes necessarily gives employment to a multitude of ale-houses." Despite the possibility of a little "decoying," the author's confidence in the wisdom of having a large number of sellers (and also a large number of buyers) remained undiminished.

Smith's support of competition was based largely on economic grounds. Under free competition a better use would be made of the factors of production, with the result that the wealth of the nation—and of all nations—would be increased. The Scottish economist probably recognized the political advantages of free competition. Certainly he inveighed against the influence, actual or assumed, of monopoly lobbies on the affairs of state. Without monopolies, and assuming no politically active trade associations, such lobbies would not exist. Smith probably felt, too, that free competition had certain moral advantages. At one point (p. 49), in a discussion of landlords, he mentions the desire of all persons "to reap where they never sowed." This universal and immoral desire which is given wide scope under monopoly is obviously subject to extensive control under competition. Of all the "institutions" contributing to the flowering of a great society—after order, security, and justice have been established—free competition, to Smith's way of thinking, ranked first.

It is perhaps possible to think of a competitive society in which the competition would be in performing acts of benevolence. But that is not what Smith had in mind, either in his model or in his description of things as they are. The motivating factor, the driving force, that he assumes was self-interest, or, to use another term, self-love. Stated still differently, and in a form that he himself sometimes used, it was "the desire to improve one's condition."

This does not mean that Smith, a most benevolent man himself, was opposed to acts of benevolence on the part of others. Far from it. His attitude toward benevolence as a principle, however, is brought out better in his *Theory of Moral Sentiments* than in *The Wealth of Nations*. As we noted in Essay 7, our author in the former book (p. 24) states that "the perfection of human nature" is found in restraining the selfish affections and the exercise of benevolent ones. We noted in the same essay Smith's definition of "superior virtue," when it is "carried to the highest degree of perfection," as "the best head joined to the best heart."

Smith taught, both by example and by precept, the great virtue of benevolence. But he was realist enough to know that benevolence could not be relied upon as the motivating factor in any economic system. His common sense (of which he had a great deal) prevented him from holding any such opinion. Benevolence is a great virtue, but in the world as it is, it is not highly developed. Nature has been niggardly in endowing man with this characteristic—in his *Theory* (p. 120) Smith refers to "that feeble spark of benevolence which Nature has lighted up in the human heart"—and, one may add, man himeslf has not reached the stage in his own development where that virtue is a pronounced human attribute.

In *The Wealth of Nations* Smith makes a number of famous remarks which indicate how feeble he felt the spark of benevolence was in the workaday world of his time, or how ineffectual he thought it was. The most famous statement is the following: "It is not from the benevolence of the butcher, the brewer, or the baker, that we expect our dinner, but from their regard to their own interest. We address ourselves, not to their humanity but to their self-love, and never talk to them of our own necessities but of their advantages" (p. 14).

The principle of self-interest, the desire to better our own condition, is the great driving force in the competitive economy.[5] It is a deep-seated and long-continuing force: it "comes with us from the womb, and never leaves us till we go into the grave" (p. 324). It is also a force that is in more or less constant oper-ation, a force so strong that it often overcomes serious obstacles in the way. As Smith himself says (p. 326), in a statement that contains some of the most characteristic features of his writing style: "The uniform, constant, and uninterrupted effort of every man to better his condition, the principle from which public and national, as well as private opulence is originally derived, is fre-quently powerful enough to maintain the natural progress of things toward improvement, in spite both of the extravagance of gov-ernment, and of the greatest errors of administration." "Like the unknown principle of animal life," our author concludes, "it fre-quently restores health and vigour to the constitution, in spite, not only of the disease, but of the absurd prescriptions of the doc-tor." (For a similar expression of opinion, see p. 508).

Smith's doctrine of self-interest has sometimes been misinter-preted. Perhaps no one has sinned more in this respect than John Ruskin. In one of his *Fors* letters Ruskin speaks of "the deliberate blasphemy of Adam Smith: 'Thou shalt hate the Lord thy God, damn His laws, and covet thy neighbour's goods.' "[6] This is a grotesque observation indeed. Smith taught no such blasphemy. His doctrine of self-interest did not imply any catch-as-catch-can philosophy; it was not equivalent to any crude form of selfishness. Moreover, it must be emphasized that in his handling of the self-interest, self-love notion Smith was dealing with only one moti-vating force, albeit a most important one, in human life. His "economic man," if we may use the term in connection with the great economist, was certainly not the whole man. And though it is the former that figures prominently in *The Wealth of Nations,* there is good reason for believing that it was the welfare of the latter in which the author was primarily interested. To Smith, it would seem, the *summum bonum* for society was not the ordinary task of "making money," nor even the more lofty Veblenian goal of "making goods," but, strange as it may seem, the Ruskinian ideal of "making men."[7] Not long after Smith died, his friend Dugald Stewart (p. 8) spoke of the famous economist's "ruling passion," which was "contributing to the happiness and the improvement of society." This is a far cry from any inculcation of the spirit of selfishness.

It is unfortunate that Smith did not embody in his great economic treatise, even in the form of a digression, an account of "the prudent man" as he strikingly depicts that personage in *The Theory of Moral Sentiments*.[8] Such a portrayal would have resulted in a better understanding of the author's general theory of human behavior, including its operation in the economic sphere. At the same time it would have made Smith much less exposed to the critical darts of Ruskin and certain other commentators. These desirable results would also have been achieved if Smith had repeated from his earlier book some of the statement he made there about self-love, statements which, we have good reason for believing, he still in general believed in when he wrote *The Wealth of Nations*. (Smith's fascinating character sketch of the prudent man in *The Theory of Moral Sentiments* is found in Part VI of the book, a part that was added to the sixth edition of the work which was published in 1790, fourteen years after the appearance of *The Wealth of Nations*.) "The man of the most perfect virtue," he tells us in *The Theory* (p. 133), "the man whom we naturally love and revere the most, is he who joins, to the most perfect command of his own original and selfish feelings, the most exquisite sensibility both to the original and sympathetic feelings of others." He refers (p. 153) to ambition as "a passion, which when it keeps within the bounds of prudence and justice, is always admired in the world." (Sometimes, however, when it goes beyond these bounds it has a "certain irregular greatness, which dazzles the imagination.") Again, he remarks (p. 79), that "Society may subsist, though not in the most comfortable state, without beneficence; but the prevalence of injustice must utterly destroy it."[9]

Smith's doctrine of self-interest extended well beyond the economic sphere. It covered a wide range of human desires. For most people at the time, however, self-interest objectives were apparently directed largely to economic ends. As Smith himself observed, in his *Wealth of Nations* (p. 325), "An augmentation of fortune is the means by which the greater part of men propose and wish to better their condition." He adds that this particular means is "the most vulgar and the most obvious."

From what has already been said, it is clear that Smith was well aware of the difference between wealth and welfare, or to state the issue more closely to his own manner of expression, between wealth and happiness. This fact is well brought out in what is possibly the most fascinating chapter in *The Theory of Moral Sentiments,* namely Chapter I of Part IV. There we find (p. 163) Smith's famous utterance about the beggar and the kings. "In ease of the body and peace of the mind, all the different ranks of life are nearly upon a level, and the beggar, who suns himself by the side of the highway, possesses that security which kings are fighting for." A somewhat similar notion is expressed in a rhetorical question he asks earlier in the book (p. 43): "What can be added to the happiness of the man who is in health, who is out of debt, and has a clear conscience?" To a person in this condition, says the author, "all accessions of fortune" are superfluous, but if, perchance, a person's happiness is "much elevated" by such accessions, it must be due to "the most frivolous levity." Smith emphasizes, however, the misery that may come to one who falls below this condition—a fall that can be "immense and prodigious" in distance.

If the accretions of wealth beyond the level that enables a person to be in health and out of debt and with a good conscience add little, if anything, to one's happiness, than why should one exert oneself beyond the level required to meet these goals? Smith has an ingenious answer, in which "nature" plays an indispensable role. Man is fascinated, he argues (p. 162), by the way wealth is produced; he is greatly impressed with "the order, the regular and harmonious movement" of the system (or machine or economy) which produces the wealth. It is the *means* of wealth production that strikes man's fancy. Looked at from this point of view "the pleasures of wealth and greatness," the author tells us, "strike the imagination as something grand and beautiful and noble," and we consider our efforts worthwhile.

It is fortunate for society that nature has tricked us—has imposed upon us—in this way. "It is this deception," Smith tells us, "which arouses and keeps in continual motion the industry of mankind."[10] This particular turn of the argument suggests that beyond a certain level of wealth attainment the real driving force behind individual effort is not economic but aesthetic. Smith realizes (p. 164) that our preoccupation with the beauty and the order of "the system" is not without its danger; our concern with means may be too large relative to our concern with ends. But he still adheres to the great significance of the "beautiful and orderly" system, or machine, in human attitudes.

Smith's support of a freely competitive economy, in which the chief driving force is self-interest, is tied up with the notion of harmony between individual advancement and the social good. This harmony-of-interest notion or principle, as it is dealt with or implied in the author's two books, particularly *The Wealth of Nations,* has given rise to considerable debate. The chief points at issue have been two in number, namely the degree of harmony that exists and the basis of the harmony.

In any society (be it anarchistic, capitalistic, or communistic) in which there is freedom of purchase and sale there is a certain amount of harmony between the interests of sellers and buyers, and hence between the good of the individual and the good of the whole group. Smith, of course, recognized this fact. But he had more than this in mind when he talked of the social benefits that arise from the pursuit of self-interest, or when, as was more frequent, he implied the existence of such benefits. He was thinking of a higher degree of harmony.

Our author does not make many explicit statements in *The Wealth of Nations* of the harmony doctrine, but there are at least two major ones, and unfortunately they are a bit confusing. The first one, which we have used at the beginning of the present essay, is very sweeping in nature. Not only does a *good* social result follow from the individual investor's self-seeking, but the *best* result. In later parlance, the social benefits are "maximized" or "optimized."

Two pages later Smith, still speaking of the individual investor, pulls back somewhat. He now says the investor "generally" does not intend to promote the public interest, nor is he aware of how much he is promoting it. Rather (in preferring to invest in domestic rather than in foreign industries) he seeks only his own security, and, in directing his investment into those channels where the value of the "produce" will be greatest, he is seeking only his own good. Then (p. 423) our author makes his most familiar, and inevitably quoted, remark. He, the individual investor, "is in this, as in many other cases, led by an invisible hand to promote an end which was no part of his intention." The limiting words, "in many other cases," will be noted. Smith continues, "Nor is it always the worse for the society that it was no part of it." Presumably there are cases when it would have been helpful to society if it had been "part of it"—but the cases, as he implies very shortly, would be few and far between. "By pursuing his own interest," Smith goes on to say, the individual investor "frequently promotes that of society more effectually than when he really intends to promote it." The word "frequently" is troublesome here. How "frequent" is "frequently?" Does the word mean in most cases, in the majority of cases, in less than the majority of cases? Finally, and shifting our attention to merchants, Smith tells us that he has "never known much good done by those who affected to trade for the public good." This aim, this "affectation," however, is not very common among the merchants, "and very few words need be employed in dissuading them from it."[11]

These two references to the harmony principle, taken together, are rather perplexing to the Smith interpreter. In the light of these statements, one might ask, how much harmony did the author imagine existed? Not (in the present instance) in any abstract sense but in actuality; specifically, in the Great Britain of his day. Some scholars maintain that the amount of harmony presupposed in *The Wealth of Nations* was quite small. Professor Lionel Robbins, for example, declares that the harmony in Smith's system was "very strictly limited."[12]

This contention receives substantial support from the fact that in his great treatise Smith gives numerous instances of disharmony —disharmony between individual interests and social interests, and sometimes between the interests of separate groups in society. Over the years a great many writers have alluded to these disharmonies, and a number have compiled collections of the examples that can be found. The best-known of the collections is that made by Professor Viner back in the 1920s.[13] Viner's list of "Flaws in the Natural Order" ("even when left to take its own course") is not a complete one, but we are still told that "it would suffice to provide ammunition for several socialist orations." The very same conclusion has been reached by Professor Macfie.

It would be foolish to deny the existence in *The Wealth of Nations* of a great many examples of disharmony. But just as there was once a tendency to exaggerate the degree of harmony found in Smith's work (and in his philosophy in general), so there now seems to be a tendency to exaggerate the amount of disharmony. A few further observations on the issue therefore seem to be in order.

While the examples of disharmony in Smith's great work are many, examples of harmony are not hard to find. We have already noted two of them, but there are others. (Additional ones can be found on pp. 326, 329, 355, 508, 594-595.) In general these examples relate to the power of self-interest to promote the general good, sometimes when confronted with formidable obstacles. This means that a certain harmony, though not necessarily the highest, exists.

The instances of disharmony found in Smith's treatise usually involve what one might call "partial" disharmony, not "complete" or "absolute" disharmony. For example, the adverse effects of the division of labor set forth in the latter part of the book (pp. 734-735), which Viner cites as one of the cases of disharmony, are indeed bad; but that fact does not mean that Smith favored the elimination of the division-of-labor principle, though he advocated some corrective steps, as we noted in Essay 6. The principle involved harmony—increasing both private and public wealth—as well as disharmony. In similar fashion one can analyze the disharmony resulting from the presence of monopolistic organizations. They are not totally bad; disharmony is involved, to be sure, but so is harmony.

Smith himself made the point we are discussing in a statement about colonial trade on the one hand and the monopolization of that trade on the other (p. 573). He looked upon the latter as "always and necessarily hurtful." But the gains of the former are so great that despite its monopolization the trade is "still upon the whole beneficial, and greatly beneficial." But, he adds, it is "a good deal less so than it otherwise would be." Smith obviously would have preferred monopolized colonial trade rather than no colonial trade—the "harmonies" involved in such trade outweighed the "disharmonies." He would have greatly preferred the conduct of that trade on a competitive basis, however, for then the amount of harmony would have been still greater; the wealth of the nation would have been still larger.

When Smith alludes to a disharmony of interests he ordinarily has in mind what we earlier referred to as "partial" disharmony. Stating the matter somewhat differently, there is similarity in the "direction" of both individual and social benefits, but in "distance" or "degree" the former exceed the latter. In at least one instance, however, he seems to have in mind a diffrence in direction: the individual in promoting his own good actually, and on balance, harms society. There is an absolute social loss.

Thus he declares (p. 250) that the interest of the dealers "in any particular branch of trade or manufactures, is always in some respects different from, and even opposite to, that of the public." As it stands this statement suggests not only different degrees of benefit to individual dealers on the one hand and society on the other, but it also points to the possibility of actual injury to society accompanying the benefits to the dealers—a situation involving not a difference in degree but in direction. What other meaning can be given to "opposite?" (Did Smith have in mind, it might be asked, dealers in some such drug as heroin?)

Our author's statement is confusing, and an examination of its context does not completely clarify the issue. His reference to narrowing the competition points to a difference in degree of benefits, not to positive social injury. However, he also goes on to speak of "oppressing" the public, a term that could connote actual harm—"to deceive and even to oppress the public." If deceiving the public causes a decrease in the benefits accruing to the society, what does oppressing the public lead to? No benefits at all, but actual injury? This is one possible meaning, although it might be argued that the statement merely implies that while all deception leads to oppression, all oppression need not involve deception, and that in either case there is simply a difference in the degree of benefits.

Whatever Smith's view was in this particular instance, in most if not all of the other cases of disharmony that he cites he is thinking of differences in the extent of the benefits accruing to individuals and to society. Mandeville's earlier statement on the issue is extreme, but Smith (recognizing possible exceptions) would undoubtedly have agreed with its general validity.

> The worst of all the multitude
> Did something for the common good.

In any human society, including the so-called natural order, there are certain to be disharmonies. This is true of market economies as well as planned economies. Some of the disharmonies are more or less inherent in "the nature of things." This is true, for example, of the conflict of interest between "masters and men." There is no economic or ethical principle for completely resolving that conflict. In general, then, one should not be surprised in finding numerous examples of disharmony in *The Wealth of Nations,* with its emphasis on the society of eighteenth-century Britain. At the same time, one should not underestimate the underlying and powerful elements of harmony. They may not be as obvious and spectacular as the disharmonies, but they are nevertheless real.

An issue related to the harmony-of-interest problem is that of the extent to which the individual is the best judge of his own interests. If there are instances in which he is not, then it follows that society's interest is not being adequately promoted. Smith makes no claim that the individual always judges his interest in the best possible manner. As a matter of fact, one can find in *The Wealth of Nations* a considerable number of examples to the contrary. A few instances may be noted. The common people of England, and of most other countries, do not rightly understand wherein their liberty consists (p. 141); "every particular banking company has not always understood or attended to its own particular interest" (p. 286); "country gentlemen" when they demanded a bounty on wheat "did not act with that complete comprehension of their own interest which commonly directs the conduct" of merchants and manufacturers (p. 483); workers on piecework "are very apt to over-work themselves, and to ruin their health and constitution in a few years" (pp. 81-82).[14]

Even though the individual may not be the best judge of his own interest, Smith felt that in most cases he would be a better judge of these interests than legislators—legislators of the kind then in positions of power. He gave special emphasis to the superiority of the individual's judgment in "local situations." Thus, in directing the pattern of domestic industry, "every individual, it is evident, can, in his local situation, judge much better than any statesman or lawgiver can do for him" (p. 423; see also p. 497 where Smith uses the qualifying word "generally.")

Returning to our central concern, the harmony of interests, there is a final problem to be noted. Assuming that there is some degree of harmony—it might be large, or moderate, or small in amount—how, one might ask, does it arise? It will be recalled that Smith in both of his books uses the term "invisible hand" to denote that influence, or set of influences, that bring individual interests and social interests into harmony. But what, specifically, does "the invisible hand" mean? What did Smith have in mind when he used the term, particularly in *The Wealth of Nations,* and what is its significance in his analysis?

This complex problem has been discussed for many years and the commentators have furnished a variety of answers to the issue.

On the basis of their answers we may divide those who have taken up the matter into three principal catgories.

In the first group are those who interpret the invisible hand, with its accompanying and inherent harmony-of-interest principle, largely if not wholly, in broadly philosophical terms. Among the representatives of this group are John R. Commons (who declares that with Smith the notion of self-interest was "subordinate to his idea of divine beneficence"); Eduard Heimann (who affirms that the invisible-hand statement is "the classical formulation of the belief in preordanied harmony, the condition of laissez-faire economy"); and Elie Halévy (who feels that the fundamental thesis of *The Wealth of Nations* is "the natural identity of interests, or, if you like, of the spontaneous harmony of egoisms," a belief that has made him a popular object of sharp criticism).[15]

In the second group or category are those scholars who take the view that Smith does not presuppose any natural harmony, any "spontaneous harmony of egoisms." Where harmony exists it is due to institutional factors. Representatives of this group include William D. Grampp (who argues that in his economic treatise Smith gave up the doctrine of natural law and presented a secular explanation of human behavior, and that the invisible hand "is nothing more than the automatic equilibration of a competitive market"); William Letwin (who declares that "To say that Smith required or even believed in natural harmony is to neglect *The Theory of Moral Sentiments* as a whole, as well as passages in *The Wealth of Nations*," and who asserts that the invisible hand is a "literary embellishment" and not "a dogmatic assertion of 'natural harmony' in economic life"); and Nathan Rosenberg (who finds that "A neglected theme running through virtually all of *The Wealth of Nations* is Smith's attempt to define, in very specific terms, the details of the institutional structure which will best harmonize the individual's pursuit of his selfish interests with the broader interests of society").[16] Frank H. Knight, whose interpretation of the invisible hand has been followed by other commentators, may also be placed in this group. Without direct reference to Smith, Knight interprets the invisible hand as "the mutual advantage of free exchange," or, in other words, as free competition.[17]

In the third group of commentators on the meaning of the invisible hand are those scholars who partially endorse the view held by those in the second group but who at the same time find some truth in the opinions of those in the first category. At least they believe there is philosophic content in Smith's use of the invisible-hand expression; it is not to be interpreted solely in institutional terms. A. L. Macfie may be looked upon as a member of this group. In one of his more recent essays Macfie refers to Smith's "semi-religious belief in the *ultimate* harmony of personal interests," and also to his "theory of a final natural harmony of interests" (though, says Macfie, the great economist's " 'Nature' is like Heinz's tins—there are fifty-seven varieties").[18] Jacob Viner should probably be placed in the third group also. In Viner's opinion, Smith's "philosophical speculations about a harmonious order in nature undoubtedly made it easier for him to reach a laissez-faire policy," but he feels that "the significance of the natural order in Smith's economic doctrines has been grossly exaggerated."[19] John M. Letiche, who refers to Smith's interest in "social arrangements" as well as to his "concept of a unified natural order," may also be placed in the third category.[20] The present writer may be included also.

In view of the differences that exist in the interpretation of the invisible hand, it is unfortunate that Smith did not state precisely, especially in *The Wealth of Nations,* what he had in mind when he used the term. Though he was averse to using footnotes, here is a case where one would have been amply justified.

Smith's support of a freely competitive type of economy, over types that were subject to substantial degrees of private and public control, was based on his belief that competition would result in a better use of the factors of production. Though he did not use the later and highly popular term "allocation," that is what he had in mind. His treatment of the allocation theme was not highly developed, however. Smith makes no use of marginalism; he gives no picture, verbal, alegebraic, or geometrical, of what "ideal" or "optimum" allocation involves; he does not discuss, at least in any detail, such nice questions as the relationship between tastes and income distribution on the allocation pattern. Nevertheless he was keenly interested in the question of allocation and had much to say about it in *The Wealth of Nations*.

The issue often arises in his discussions of governmental interference in the free market and in his treatment of monopolies (which at that time also involved governmental interference). In all cases the allocation pattern was distorted, or, to use a term Smith liked, "deranged." Thus, he says (p. 473) that bounties, like "all other expedients of the mercantile system," force the trade of the country "into a channel much less advantageous than that in which it would naturally run of its own accord." Speaking of the monopoly of the colonial trade he declares (p. 576) that the effect has been "not to augment the quantity, but to alter the quality and shape of a part of the manufactures of Great Britain." A few sentences later he speaks of "the whole quantity of manufacturing industry" in Britain having been diminished (from what it otherwise would have been).

In some instances the amount of capital, and of labor, drawn into a particular use by governmental interference may be decreased instead of increased. This is true where monopolies are granted to carry on the trade with rich countries (p. 596). Again, under the severe rules of the Statute of Apprentices, the number of young people entering industry is insufficient (pp. 120-123). Similar undermanning results from the exclusive privileges of trade corporations (p. 129). But whether too much labor and capital is drawn into particular uses, or too little, society is injured (p. 597). The wealth of the nation is less than it otherwise would be.

Though he does not develop the point with any analytical finesse, Smith favored that kind of resource use, or allocation, that would maximize output. He does not use the word "maximize," however, but that is the concept he appears to have had in mind. Some of his remarks in *The Wealth of Nations* point to this fact. "The most advantageous employment of any capital" in a country, he says (p. 566), is that which increases the country's output "the most." In another instance (pp. 594-595) he uses the words "most advantageous to society" ("in ordinary cases") and "most agreeable to the interest of the whole society."

Both as a theoretical phenomenon and as a matter of applied economics, allocation has to do with the use of *given* resources. As such it does not involve the question, so important in Development Economics, of increasing the quality and quantity of the resources. As a consequence there may arise a clash between "choice" and "growth," as we noted in the previous essay. Such a clash is not found in Smith's book, however. The author was interested in *both* allocation and development. And interestingly enough, he made the point that, as a practical matter, the former has a bearing on the latter. In speaking of the monopolization of the colonial trade (p. 574), he refers to the adverse effect that such a policy has on the national output, and then he points to the harm this does to the "power of accumulation." The power of accumulation is of immense importance in Smith's discussion of growth.

With his strong support of a freely competitive economic system, Smith favored the curtailment or elimination of many of the governmental policies of his day. Among these were tariff restrictions, bounties, the granting of exclusive trading privileges, restrictive apprenticeship rules. It was his firm belief that the market should be free, or at least as free as possible. In this way decision-making in the economy would be greatly diffused instead of concentrated, and the wealth of the nations would be enhanced.

With decision-making diffused, a vast amount of actual or potential governmental interference would be done away with; a large degree of laissez-faire would prevail. But by no means was Smith a believer in complete laissez-faire. The philosophy of anarchism had no appeal to him. He recognized a wide range of matters in which it was quite proper, and desirable, for the government to intervene. To say, then, that "Like the Physiocrats, Adam Smith believed that the government which governs least governs best,"[21] is clearly an exaggeration.

Smith believed that even in a society of "natural liberty" there would be a number of important functions for the government to perform (p. 651). These are: the protection of society from external foes, the establishment of a system for dispensing internal justice, and the erection and maintenance of certain public works and institutions—ventures which individuals could not profitably conduct. In the actual society in which he lived, Smith recognized the value of other types of governmental intervention.[22] These are too numerous to be mentioned here, but a few examples may be noted. Although, in general, he was opposed to tariffs and other commercial restrictions he recognized that there were circumstances under which such restrictions were desirable. Thus he spoke (p. 431) favorably of the Navigation Act—because he felt that defences was "of much more importance than opulence." To help overcome the deleterious effects of the division of labor, and for other reasons, he advocated governmental activity in the realm of education. Smith favored a ceiling on interest rates—giving Jeremy Bentham the opportunity to write his essay in opposition to such a policy.[23]

It is well to emphasize that Adam Smith favored a rather extensive range of governmental activities, that he was by no means in favor of a universal hands-off policy. It would be undesirable, however, to overstate the case. Despite all his concessions, Smith felt that such crucial economic decisions as to what should be produced, how much should be produced, and what prices should be charged should be left very largely to the market. He was strongly opposed to centralized planning, to the establishment of a "Gosplan," and even to "NRA codes." He did recognize, however, the need for, and the importance of, a "public sector" in the economy. That is what he had in mind in his third function of government under natural liberty.

Smith's advocacy of an essentially free, unplanned type of economy was based on a number of considerations. For one thing the experience under Mercantilism, with its extensive controls, argued for economic freedom. Smith has much to say in *The Wealth of Nations* about the bad effects of governmental intervention, particularly as it involved monopoly. The monopolists, operating under a variety of aids from the government, distorted the pattern of production, charged high prices, made excessive profits, and in general had an adverse effect on the growth of national wealth. Without governmental assistance the monopolists would disappear, or greatly diminish in number, and free competition with its beneficent results would take over.

Closely allied to the economic benefits to be derived from the elimination of the monopolists was a very substantial political gain. The growth of the monopolists had been fostered by the government, but at the same time the government had been greatly influenced by the monopolists—an intricate, two-directional cause-and-effect relationship. A recurring theme in Smith's book is the practice of business lobbying, the "clamour" (a favorite term of the author's) of merchants and manufacturers seeking favorable legislation, some of which, says Smith (p. 612), may be said to be like the laws of Draco, "all written in blood." Monopoly-controlled government was, in Smith's opinion, poor government. He was not, of course, opposed so much to government as such, but to the government such as it was.

And the government "such as it was" had still other characteristics, in part no doubt due to the control exercised over it by monopolistic, special interest groups. Smith speaks (p. 326) of "the extravagance of government, and of the greatest errors of administration." He refers (p. 329) to kings and ministers who "are themselves always, and without any exception, the greatest spendthrifts in the society."

If, through the elimination of monopolies and other means, the operation of government were improved, then Smith would undoubtedly have approved an expansion in its functions. As Professor Viner points out, Smith, who "saw a wide and elastic range of activity for government" was willing to extend the range still farther if the government, "by improving its standards of competence, honesty, and public spirit, showed itself entitled to wider responsibilities."[24]

Smith's view of the government "such as it was" may have been distorted. His opinions on Mercantilism were extreme, a general fact that has long been recognized. In more recent years scholars have subjected these opinions to an increasing amount of critical appraisal, and this appraisal has been to the advantage of the Mercantilists and the disadvantage of Smith. For one thing it has been argued, notably by Professor Charles Wilson, that the influence of political lobbies during the period of Mercantilism has been exaggerated.[25] While recognizing that active pressure groups existed, Wilson believes that the notion that governmental policy was a product of "the irrestible pressure of private interests on a supine and ineffective government" is a view that is "historically casual and logically inadequate."

It may well be that just as Smith underestimated the force of the economic case for Mercantilism, so he overestimated the influence of Mercantilist lobbies on governmental policy. This is not a point at issue, however, in our present discussion. Smith's attitude toward governmental intervention was influenced by what he *thought* was the effect of lobbies—it makes no difference to our argument if his views were unbalanced.

Smith's support of limited governmental intervention was probably associated with his ideas concerning the existence of harmony in the economic order. The harmony, whatever its extent and origin, was in his estimation greater under individual freedom than under governmental control. And the greater the degree of harmony the better off the society.

Finally, Smith felt that the central economic problems facing society could be more effectively handled in a free, market economy than in one in which the major economic decisions were made by governmental bodies. The market was a better organizer of production than any conceivable planning body; it could make better shifts on "the great chess-board of human society" than any alternative agency.

Professors Viner and Macfie both speak of Smith as furnishing (in his numerous examples of disharmony in the economic system) material for a number of socialist orations. As a matter of fact, however, Smith's relation to socialism was much closer, and much more influential, than this whimsical observation suggests. One cannot say with any degree of precision what effect Smith had on the development of socialism, but some writers believe it was very substantial.

In *The Wealth of Nations* Smith remarks (p. 64) that "In that original state of things, which precedes both the appropriation of land and the accumulation of stock, the whole produce of labour belongs to the labourer." This statement (somewhat enlarged), says Professor Cannan, "became the foundation stone of the nineteenth-century socialism."[26] Max Lerner asserts that in setting forth the labor theory of value—"which is the core of Smith's economics"—our author "became the forerunner of Bray and Hodgskin and eventually of Marx."[27] A. W. Coats, pointing to one of the disharmonies mentioned in *The Wealth of Nations,* declares that Smith "laid the foundations of nineteenth century socialism by underlining the conflict between labour and capital."[28] Bruce Mazlish finds Smith to be "the central link in Marx's synthesis of philosophy and economics."[29]

If *The Wealth of Nations* paved the way to socialism, or had a pronounced influence on socialism, as these writers suggest, it is indeed one of the great ironies of history. Certainly Smith, with his strong support of private enterprise, did not intend it that way. But unexpected results can easily follow from given causes.

Ordinarily Smith's name has been linked with the development of capitalism rather than with socialism. Indeed, it has sometimes been said that he was an apologist for capitalism, and a man with a definite class bias. On this issue there has been some difference of opinion.[30] If Smith had a class bias—and there is some evidence that he did—it was not one of his marked characteristics. Moreover, he was by no means an uncritical supporter of capitalistic enterprise, not as he saw it in operation. It should also be added that Smith's primary "point of reference" was not the good of any class or of any group in society but the good of society as a whole.

In discussing various aspects of Smith's market economy we have given primary emphasis to what the author himself had to say about such an economy. While we have noted some of the present-day features and implications of his analysis, we have made no extensive attempt "to bring Smith up-to-date." On a very modest scale we shall now undertake that task, devoting most of our attention, however, to two aspects of that analysis: the issue of harmonies and disharmonies, and the question of governmental intervention.

For a long time after the publication of *The Wealth of Nations* the general rule among economists in discussing price determination was to follow Smith with his great emphasis on a competitive model, supplemented by references to monopoly markets. In other words, the discussion was directed to "pure competition" and "pure monopoly." During the 1920s and 1930s a very significant change occurred, a change in which such persons as Piero Sraffa, Roy F. Harrod, Joan Robinson, and Edward H. Chamberlin played highly important roles. New models, relating to the area between the two market extremes, an area that the older economists had neglected, were constructed, and new terms and analytical techniques came into general use. Such terms as oligopoly, duopoly, product differentiation, imperfect competition, marginal cost, and marginal revenue became an essential part of the economist's vocabulary. These changes in the analysis of price were revolutionary in nature and took economics very far beyond the point at which it had arived in 1776, and even in 1926. The simple model that Smith wrote about was superseded by a host of highly sophisticated models, models requiring the artistry and precision of the draughtsman (in the construction of graphs) and the vision and accuracy of the mathematician (in the formulation of equations).

To Smith the driving force in the economic life of a nation was self-interest. Though he taught, both by example and precept, the virtue of benevolence, he felt that in the business affairs of the country benevolence was a feeble spark. Today a great deal of the price analysis in economics is still based on the notion of self-interest, as it was in 1776, but other motivating factors are being given increasing attention. These other factors are indefinite and nebulous in nature and do not lend themselves to the nice type of analysis that accompanies the assumption of self-interest and profit maximization. Whether self-interest is as potent a force in the economic life of the free economies of today as it was in Smith's time is a debatable issue. In communistic nations, on the other hand, vigorous attempts are being made through institutional and other means to diminish the force of self-interest and increase the power of public interest. So far, however, only limited progress has been made.

As we noted earlier, Smith recognized the existence of numerous instances of disharmony in the economy. With the great technological, economic, and social changes that have occurred since the 1770s, many new kinds of disharmonies have developed, and today we are more conscious of these disharmonies than ever before. Indeed, the particular type of disharmony embraced by the now popular term "pollution" has become one of the great social and economic problems of the day.

The present wave of interest in pollution, however, was preceded by an increasing awareness among economists of the importance of disharmonies in general in the system. In recent decades new analytical approaches for examining these disharmonies have been developed, and to such older concepts as "marginal individual net product," "marginal social net product," and "social costs" have been added such newer terms as "side-use effects," "spillovers," and "externalities."

The types of disharmony that exist in the economic order today are numerous and complex. It will be helpful to our understanding of these disharmonies, and of those Smith had in mind, if we try to classify them. Such a classification, based on the persons or groups involved, follows. The entries in our classification are not mutually exclusive, however, nor, considered as a whole, are they all-inclusive.[31]

Classification of Disharmonies

(1) Between Producer and the Public (Social Costs)
(2) Between Producer and Producer (External Diseconomies)

(3) Between Consumer and Consumer
(4) Between Factors of Production

(1) Many of the examples of disharmony found in *The Wealth of Nations* can be placed in the first category of our classification. As we have already noted, Smith has much to say about monopolies, and the bad effects they have on prices and the use of resources. Much of the disharmony between producers, and here we are thinking particularly of manufacturers, and the public manifests itself in the operation of the price mechanism. In other words a pecuniary social cost to society is involved. But today many of the social costs associated with production also involve nonpecuniary costs (which may, indirectly, lead to pecuniary costs as well). Water and air pollution are outstanding examples. These costs now bulk large in American society and the country is faced with a mammoth task trying to cope with them. In Smith's day what we have called nonpecuniary costs were of small significance, and they do not seem to be involved in any of the examples of disharmony found in his book.

(2) When a monopolistic producer sells, say, raw material to another producer who is operating under competition, the latter may be charged an excessively high price. Thus there may be disharmony between them. The situation would be different if the latter were the sole buyer (a monopsonist). Smith did not discuss this type of disharmony. Nor, it would seem, did he take up the type of disharmony involved in what is sometimes referred to as "external diseconomies" (a concept that is currently used with considerable flexibility). He does not mention the case of the steel mill, the smoke from which might interfere with the operations of an adjacent plant.

(3) Smith gives very little attention to the disharmony that exists between consumers and consumers, a type that is now becoming increasingly common. Outboard motors, motorcycles, and pleasure cars were nonexistent in his day. However, in straining to find examples of this type of disharmony in *The Wealth of Nations,* one might mention the prodigal person who spends too freely on consumption goods, thereby harming capital accumu-

lation and, ultimately, the well-being of other consumers. One might also point to Smith's Veblenian utterance about "the parade of riches" by wealthy persons, a type of behavior that could easily dissatify the members of "the inferior ranks."

(4) Clashes of interest between the factors of production, including "masters and men," were present in Smith's time just as they are present, and in a more extreme form, today. As was indicated earlier in our discussion, there is no satisfactory formula for determining how the fruits of productive effort should be distributed among those who cooperate in the effort. Disagreements —disharmonies—can easily arise. Sometimes, as in a strike by tugboat operators or railroad employees, the disharmony can lead to serious social as well as private losses. The disharmony that exists between productive groups or classes can relate to nonpecuniary matters as well as to "fatter pay envelopes." Today the whole question of management prerogatives is a cardinal issue in industrial relations.

Earlier in our essay we referred to Smith's views on the question of whether individuals (or groups of individuals) are the best judges of their own interests. With the passing of the years has any change taken place in this matter? In the free economies of the world, and particularly in the United States and Canada, are individuals today better, or poorer, judges of their interests than were the individuals in the eighteenth century? That question can easily be asked but not easily answered. The complexity of the issue is obvious when one considers a few of the subordinate questions that arise in the general area of consumption. What has been the effect of modern advertising on the ability of the consumer to make rational buying judgments? Has advertising increased the efficiency of consumption by decreasing the gap between "desire" (which it tries to stimulate) and "satisfaction"? And, though it may be a rash question, has advertising led to any qualitative improvements in the individual's scale of interests or wants?[32] What, one may further ask, has been the effect on the consumer's discretionary ability of the great proliferation of products? Of increased general education?

Is the individual today any more adept at choosing his occupation than he was in Smith's time? In starting a business? In making an investment? These are all difficult questions. Of one thing, however, we may be certain: assuming a harmony of interests, the better is the individual in judging his own interests (and then acting upon them), the better will a free economy operate. This, of course, does not rule out the virtue of having "a good heart" as well as "a good head."

The question of resource allocation, to which Smith gave a great deal of attention, continues to be a highly important matter today, both in economic theory and in the actual functioning of the world's economies. Since Smith's time the analysis of resource use, including the use of the concept of an "ideal" or "optimum" pattern of usage, has been highly refined. The notion of marginalism has contributed indispensably to the progress of analysis. New aspects of the problem have come into the forefront, including the presence of economic inequality among the consumers (among those who cast the "dollar votes") and the vast and complex issue of so-called consumer sovereignty.

As a result of a variety of influences there is a widespread feeling, in the United States and other countries, that more of the productive resources of the economy should be allocated centrally, rather than through the operation of the price system; in other words, that the Smithian system of allocation should be considerably modified.

This opinion raises again the question of governmental intervention, to which we gave attention some pages back. The policy of limited governmental authority, endorsed by Smith, has become increasingly unpopular over the years. The best illustrations of this fact are found, of course, in the communistic nations of the world. In such nations the market, with its outstanding characteristic of diffused decision-making, is largely replaced by extensive planning under which the chief decisions in the economy are made centrally. To be sure, certain aspects of the market system— certain features of free enterprise and capitalistic competition— are being reintroduced into some of these economies. But for the most part the major economic policies are made by the government.

And interestingly enough, in these economies two of the features of the Smithian system have experienced an interesting reversal. First, the notion of a harmony of interest is still present, but the "direction" of the harmony is turned around.[33] In Soviet Russia, for example, instead of each individual seeking his own good, as Adam Smith would have it, the people are encouraged to seek the good of society. In this way they will promote their own individual interests and well-being. Slogans, publicity, education, medals, and other means are used to develop a social consciousness. That the new philosophy has not been adequately successful is suggested by the extensive use in the Soviet Union of the piece-rate method of wage payment.

In the communistic, highly planned economies the Smithian notion that, on the whole, the individual is the best judge of his own interests, is replaced by the notion that the government is, on the whole, the best judge of the individual's interests, at least in terms of ultimate results. It is better fitted to decide the general course of production, the price structure, the rate of growth. The individual has certain discretionary powers, of course, and the planners cannot be oblivious to the judgments he expresses. But the fact still remains that these judgments are of limited influence, particularly of direct influence, in guiding the economy. As time goes on, however, this situation will probably change. A higher degree of "consumer sovereignty" will likely prevail. But the "seen hand" of the government, rather than the "unseen hand" of the market, will continue to be of predominant importance.

If the communistic nations have moved very far from the noninterventionist policies of Adam Smith, the so-called free economies have also departed, in varying degrees, from these policies. This has been due to a number of factors, including the presence of widespread disharmonies in the economic system, and the recognition of the fact that if these disharmonies are to be lessened governmental action is necessary. An outstanding example is the pollution problem. But this is not the only problem in which state intervention is advocated in this country. For others one need only mention housing, schools, hospitals. The "public sector" in the traditionally free economies has been steadily growing. In all such economies—indeed in every type of economy—there is a nice question as to how large this sector should be. A few years ago the issue was described as "The Great Debate." More recently it has been spoken of as "The Social Balance Controversy." The term "National Priorities" has also been used.

Despite widespread differences of opinion on the issue of the public sector in the economy, there would be general agreement—except among the new anarchists—that this sector should now be larger than the one envisaged in the eighteenth century by Adam Smith. Even the members of "the Chicago School," with their strong support of the price system and their admiration for Adam Smith, would likely agree.[34] In view of the technological, economic, and demographic changes of the past two centuries one would expect such general agreement. Moreover, Adam Smith, could he be consulted, would undoubtedly go along. But just how far he would be willing to move in the direction of "the positive state" is a debatable issue. Smith believed strongly in "the remoulding of a State by a powerful Society," not "the remoulding of a Society by a powerful State."[35] Today, however, he would undoubtedly be willing to grant a considerable increase in the leeway the state has to influence and improve the well-being of society.

NOTES

1. G. L. S. Shackle, *The Nature of Economic Thought* (Cambridge at the University Press, 1966), p. 8. Shackle goes on to point out, however, that the Walrasian model is not now looked upon as adequate. Among other things it does not give proper attention to the influence of money, and it omits the operation of uncertainty.

2. Fritz Machlup describes Quesnay's *Table* as "one of the most remarkable macro-models that has ever been produced." *Essays on Economic Semantics* (Englewood Cliffs, N.J.: Prentice-Hall, 1963), p. 103.

3. *The Impact of the Social Sciences* (New Brunswick, N.J.: Rutgers University Press, 1966), pp. 24-25.

4. Neil W. Chamberlain, *Private and Public Planning* (New York: McGraw-Hill, 1965), p. 3. Smith, says Chamberlain, "epitomized a system as neatly as has ever been done: 'A system is like a little machine.'"

5. Milton Friedman, one of the leading contemporary admirers of Adam Smith, gives a broader interpretation to self-interest, to "private interests," than the great Scottish economist did (and his interpretation was by no means narrow). In Professor Friedman's opinion, "The man who devotes his life to religious evangelism under a vow of poverty is pursuing his private interests no less than the man who accumulates money with an eye to wine, women, and song." *The National Review,* August 24, 1965, p. 723. It would seem that according to such a view, all interests are private interests, or self-interests; and all benevolent, sympathetic, and unselfish acts if not wholly directed to the gratification of private interests have a private-interest foundation. If one accepts this notion, it would seem desirable, for the sake of analytical clarity, to speak of "benevolent self-interest," and "nonbenevolent self-interest."

6. *Fors Clavigera,* Letter 72, in *John Ruskin's Works,* 26 vols. (Boston: Estes, St. Mark's ed., 1898), 9, p. 355. In an earlier letter, No. 62 (p. 125), Ruskin referred to Smith as a "half-bred and half-witted Scotchman." In appraising Ruskin and his remarks about Smith one should perhaps make some allowance for his mental problems during the time the *Fors* letters were written. Ruskin, however, was not alone in his virulent criticism of Smith's self-interest doctrine. G. R. Stirling Taylor declared that "the so-called philosophy of Adam Smith and his followers was little more than a creed for highwaymen and gangsters." *Great Events in History,* ed. by G. R. Stirling Taylor (London: Cassell, 1934), p. 652. More recently, and in less extreme terms, J. M. Reid alluded to Smith's "gospel of greed." *Scotland, Past and Present* (London: Oxford University Press, 1959), p. 41.

7. T. W. Hutchison declares that "As regards Adam Smith, there is certainly much truth in the proposition that 'the desire for better men, rather than for larger national incomes, was a main theme of the classical economics.'" *"Positive" Economcis and Policy Objectives* (Cambridge: Harvard University Press, 1964), p. 132. The "proposition" had been advanced by George J. Stigler, in *Five Lectures on Economic Problems* (New York: Macmillan, 1950), p. 4. That Smith was a welfare theorist as well as a wealth theorist is argued by J. M. A. Gee in his discussion of "Adam Smith's Social Welfare Function," in the *Scottish Journal of Political Economy,* November 1968, pp. 283-299.

8. A discussion of the relationship between the prudent man and the economic man, and of Smith's treatment of self-love in general, will be found in A. L. Macfie's article "Adam Smith's *Moral Sentiments* as Foundation for his *Wealth of Nations*," reprinted in *The Individual in Society*, pp. 59-81. Smith's economic man is less "economic" than the traditional economic man of the later economists. On this point see Macfie, pp. 112, 121.

9. On the matter of justice, see Quotations 19, 20, 23, 24 in Essay 7.

10. For further discussion of "the deception idea" in *The Theory of Moral Sentiments* and *The Wealth of Nations*, see Macfie, *The Individual in Society*, pp. 47, 52-54, 60-62, 122-125.

11. Smith's contemporary, Adam Ferguson, made a somewhat similar observation. "When the merchant forgets his own interest to lay plans for his country," said Ferguson, "the period of vision and chimera is near, and the solid basis of commerce withdrawn." *An Essay on the History of Civil Society* (Boston: Hastings, Etheridge and Bliss, seventh ed., 1809), p. 235.

12. *The Theory of Economic Policy in English Classical Political Economy* (London: Macmillan, 1952), p. 25.

13. *Adam Smith, 1776-1926* (Chicago: University of Chicago Press, 1928), pp. 134-136. An earlier collection of disharmonies was compiled by the German economist Karl Knies (1821-1898). See Alfred Marshall, *Industry and Trade* (London: Macmillan, 1923), p. 748.

14. J. M. Clark, in discussing Smith's "economic man," declares that "Smith was as far as possible from holding that individuals intelligently chose and successfully pursued their own interests." Carl Becker, J. M. Clark, William Dodd, *The Spirit of '76 and Other Essays* (Washington: Brookings, 1927), p. 86. Professor Clark's statement is exaggerated. "As far as possible" is a long way.

15. Commons, *Institutional Economics* (New York: Macmillan, 1934), pp. 159-162; Heimann, *History of Economic Doctrines* (New York: Oxford University Press, 1945), pp. 64-65; Halévy, *The Growth of Philosophic Radicalism* (New York: Macmillan, 1928), pp. 89, 107.

16. Grampp, *Economic Liberalism*, 2 vols. (New York: Random House, 1965), II, pp. 4, 34; Letwin, *The Origins of Scientific Economics* (London: Methuen 1963), p. 225; Rosenberg, *The Journal of Political Economy*, December 1960, p. 559. The wide gap that can separate the interpreters of Smith is suggested by a remark made by Edwin Cannan concerning "institutions" and the harmony of interests. Cannan speaks of "the very fact which Smith *ignored*, namely, that such harmony as is found between the pursuit of self-interest and the general good is dependent on the existence of suit-

able human institutions." *An Economist's Protest* (London: King, 1927), p. 428. Italics added.

17. *Freedom and Reform* (New York: Harper, 1947), p. 377.

18. *Scottish Journal of Political Economy*, February 1967, pp. 3, 7. Earlier, Macfie referred to "the almost theological view of the invisible hand." *The Individual in Society*, p. 61. Professor Macfie has an excellent discussion of the invisible hand, as the concept is used in both of Smith's books, in *The Individual in Society*, pp. 101-125.

19. *Adam Smith, 1776-1926*, p. 140. More recent observations by Viner on the issue here discussed will be found in his article on Smith in the *International Encyclopedia of the Social Sciences*.

20. *Theories of Economic Growth*, ed. by Bert F. Hoselitz (Glencoe, Illinois: Free Press, 1960), p. 70.

21. John H. Hallowell, *Main Currents in Modern Political Thought* (New York: Holt, Rinehart and Winston, 1963), p. 139.

22. Jacob Viner has an extensive list of the kinds of governmental intervention mentioned in *The Wealth of Nations*, and which Smith favored. See *Adam Smith, 1776-1926*, pp. 138-155.

23. *Defence of Usury*, in *The Works of Jeremy Bentham*, ed. by John Bowring, 11 vols. (reproduced, New York: Russell & Russell, 1962), 3.

24. *Adam Smith, 1776-1926*, p. 154. See also Alfred Marshall, *Industry and Trade*, pp. 744-745. George J. Stigler in commenting on Smith's distrust of the state contends that the distrust was primarily one of motives, of self-serving groups, rather than of governmental competence. *The American Economic Review*, March 1965, p. 3. The "motive" element was also stressed by Marshall, who speaks of the corruption of the government of the time and Smith's practice of looking "with suspicion on those who invited the government to new enterprises for the public weal." *Memorials of Alfred Marshall*, ed. by A. C. Pigou (London: Macmillan, 1925), pp. 334-335.

25. See Wilson's chapter on "Government Policy and Private Interest in Modern English History," in his *Economic History and the Historian* (New York: Praeger, 1969).

26. *A Review of Economic Theory* (London: King, 1929), pp. 338-339. Cannan also includes Smith's preceding sentence—"The produce of labour constitutes the natural recompence or wages of labour"—as well as the following one: "He has neither landlord nor master to share with him."

27. Introduction to *The Wealth of Nations*, ed. by Edwin Cannan, p. x.

28. *Renaissance and Modern Studies*, 1962, p. 45.

29. *The Riddle of History* (New York: Harper & Row, 1966), p. 254.

30. See Eric Roll, *A History of Economic Thought* (Englewood Cliffs, N. J.: Prentice-Hall, 3rd ed., 1956), pp. 149-151; Hla Myint, *Theories of Welfare Economics,* p. 26; and Lionel Robbins, *The Theory of Economic Policy in English Political Economy,* pp. 20-22.

31. In attempting to use the Classification of Disharmonies one runs into the difficult problem of definition. What, precisely, is meant by "social costs"? By "external diseconomies"? These questions cannot be probed here. Discussions of the problem can be found in William J. Baumol, *Welfare Economics and the Theory of the State* (Cambridge: Harvard University Press, 1965); E. J. Misham, *Welfare Economics* (New York: Random House, 1964); Tibor Scitovsky, *Papers on Welfare and Growth* (Stanford University Press, 1964).

32. Philip H. Wicksteed acutely observed that "The man who can make his fellows desire more worthily and wisely is doubtless performing a higher task than the one who enables them more amply to satisfy whatever desires they have." *The Common Sense of Political Economy,* 2 vols. (London: Routledge, 1933), I, p. 123. To what extent, one might ask, can one reasonably expect private entrepreneurs to promote the end Wicksteed had in mind?

33. Where Smith speaks of, or implies, a harmony of interests it is a harmony that moves, in specific instances, from the good of the individual to that of society. But, in a very general sense, he recognized a reverse type of harmony. Man, he says (*The Theory of Moral Sentiments,* p. 81), "is sensible too that his own interest is connected with the prosperity of society, and that the happiness, perhaps the preservation of his own existence, depends upon its preservation."

34. Milton Friedman and George J. Stigler are the leading members of the "school."

35. The quoted words are those of George Unwin. See his *Studies in Economic History: The Collected Papers of George Unwin,* ed. by Richard H. Tawney (London: Macmillan, 1927), p. 28.

Index